"Beyond the brilliant business and life lessons, *Fifteen Minutes of Shame* is an unflinchingly honest portrait of a good man, lifelong learner, and friend who is so much more than his worst day."

James White, board chairman, the Honest Company; lead independent director, Affirm Inc.; and former chairman, CEO, and president of Jamba Juice

"*Fifteen Minutes of Shame* is an exhilarating, authentic read. From the first page, the book underscores how Des thinks differently—unburdened by convention, inspired by the lure of the possibility, and led by an unrelenting drive to help others excel. It's a great read for anyone facing adversity and a lesson to never give up."

Diane Ellis, former CEO, the Limited, and president, Chico's FAS and Brooks Brothers

"In *Fifteen Minutes of Shame*, Des courageously bears his soul with such openness and authenticity that you cannot help be drawn in from the first page. It is a master class for anyone facing adversity in how to own your mistakes but not let them define you."

Monica Woo, former president, 1-800-Flowers

"Des is a compelling and courageous business leader who through endless pain and some significant mistakes has the fortitude to share his story honestly. His is a story worth telling and most importantly worth reading. There is not a single professional who has not made mistakes along their climb, but there are few who are willing to share them so openly. In a world more interested in 'headlines' than long-term values, Des reminds us to walk with our heads high and our hearts open."

Bonnie Siegel, founder of ASE Group and former presidential campaign strategist

"I have known Des for over twenty years and seen how he faces adversity head-on and brings out the best in everyone. After reading *Fifteen Minutes of Shame*, my respect for him is even greater. The life lessons laid out, page after page, are profound, riveting, and delivered with an authenticity that make Des special."

Jeff Hamill, former senior executive, Starbucks, 7-Eleven, Smile Brands, and author of *Taking Responsibility*

"Des's story proves it does not matter where you start in life but what you do with your life that counts. We all face adversity, but staying in the fight, no matter the odds, is critical. The book is filled with countless life lessons, but the most profound is that your worst moments do not have to define you. It is your will to learn, evolve, and your ability to grow that make the difference. In *Fifteen Minutes of Shame*, Des illuminates that and so much more."

Keith King, special advisor to president of OVG, former president of Centerplate International, and Team USA Olympic member

"I have seen Des's impact firsthand. He thinks differently. *Fifteen Minutes of Shame* captures why and more with refreshing candor, self-awareness, and brutal honesty."

Hal Handel, COO, New York Racing Association

"In *Fifteen Minutes of Shame*, Des lays out his life story with the kind of candor and honesty I have come to expect from him. Des holds nothing back and underscores how we are all better than our worst moment and that we all face adversity, but giving up is never an option. Des is the rare person who enables the type of adrenaline boost that we all dream about injecting into our lives. The learnings throughout the book, from one of best leaders out there, are priceless."

Johnny Custer, senior executive, advisor, and author

"I have worked with many great leaders, but Des has set the standard that I use to compare all others. *Fifteen Minutes of Shame* is an emotionally charged story that is both terrifying and inspirational. It is exactly what I would expect from Des."

Roger Glenn, senior human resources executive, Safeway and Target

"Des has proved to be a great business leader—his empathy and emotional intelligence ensure that all who come into contact with him believe they are part of the solution and not part of the problem. *Fifteen Minutes of Shame* shows how these traits mean you are not defined by the lows but can be inspired to overcome them."

Simon Cohen, former CEO, Leicester Tigers

www.amplifypublishinggroup.com

Fifteen Minutes of Shame: How a Twitter Mob Nearly Ruined My Life

For more information, please contact:
Amplify Publishing, an imprint of Amplify Publishing Group
620 Herndon Parkway, Suite 320
Herndon, VA 20170
info@amplifypublishing.com

Library of Congress Control Number: 2022922123

CPSIA Code: PRV0423A

ISBN-13: 978-1-63755-659-7

Printed in the United States

Music has played a powerful role in my life.
Not because I'm in the business. I'm not.
Music has been ever-present in my life.
It was there to celebrate my successes,
and more importantly, music has gotten me
through moments when I was not sure
if I would or could.

Therefore, it's only fitting I put my dedication
to my true love, Carol, into song.
I created this song in 1995 and released
the remix in 2022.
It may not win a Grammy anytime soon, but here goes . . .

Carol,
I love you and nobody else.
I can't understand the feelings that I possess.
I love you, my green-eyed bride.
I'll love you until the end of time.
Because you make my life complete.
Because you are my everything.

15
HOW A
TWITTER MOB
NEARLY RUINED MY LIFE

MINUTES OF
SHAME

DES HAGUE

an imprint of Amplify Publishing Group

CONTENTS

FOREWORD

Life sometimes takes unexpected turns and leads us on unanticipated journeys. That certainly has been the case for Des Hague and myself.

Back in 2006, writing a foreword for his book was something I could not have imagined in my wildest dreams!

Before meeting Des, I saw him as potential competition. I was the CEO of Safeway's multimillion-dollar e-commerce business, Safeway.com, when Des joined as the president of Safeway's perishables business. Simply put, he landed a great job! I reported directly to Brian Cornell during those days and was considered an up-and-coming executive. Des was going to be my future competition to take the next big opportunity on Brian's team.

Des and I were about to face off in a corporate race to the top . . . or so I thought.

Like so many others, upon meeting Des in person, I was quickly drawn to him. I witnessed firsthand how he worked collaboratively and with unique authenticity. From those early days at Safeway, I knew Des was a special human being who had leadership traits that I could learn from. The way he motivated people and his approach to servant leadership were refreshing, and they set him apart from other leaders on the senior leadership team.

Retail was very segregated at that time. Perishable team members were not very motivated to work with the Non-Perishable team, let alone a dot-com guy! Des always approached the business with a "we" rather than a "me" mentality. It was always about finding solutions that created upside for everyone, not just himself or his direct team.

He routinely facilitated alignment for organizationwide, cross-functional initiatives. He was able to achieve this much quicker than his peers, and having the opportunity to observe and learn from this skill has helped me to this day. It was amazing to see. The man I thought would be my nemesis had become a lifelong friend.

In 2014, years after we had both moved on from Safeway, a video clip surfaced on my Twitter feed showing Des kicking a dog for no apparent reason—according to the narrative. As I watched that short clip, I immediately reflected back to our days together at Safeway and felt profound sadness. Candidly, *nothing* on the clip represented the man I knew. I had now known Des for almost a decade, and I had seen him in some of the most stressful professional situations that one can be placed in. I had shared numerous dinners and long conversations with this man and his family. Watching that clip, I knew something was very wrong. For Des to act so out of character, I knew he was in pain, and I reached out to him to offer my support.

He immediately took full responsibility for his actions. There was zero deflection and no excuses. He owned it! His next words shocked me to my core. He informed me that he had resigned. His family was receiving death threats, and his youngest son had been physically attacked. As he poured out his soul, the anguish he felt for his loved ones and the company he led was obvious.

I vividly recall the deep sadness I felt for Des. I hoped he would not allow this incident to destroy him. I must admit—due to the viral nature of that video clip, I gave Des slim odds of making it to the other side. I thought his career was probably over. If only people knew Des for the man he was and not for what was shown on that forty-two-second video clip. It made me sad to think that an unfortunate moment on social media could have the power to ruin my friend, who had done so many good things for other people.

In spite of the social media frenzy and the circus that followed, I am thankful that my concerns for Des proved unfounded! If anything, I have an even greater respect and admiration for him seeing how he overcame this challenge in his life. Over the past eight years, he has shown how one should accept responsibility for their actions and has demonstrated how to deal with adversity with class and character. Des would be the first to tell you that his actions on that fateful day have had a profound impact on his life, but it has not defined who he is as a person and a leader.

Des is a shining example of why you should never allow yourself to be defined by your worst moment. Over the years, we have worked on a number of business ventures together. Most recently, I proudly served as one of his advisors to a tech start-up that helped retailers eliminate operational inefficiency from their businesses.

As with many things in our society, social media was originally developed as a platform to promote and enhance all the good in our community. Staying in touch with old friends, sharing moments from your families' lives with loved ones, and, of course, making others laugh!

Unfortunately, this platform also reveals the dark side of humanity. We have all had "bad days" and have done things we would never want the public to see. Unfortunately for Des, the public saw his "bad day," and the dark side of social media created a narrative that was particularly destructive to his family. We often forget there are people with loved ones on the other side of that tweet. Our society is a much better place when we engage in dialogue from a perspective to understand, not tear down. Engage in conversation with grace and not vitriol. In all situations, life is much more complex than can be appropriately expressed or explained in a headline or 140-character snippet of truth.

I have the awesome responsibility of raising a family that earlier this year expanded with the arrival of our latest baby boy. It is a time for hope and at the same time concern. I want to make sure my family minimizes the downside of social media as they move through this life. Cyberbullying in any form is evil. We have to be kinder and more forgiving. More compassionate. Strive to argue less and never hate. Overall, become less hostile and judgmental. For my family, we leverage social media as it was originally intended—to highlight the good in our world!

Finally, I hope I am a small reason why you are reading this. Several years ago, I told Des he needed to write a book on the whole incident and his life story. I made a promise that if he did write his story, I would gladly contribute to the book and write his foreword. I have delivered on my word.

In this book, Des will lay out the lessons he has learned during his life journey, from the unimaginable adversity to a myriad of successes, both personally and professionally. In spite of the ups and downs, he has persevered and found the strength to continue to serve others along the way.

I am delighted that you now get to know the man I know and proud to call Des my friend. Who would have thought that? It's indeed serendipity at play. I know I am a better man for it. Des has been an inspiration to me, and I am certain he will inspire you as well!

Enjoy his story.

Matthew Gutermuth

CEO of iControl Data Solutions and former CEO of Safeway.com

INTRODUCTION

Saturday, August 23, 2014, is a day I will never forget. In fact, it is etched deeply into every fiber of my body. Sadly, this fateful day will go down in the annals of history—at least mine—as the worst day of my professional and personal life. Ironically, for totally different reasons, it was all inexplicably linked to one painful event.

I had taken the red-eye back, with no Wi-Fi, from Vancouver and touched down in Newark in the early hours of Saturday morning. While I may have been out of touch, that did not mean the world had stopped. The world had been busy. Very busy! I knew something was wrong when I turned my phone back on.

I had received so many messages that they filled my inbox. A news story had broken. Someone in Vancouver had leaked a video of me kicking a dog in an elevator to the BC SPCA and the media.

Without the appropriate context, the story looked horrible. The forty-two-second clip did not show things for how they were—me disciplining a poorly behaved dog—but rather gave the illusion of me abusing a dog.

Twitter and its shapeshifting minions did their thing of driving hate. No one, including me, was ready for the sheer pandemonium that it set up in its wake. It was like watching a total deconstruction of reality—my reality.

I rode home lost in my thoughts, none good. I arrived home at around three o'clock in the morning. I went to see Carol, my wife, who was sound asleep. I sat at the end of the bed and gently woke her. I had been dreading this very moment. I said there was a problem.

Carol, waking up, asked what it was. I said I was the problem and that a story was going to break about me mistreating a dog. I also told her that I was ill and that I was trying to handle it without causing the family any more pain. I then took a deep breath and confessed to her the hardest thing I have ever had to tell someone in my life—I had been unfaithful.

In a matter of days, the story about the dog went national and then international. A rabid band of the loudest, shrillest blue-checkers on Twitter, for which a skull and crossbones is a more appropriate designation, was driving the story.

They saw me in a grainy feed, in a completely out-of-context situation, and simply determined my total destruction was the only thing that could right the world. They tasted blood in the water and wanted nothing but vengeance.

A petition for my immediate firing from my job as CEO of Centerplate, one of the world's largest hospitality providers, yielded more than a hundred thousand signatures. Major media outlets joined the fray. Even *Sports Illustrated* was calling for my head.

Eventually, I was forced to resign. And even though I had publicly apologized, the backlash didn't stop there. My home was raided. My life was threatened. My family was threatened. My son was attacked.

I later found out it was a pathetic scumbag who worked at the residential building in Vancouver and had wanted to get his boss fired from the building's security team who leaked the video and my personal information. This was not done for moral outrage but for personal ambition.

Overnight the endless pages of positive press I had accumulated—and more importantly, the reputation I had built as a caring father, loving husband, and upstanding community leader—over decades were replaced with the "dog incident."

If I did not see it firsthand for myself, I would have thought it was not possible. You could not do any type of search without my worst moment being center stage.

What the mob didn't know was everything that happened before those forty-two seconds.

In my life, I had faced daunting odds too many times to remember. I had been punched, beaten, bitten, kicked, pushed down, beat down, mugged, raped, stabbed, and stomped on. I knew what it felt like to be hurt and worked my entire life to keep others from that fate.

But I had never been broken. For the first time, I thought broken was coming. It was a terrifying, paralyzing feeling.

My story is proof that we now live in a world where, no matter who you are, you can be canceled and are routinely judged by your worst moments. There is no gradation of response in relation to the severity of any situation. And you can forget about redemption.

I'm not suggesting that social media should be eliminated. People should have freedom of choice. But how do we lessen its negative impacts?

Information broadly assimilated is a good thing. No one wants to go back to when a handful of national papers and even fewer media networks controlled the narrative.

We all have the right to voice our opinions, but reacting without a full review should be vehemently guarded against. I am asking us to step back and think for a moment about any issue and ask does the punishment match it or have we allowed the mob to exaggerate any situation.

A mob mentality is known to lower a group IQ by fifty points. And Twitter is nothing if not a mob. There is also debate that bots are anywhere from 5 to 50 percent of Twitter accounts. Step back and think about that. The town square topics are being manipulated by those with a nefarious agenda almost half of the time. You are left questioning what is real and what is deep fake. Unrest is being sowed.

To me, it makes the case that anonymity should no longer be an option. Your profile should be clearly identified. If you state it, stand by it publicly. No more hiding in the shadows.

Below I have highlighted just a handful of social media-led high-tech cancellations. Out of respect to the individuals, they will remain nameless as to not see their names tarred further. Plus anonymity is how you roll on Twitter.

- A PR expert was fired while traveling back from Africa for a tweet about catching AIDS and not to worry, because she is white. Insensitive. Yes. Worthy of being fired? Receiving death threats? Come on.

- A CEO was placed on administrative leave when he laid off nine hundred employees by Zoom. Again, clumsy, but even if he had called in all and managed that logistical nightmare, he would have also been called insensitive and out of touch for flying people in only to fire them. Also, don't forget the issue was cash flow. That cost would have run in to the millions of dollars. To me, this is a case of heads you lose and tails they win.

- Another CEO was forced off LinkedIn—of all places—and his family was sent threatening messages. His crime was suggesting new hires needed to put in twelve-hour days. Interestingly, the richest man in the world stated he wanted to reduce his own weekly schedule to eighty hours a week. Is this worthy of threatening behavior? Should this be the accepted norm?

- Just last year, students petitioned that a long-tenured professor be fired because his class was too difficult. What was the outcome? He was fired, of course!

This all comes back to asking, "What world do we want to live in?" The scary version of reality today is one that allows us to be led by an IQ-lowered mob that in turn may be manipulated by bots to drive engagement.

One authoritative voice on the value and relevance of social media, and Twitter in particular, would be Jack Dorsey, one of the credited cofounders of Twitter, who stated his biggest regret is that Twitter was ever a company.

After barely surviving my own social media mauling, I'd have to agree with Jack. I truly hope the new owner can manage the platform better moving forward.

This book lays out my life, highlighting my challenges, successes, and failures—hopefully, it will be both enjoyable and provide learning experiences. It underscores how adversity visits us all, but defeat is optional if you possess the right mindset. It does not matter where you start in life but what you do with your life that counts. My wish for you is that you live it fully!

PART 1

SURVIVING
THE CAULDRON

The Early Years

My start to life on earth was anything but typical. But before we get to that, let's get some of the basics out of the way. My father was English, and my mother was Irish. Nothing strange about that, you might think. But the 1960s were a different and much more complicated time.

My parents met in Rotherham, South Yorkshire, which is a small dot of a town in northern England. For my parents, it was not love at first sight. In fact, it was anything but. My mother had been dating one of my father's friends, and they split up. My father built up the courage to make his move, resulting in my mother bolting back to Belfast—wise woman. I always imagine her legging it down the road screaming, "Run, Forrest! Run!" My father, being stubborn, and maybe a bit of a stalker, pursued her and eventually wore down her resistance. They began to create a life together, and in 1965 gave birth to my elder brother, Paul.

I came along in July 1967, aptly named the Summer of Love. Mine was not a smooth arrival. I pitched up in Belfast, not quite the bundle of joy advertised but with yellow jaundice and a little ahead of schedule. Rather fitting for someone who has always been accused of being in a hurry. I was whisked off to the ICU, where I was shoved into a steaming "sauna." Allegedly, I spent my first week or so chilling out, working on my tan in a glass jar covered in wires. Maybe this is where I picked up my love for sunbathing.

Not that I was aware, but this was a period of deep unrest in Ireland. The Irish were in a heated terror war with the English. In fact, it had been going on for over half a century. Apparently, both sides knew how to carry a grudge. The relationship between my father, being English, and my mother, being Irish, was very much frowned upon in Northern Ireland—one could say as popular as a turd in a punch bowl. Yes, that appealing. Tensions (always fraught) boiled over in 1969, along with the birth of my younger brother, Dominic, who is the brain of the family. But that's not saying much.

In late September 1969, my father was traveling to his workplace—a small brewery, I'm told. Ironic, as Dad was a teetotaler. Turning the corner, my father saw his building and livelihood go up in smoke. He had been repeatedly warned that "his kind" were not welcome, but as previously mentioned, he always was a little stubborn.

Regardless, this time my father took the not-so-subtle hint and fled for his life. Upon racing back home, Dad dashed into the house. Moments later the Hague family was making our Great Escape. I can see myself clearly riding a motorbike like Steve McQueen. The ultimate Boss Baby. Okay, that did not happen, but we did race to the coast and flee across the channel to England. Candidly, at two years old, I have no recollection of this. But I like to think I was saved like baby Moses. Well, I do have a healthy ego.

The Dash to Safety

My parents had split up for our "get-out-of-hell" journey—the thinking being it would make us less of a target and increase the chances of a successful escape. My father took Paul, and my mother ushered Dominic and me. We met back up at the docks, where we took the ferry over to the mainland. I have visions of a Viking-like crossing, with me at the front of the vessel looking for the shore, but it may have been a little more pedestrian. Not to mention I get seasick just looking at water. We were Rotherham bound. This must have been less than a joyous moment for my mother, in light of her bolting from there previously.

My first recollection of life came a few years later, when we moved to Ewers Road in Kimberworth. It was a three-bedroom, midblock, brick home. I loved that place. There was nothing fancy about it. Your typical working-man's place. Luxury accommodations it was not. A Realtor would kindly refer to it as a fixer-upper.

There was a little park down the road, where my brothers and I would climb trees for hours. Truth be told, we got into fights almost daily, and not the polite kind. We only stopped when blood was drawn or limbs were damaged. My brothers were terrible!

One of my favorite battles with Paul came a few years later, when I was around ten. I was standing at the top of the stairs, and Paul was standing at the bottom. We were arguing about who was going to run to the shop. I had done more than my fair share. Paul disagreed and thought he was in charge. I wanted to cast my vote on the matter to make my feelings clear. I raced into my bedroom and picked up my alarm clock. It was one of those metal ones with the three-pronged legs. It weighed a bloody ton.

Without thinking, I wound up like I was going to deliver a fastball and launched the clock down the stairs. I was hoping I'd hit in the strike zone, maybe his chest or something. I wanted to leave a mark, but I stared in slow motion as the clock sailed down the stairs and hit my brother right in the kisser. It got worse—one of the metal-pronged legs had stuck into his forehead. For a moment I thought I had killed my brother. Then he looked up at me. The clock stuck right there in his forehead was quite the sight. All I could do was laugh. Next Paul was charging up the stairs, and I knew I was going to get a right old MMA-style beating. I offered no defense, and he did not hold back. Paul pummeled me for ten minutes flat. I admired his stamina. The result was that my ears were boxed blue and stayed that way for weeks. It was not the last of our duels, however.

In 1972 another addition to the Hague clan was introduced, Damian. Apparently, my mother seemingly wanted an all-boy team of ruffians. One could say my parents clearly did not watch much television at night. Now we had Desmond, Dominic, and Damian, with Paul being the odd *D* out. We used to tease Paul, stating his name was really Dale, but he was too thick to remember.

This is also the moment of my first epic embarrassment and meltdown. My mother would host luncheons. Not the posh type with the champagne flutes. We were northerners. We served biscuits and tea with a lump of coal on the side. Who needs lemon? We were tough.

At this particular bash, I vividly remember my mother showing off our newest addition, Damian. For the life of me, I had no idea what the fuss was all about. To me, this thing was a monster. It cried constantly, stunk awfully, and couldn't even speak or walk. I was about five years old and apparently still a bed wetter. I know. Who can believe it? To my utter disbelief, my mother proceeded to whip me up in the air like a gymnast and incredulously in front of these ladies pulled off my flannel Tarzan nappy and proceeded to expose my junk to the world. I was mortified. I stormed off in a huff, wailing. What was my mother thinking? The indignation of the thing was too much for me. The only silver lining is from that day on I moved forward sans my flannel friend. A man's got to have his privacy, after all.

Barring my indecent exposure incident, life was actually great for the family. My father was now the manager of a betting office. I'm told that was quite the accomplishment. The man was a math genius. He could tumble numbers in his head at a speed that would make most go dizzy. I picked up a little of that talent myself later in life. My mother worked at the local library about two blocks from where we lived. After school I would love to go visit my mother and wait for her to finish and walk her home. I loved those afternoon walks, but this was when I realized I had a problem.

There were several other children who were also at the library, many much younger than I. They were reading. I was not. It was not for lack of trying, but every time I picked up a book, the words on the page appeared scrambled to me. I could make no sense of them. To not appear stupid, I would pick out picture books and read along with the other kids. I became a master at making up elaborate stories and regaling my audience with them.

I got so good that I almost forgot I was not reading the actual words. That did not last long.

My first day at infant school, the teacher announced it was a reading day. He wanted to see what he had to work with. *You have to be kidding me*, I thought upon hearing that unexpected news. I was mortified as I sat there and knew the jig was up. Things got worse when I saw that the teacher actually sat next to each pupil and had them take turns and read out loud. There would be no way for me to regale him with a made-up story. The knot in my stomach tightened. The teacher finally sat down next to me. I mumbled softly so the other schoolkids could not hear that I could not read. The teacher, Mr. Scarsdale, just looked at me, smiled, and said, "That's what I am here for." It did not stop me from feeling six inches tall. I could feel my face had gone beet red.

It was not that simple, however. Mr. Scarsdale, a few days later, met with my mother after school and stated that I needed to be tested. I was horrified, thinking I was a simpleton. Mr. Scarsdale suspected something was wrong with me. No kidding! I could have told them that and saved them the money. "Full-on fruitcake," I'd say. The tests revealed I suffered from dyslexia. Ironic that I could not spell out my own disability.

At least the diagnosis allowed me to realize why I was so far behind the other kids in my class. Mr. Scarsdale agreed to work with me every day after class for thirty minutes. My thought was that the extra half hour would cut into playtime. But those sessions were fantastic and oftentimes stretched to an hour. While initially unbelievably frustrating, I muscled through. Finishing my first *Treasure Island* book was a momentous occasion for me. From that time onwards, reading has been a central love of my life. Thank you, Mr. Scarsdale!

Through it all, my mother was amazing. This woman went out of her way and made me feel good about myself while at the same time encouraging me to push myself. One of her challenges to me was to read ten books in a month. I did say she was a cunning feline. The prize, which she knew I'd bite at, was a trip to the fair that was coming to town the next month. I loved the fair and eating candy floss. Riding the teacup with my mother is one of my most special moments to this day. At this fair, I had also won a prize, which was a vinyl record. It was "Jolene" by Dolly Parton. I had never heard of her or the song before, but I played that record so much my mother would ask me to stop, or I'd wear out the needle. It was more likely her patience wearing thin, but she was always smooth. From that time on, listening to music joined reading as a constant companion.

Trouble in Paradise

"Two days ago, I had this nice, simple life. And now it's a nightmare."
—Dani Ramos in *Terminator: Dark Fate*

Around my seventh birthday, life turned. My mother became ill. I was too young to comprehend the magnitude, and sadly no one sat us down and explained things. I was blissfully unaware. My mother had a series of health issues; first she had a metal rod placed in her knee for God knows what reason and then was diagnosed with late-stage cervical cancer. Again we were left in the dark. I will never forget seeing my mother cry as she stared at her bald head in the mirror. I recall racing over and rubbing the top of her head like a genie's lamp, kissing the top of it, and stating she was beautiful. I was not lying—my mother was beautiful. My dad won the lottery with that lady.

Over the next several months, my mother grew weaker and weaker, and most afternoons I would lay in bed with her and cuddle. I knew something was not right and did everything to comfort her. I even started to behave and not fight incessantly with my two thug brothers. Well, I at least tried to refrain from those dustups.

On May 1, 1976, my father came into our bedroom in the early hours of the morning and stated he was taking our mother for a checkup and instructed us to behave. *Like he had to say that*, I thought at the time. We'd be back fast asleep in moments. I should have known something was up because recently family from Australia and Ireland had turned up for visits. Another telltale sign was when our priest, Father Burke, appeared later that morning and started performing magic tricks with his silver coins.

Ironically, that afternoon was the FA Cup Final—a Super Bowl of sorts. Manchester United, my team and clear favorites, were playing Southampton, a team in the lower divisions. Southampton beat Manchester United and lifted the trophy. It was an omen of things to come.

A few hours later, my father returned and went straight to his bedroom. I only saw the back of his head as he staggered up the stairs. My father was a weak man, but we had no idea at the time how this was going to affect our lives. So, with my father holed up in his bedroom, the priest was left to handle the conversation. Father Burke sat me and my brothers down and told us that our mum was in heaven. I was thinking, *That's impossible. She just went for a checkup. How did that happen?*

Later that same afternoon was the start of my athletic life. I would run around the local school track, which was one block over from our house, crying my heart out, praying to see my mother again, and asking God to bring her back. I sobbed more with every lap around the track, realizing the "Big Guy" was not going to deliver. Those daily runs became the norm, and over time the sobbing lessened, but the feeling of utter loss remained. My family was deeply religious, especially my mother. She had slated me to become a priest and likely had visions of Cardinal Hague. The Catholic Church dodged a bullet there.

In all seriousness, though, on that first day my heart hardened, and I rejected God's existence. If he could take my mother, the most kind and precious person in the world, then I had no purpose or desire for him. Bye-bye, God. That night, as would become habitual, and to my brother's dismay, I played "Jolene" on constant repeat. It was my way of keeping close to my beautiful mum.

Around this time, in addition to the daily runs, I became very interested in sports. Paul became my archrival in all sports and still is to this day. He was also very good for me, as he was bigger and better. I had to work hard to win. In the early days, out of a hundred games, I'd lose ninety-nine of them. We had epic tennis matches, akin to Borg and McEnroe. I took on the persona of McEnroe. I never stopped trying to register a win though. I confess that I smashed my fair share of rackets out of sheer frustration.

This is where I developed my competitive spirit. I wanted to win. I never gave up, and oftentimes in neighborhood competitions I would face off against my nemesis in the finals after beating out the other older kids.

As the saying goes, "When it rains it becomes a shit show." That's not really the right phrase, but this is my story. Shortly after, my father was let go from his managerial position at the Ladbrokes betting shop. Looking back, I think he was fired because he simply could not get his act together. By this time I was now what could loosely be termed cooking and cleaning the house. Needless to say, our place looked like a tornado had ripped through it, and the quality of cuisine, shall we say, was less than desirable. I was nine, after all. Cut me a little slack!

Not long after this, we moved into a council estate and a state-subsidized home. Think rough inner city and then go down a few notches. My father was really lost without my mother. I wish I could have seen this coming, but looking back, this was his demise. We were no help.

My father pivoted for a while and took on a job in the ironworks. It was brutal manual work, but he never complained. He was trying to provide for the family and vowed he'd get us back in a nicer home. He eventually did so, but I truly wish he never did. His desire led to the evilest person in the world entering our lives and bringing utter, unmitigated chaos with her.

Enter the Darkness

"The world is a dangerous place to live—not because of the people who are evil, but because of the people who don't do anything about it."
—Albert Einstein

Diamonds, I'm told, are created under incredible pressure. I know some humans are as well. Surprising things can take root and flourish in the toughest and most inhospitable environments. That's how I sum up the balance of my childhood.

For me, this was the beginning of the worst of times. A cold season, for sure. The windows-frosted-with-no-light kind. The possibility of sunshine was not in the forecast. I did not realize at the time just how bad it would get. It would not take long though.

The worst of times came in the guise of the live-in help. By now my father was working nights in the mill and had four young boys to take care of. Honestly, my skills were not improving, and my father was not up to the task of caring for four young boys. While we were choirboys at the church, we were not choirboys at home. Looking back, we were a handful. To remedy this after tiring out our grandparents, my father placed an ad for "live-in" help. Little did we realize at the time the profound impact this would have on our lives.

Here enters Mary Poppins (MP), real name Veronica, full of smiles. MP came as part of a package deal with her youngest son, Neil. Now there were five boys in the house. Not like our small home needed another two bodies! At first things started off well, and then MP began to morph into her real character, the Darkness. In no time, the Darkness took to punishing us—namely, me, as I was emerging as someone who protected my younger brothers. It was declared that I no longer liked french fries, which were my favorite food. The Darkness moved on to add chocolate to my growing "cannot eat" list. That was a low blow, but in fairness to her I had covertly been engaged in my own psychological warfare. To even the playing field, I had placed worms in her coat pocket and mud in her purse. I denied these allegations under intense interrogation, but I think the jig was up.

In the coming months, the list of things I used to love but that I'd never get my "nashers" on again, as decreed by the Darkness, lengthened. The punishments did not stop at my diet. Worst of all was the monthly haircut. Boy, did she go to town. The embarrassment of her bowl cuts was mortifying. I was laughed at mercilessly by my fellow students. They thought I asked for this style. I suffered in silence.

My father walked around oblivious, on cloud nine and thrilled with his newfound relationship. To my horror, they had become intimate. I found out by walking into dad's bedroom one morning to see her in bed with him. My eyes could not unsee that. I honestly thought she was a witch and had cast a spell on him. I often went to find her cloak and black cat as evidence. While my father was infatuated with the Darkness, I was starting to live in fear. I was not being physically abused but more mentally tortured. My luck was going to run out.

Around this time my father had shifted to permanently working nights to earn more money on his mission to get us into our own home. This left us exposed every night. That's when things turned ugly. The Darkness liked her drink, and not the Shirley Temple type. To be clear, she was five feet tall and ninety pounds soaking wet; however, after knocking a few bottles of cider down nightly, what she lacked in stature was made up in pure evil. This person morphed into a demented goblin. I will never forget the look in her eyes as she scowled and sent us to bed. It was the look of a demon, maybe the devil himself. But up to this point, apart from a few swats on the rear end, there still had been no violence—just an ever-growing list of petty restrictions.

Into the Garden of Evil

"It is our moments of struggle that define us."
—President Trumbull in *Angel Has Fallen*

On one late Saturday afternoon, mental abuse turned physical, and in a really bad way. Escalation time had arrived. It was not a slow progression but went ultraviolent and quickly. The Darkness came screaming into the small living room, where my brothers and I were sitting on the couch. The Darkness demanded to know who had taken the last slice of bread. My father did not work weekends and walked in behind her like an obedient lapdog. The reality was, I had taken it.

I was on the sofa thinking, *Why is she waving a small saucer above her head like a lunatic?* I copped to the infraction. "Do I not like bread now as well?" I wanted to ask but did not have the time to form the words.

Seconds later that ceramic plate came crashing down on my right kneecap. I had slightly less than a second to shift from frowning like she was crazy to gaping like she was crazy. *Off-her-rocker crazy*, I thought as the plate shattered and the broken pieces sliced through my skin, hitting bone. I remember seeing the bone of my kneecap become visible. Then, as if in slow motion, blood spurted out. I remember looking at my younger brothers, who all were clinging to one another in abject fear.

Even then I was looking down at my knee thinking she did not mean that to happen. Wishful thinking on my part, and my error was swiftly corrected. I tried to grab my kneecap, but the blood made me pull away. That's when I realized the Darkness was not done. Her fists rained down, flying into my face, followed by a few kicks a professional football player would have been proud of. I was knocked on my back, spread out on the sofa and anticipating the next blow when thankfully my father grabbed her from behind. Dad pulled her off me, but not before she got a few last kicks in for good measure. It is so hard for me to understand why my father did absolutely nothing. It ranks up there as one of the biggest disappointments in my life. If your only living parent does not care, who will?

Do You Really Want to Hurt Me?

"Life without hope is no life."
—Unknown

The next moments are a blur to me, but I remember my father, along with the Darkness, drove me to the hospital. I vaguely remember my brothers all crying, especially Damian, who looked terrified. My father, incredibly, had not said a word. As we pulled up to the hospital, his words shocked me: "If asked what happened, say you fell in the garden over the vegetable boxes." I then moved to get out of the car but due to injury could not. My father picked me up and carried me inside.

A few months later, my father had saved up and made good on his promise that we would get our own house. We moved to West Hill estate. It was a three-bedroom semidetached place. Life got better, but the plate incident was merely a warm-up for violence to be unleashed. From this point on, I knew I had to get comfortable with the uncomfortable.

Over the next few years, the beatings would occur proportionally to the number of bottles the Darkness guzzled. Her poison of choice was typically cider or sherry. When the brandy was cracked open, that's when my fear shot to another level. To compound the misery, my younger brothers were also beaten. Paul had the awful experience of one time of having a cigarette stubbed out on his bare chest. Neil, her son, was always spared. This was not indiscriminate rage; it was focused. This so-called woman knew whom she was targeting. This was not blackout drunk rage. This was evil. For all the pain and suffering, however, the Darkness did not stop me from loving Neil, and I never held him accountable for the actions of his wicked mother. The child should never be blamed for the sins of their parents.

My father was injured in a bad work accident and shattered several of the vertebrae in his back. This resulted in a lengthy hospitalization and recovery period. This also exposed my brothers and me to increasing danger. Over a period of nights, the Darkness would enter the bedroom where everyone except Paul was sleeping. By this time Paul was wisely spending most nights out at a friend's house. Great parental supervision. Anyway, in a mad rage, the Darkness grabbed each of us and beat us badly.

After the third night, I decided this could go on no longer. I went to bed with my brothers and got them all settled. Then I stood guard and waited for her to come up the stairs. I was only eleven years old—a mere child and not really big enough for the task at hand, but I was committed. I remember the first time she saw me there as she rounded the top of the stairs, swaying from overimbibing, with rage in her eyes. She asked menacingly, "What the fook you think ya doing?" Darkness was from the Liverpool area.

I remember saying calmer than I felt, "You need to go to bed."

She was freakishly strong. Think the possessed child in *The Exorcist*. I was also ready for her attack. I took it well and never allowed her to enter the bedroom. Every attack she made was successfully pushed back. That's not to say I did not take a right old beating, because I did. My nose was bloodied. My face was torn up, as her long fingernails had dug in to my cheeks, and my left eye was swollen from her sick attempt to gouge it out. I took her punishment, but I did not hit back. I often wonder what would have happened if on that night I would have fought back, but my mother had raised me to never hit a lady. I should have qualified that by asking, "What if she was also the devil? Would it still count?" From that night on, the Darkness never broke through my defense of my brothers again. Not through lack of trying on her part, I might add.

I always thought I had taken the brunt of the rage, which was true physically. But my brothers were equally affected. Lying there, hearing fight after fight, I realize the anguish and mental torture my brothers went through fearing they were next. Maybe it was worse for them.

Land of Confusion

"*Trouble* is a polite word for what I am."
—Gabrielle in *Xena: Warrior Princess*

This was *Full Monty* land. Seriously, the film was based in my neck of the woods. The joke is that half the people were all fur coat and no trousers. Half were as dumb as a bag of rocks, and the other half were mental.

This was a scrappy area, and from an early age I was no stranger to work. My first job was as a paperboy, when I had just turned nine years old. I was following in the footsteps of my brother. I remember the pay well. It was a pound weekly, roughly $1.20. It meant the world to me. My father was not a generous man, and I would never receive a penny from him in all my childhood after my mother's passing.

We had been on the council estate for a few months. It was a rough existence. So much so that on many a day I would have to fight my way through a few thugs just to get to school. Ridiculous to think of. I suppose it could have been worse; I could have had to endure critical race theory or sexual orientation classes.

Anyway, the newspaper round was great for me. My fondest recollection is on the Sunday of my first week. I carried my paper bag from the previous six days with no issue; however, I learned painfully that on Sunday the advertisements and special edition catalogues doubled the weight of my bag. My brother Paul carried my bag at the start of my round and then started to walk away to start his own round. He turned around to see me stumbling and collapsing under the weight of the bag into the deep snow. I will never forget how he came back and carried my bag and started delivering a dozen of the papers until such a time as I could continue myself. No matter how I jest, my brother was awesome. The next Sunday I was prepared and carried my own bag.

Throughout this time, to try to forget about the constant beatings, I lost myself in sports, reading, and music. Football, cricket, and tennis were by far my favorites. There was not a sport I did not like. I would play tennis for eight hours straight on weekends and during holiday breaks, weather permitting. I loved walking up with my one well-used racket, wearing only a torn pair of shorts, and beating all the kids and many of the adults. Their twenty rackets and Wimbledon-approved all-white fancy getups were no match.

I had also become quite a good little football player. So much so that the scouts at Rotherham United came to watch one of my games at the local park. These were the very same scouts who had picked out David Seaman, who went on to be the keeper for Arsenal FC and England. I held similar aspirations. After the game, they pulled me aside and asked to speak to my parents. By this time my father had married the Darkness. Dad was all in, and for me it was about surviving. I remember the day well, as Elvis had died a few days earlier, and I played his "Suspicious Minds" track repeatedly. My head was always on a swivel, so a very fitting song for the time. How I wished I could have retuned the Darkness to sender.

I walked with the scouts excitedly back to my place. In those days, it was safer to be around strangers, not that my father and his evil bride cared. Anyway, I introduced the scouts to my father and the Darkness. The scouts asked for me to be allowed to come and try out for the youth team. I was so excited for a second after hearing those words—*special*, *talented*, and *could make it big*. Then my stepmother stood up, crushed my dreams, stated this is not possible, and marched them out the door.

After the scouts left, holy hell broke loose. The Darkness immediately attacked me with a hot pair of curling tongs—you know, the ones with the sharp, pointy tips. How she got them so quickly, God only knows. She demanded to know why I dared to bring people home. She was clearly frustrated I had the temerity to make something of my life. I pulled myself away, but not before the top of my head was running red with blood. I can still feel the indentations on my scalp to this day. I remember crying that night so hard I thought I would never dry my eyes again. Not because of the beating but because my dream of being a football player was shattered. Looking back, I believe I would have given Ronaldo a run for his money—at least that's my story.

Fight Club

"You could fight for God, or country, or family. I do not care, so long as you fight!"
—Robert the Bruce in *Outlaw King*

As I mentioned previously, life on the council estate was tough. Edward Norton would never have survived. Make no mistake, you did not have to go out of your way to find trouble. Trouble would find you. And often. I remember transferring to a new junior school. Anthony Ling was the top dog and made sure everyone knew it, especially me, being the new kid.

I quickly made a name for myself when three of my classmates slapped Dominic, my younger brother, and informed him that Father Christmas was made up. I'd just graduated to knowing the truth about Santa and was not happy either. I remember Dominic crying, but I made those three bullies cry more. Ling did not take kindly to someone administering justice on his turf. Even though I tried to mind my own business when leaving school one day, I was attacked from behind by the aforementioned Mr. Ling. All the other kids seemed to be in the know, as they were all there screaming for Ling to not so kindly remove my teeth. It's always tough being the new guy. I thought, *Sticks and stones may break my bones, but words will never hurt me.* I zoned them out and had the fight of my life. We spun around like alligators killing prey, but I got the better of the exchange and emerged victorious but bloodied. There was a new cock in town—the Desmond.

From there a series of fights sprang up. Another time walking home from school a kid from a nearby Rockingham school named Gary was waiting for me. He was allegedly the cock there, and unknown to me at the time he greatly frowned upon me having the gall to walk through his kingdom to get home. That point was driven home when I walked around the corner of a building, and a house brick was slammed into the side of my head. How my skull took that hit is beyond me. I remember seeing sparks, and I am confident this was my first of many concussions. I was disorientated but managed to keep on my feet.

Gary then attacked and landed a few punches. I was bigger by several inches and tried to jab him back and keep him at arm's length, but my legs were weak and felt like they were made of jelly. Every time I tried to land a punch on him, he countered and made me suffer. After a few moments, I stepped back and can say honestly this was the first fight I had ever run away from—the rationale being he had an unfair assist with the brick. Needless to say, from that day on, I also never took that path home again.

There are so many other scrimmages where I lost teeth, got black eyes, cuts, deep wounds, and more cracked ribs than one might think possible. Looking back, I also had many a concussion. But for the sake of brevity, I'll leave it there. Suffice to say, the trauma at home and violence outside the home was not a good recipe for my educational development. Looking back, it is amazing I really cared, but deep down I always wanted to make my mother proud. I was failing miserably at junior school though. My grades were atrocious. By no stretch of the imagination was I a model student.

You Spin Me 'Round

"Reality is fabricated out of desire."
—Man Ray

I moved on from junior school to Wingfield Comprehensive School. I woke up on the first day of school and was excited. Even the beating administered by the Darkness the previous night did nothing to dampen my enthusiasm. I walked to school with my brother Paul, who was already attending there. Anyway, I got to the assembly, and the principal was welcoming us all and talking us through the process. The first-year students were being split into three groups: A, B, and C classes. A being the high achievers and C, the strugglers.

Even though I had not really applied myself, I had made steady progress. I did not expect to be assigned the C class, also known, and not so kindly, as the Dunce Squad. How could they make such a mistake? Looking back, I was clearly in denial and thoroughly deserved the placement. I remember looking around the class at my fellow C students. My fighting partners, Mr. Ling and Gary, the infamous brick thrower, both were there. *At least they got that one right*, I thought. Several others in the class had severe learning and physical disabilities. I looked in horror and thought, *Why am I here in this freak show of a group?* I even went up to the teacher and asked why I was with this group. I know I did not ask it that politely, but the answer was I was where I was meant to be. I never liked that teacher, Mr. Ralph. In the coming weeks, I became close friends with his wooden cane, which he used to rap my knuckles for misbehaving.

Despite my inexhaustive indiscretions that resulted in punishment, all richly deserved from that first day, I started to apply myself to schoolwork. I am proud to say, in spite of the constant canings, I quickly moved from 1C, the Dunce Squad, to 1B and then on to 1A, the Brain Trust, by the end of the first year. It was a meteoric rise. It helped that Ms. Reynolds taught two of my classes, and I developed a crush on her. I don't think the teachers or my fellow students could believe it. Who could blame them?

While the beatings at home and fights did not lessen, I had finally found the ability to apply myself to school. I became a master of compartmentalization. That class advancement was probably one of my biggest awakenings—the realization that I was smart, but I needed to apply myself. Who knew all that was needed was the power of a beautiful woman?

Walk through Fire

"Anywhere is dangerous if you carry danger with you."
—Iris Murdoch in *The Message to the Planet*

I truly believe my love of sports and losing myself in music and reading gave me the ability to survive. They were my safe space. I went there daily. It helped that the teams I was on were good. We won and won often. For football, we won citywide tournaments, and in cricket we made the county semifinals. I was a first-team player and was very engaged.

Unfortunately, the Darkness had upped her ways and schemes to hurt me. By now she had taken it upon herself to ban me from playing sports as part of her psychological warfare campaign. Many times she would turn up as a sports event was going on, and after she gave me permission to play, she would force me to leave the field. These moments were equally embarrassing and soul-crushing; however, I was not always successful at blocking out my home life when playing sports. I remember one occasion we were playing in an important football match. I got the ball and suddenly had this jarring thought: *Why am I even doing this? It means nothing, and I'm going to go home and be badly beaten.* I recall trying to shake this off and just starting to silently cry on the pitch. The thought chilled me to my core.

I am very thankful that for the most part I kept myself together and was able to protect my brothers and myself the best I could. These sadness attacks picked up in intensity and came out of nowhere. It was like a dark veil sliding over me an inch at a time.

Up until this time, none of my friends had seen any of the abuse taking place. I never talked about it to anyone. At school I was the life of the party. No one would think my life was in turmoil. It was a deep source of shame I kept concealed. But at least it was not known. That soon changed, unfortunately.

One night I was walking home from a friend's house with Colin Smith, who lived a few streets down, when the Darkness walked up the street. From her swaying demeanor, I knew she was looking for trouble. The Darkness just started wailing on me, pulling my hair, and simultaneously punching and kicking me. Colin stared on in shock and me in shame as I silently took the beatdown. The thought that consumed me was not that it hurt. It was more painful than that; now my friends would know. I eventually untangled myself and walked ahead, out of her reach, with Colin. Colin was silent. He clearly could not believe what he had witnessed and obviously had immense trouble processing. What normal young kid would not? The next day I made sure I bumped into Colin early and asked him to keep what he had seen between him and me. Colin asked why she would act like that and if I wanted him to tell his parents. Honest questions of a child that really cut like a blade. I said I would handle it myself. We never spoke of it again, but Colin's kindness inspired me to always look out for others.

Straight to Hell

"It's always darkest before the dawn."
—Florence + the Machine in "Shake It Out"

I thought we had reached the apex of the abuse front, but sadly that was another misjudgment on my behalf. The correction came swiftly. For my fourteenth birthday, I remember walking home from school and thinking what if anything would be in store for me. Maybe this year I'd get a present. One can still dream, right? I walked in the back door of our home.

Immediately, it was obvious the Darkness had been on her poison. She was screaming at my father as she stood in front of the hot chip pan on the gas stove. Incredulously, without a word, she grabbed the pot holders and lifted the chip pan and came my way. Luckily, I reacted quickly and managed to push her arms across her body. She lost control of the pan, and its boiling-hot contents spilled across the carpet inches away. I was stunned but also thankful to not be a major burns victim or worse. But she was not finished. She picked up a stainless-steel fork and threw it at my father. It embedded deeply into his upper arm, and blood started to seep out where the metal teeth of the fork had penetrated deeply. After all, Sheffield, a neighboring city, is famous for steel, and their craftsmanship held up. I stood speechless and then ushered myself to the only bathroom that was upstairs and threw up. I was so numb to the madness but did not know how to escape. That episode was never acknowledged.

Cup Final

Our football team had made it to the county finals. We were playing a local rival, Oldham. The night before the game we should have done what any normal athlete would do—go to bed early. But we were not normal. We prescribed to the Gascoigne, beer-drinking, out-of-control regimen. It's funny because my tolerance for alcohol was ridiculously low, but I made up for that with commitment.

That night we partied hard. We had consumed all the lager in a friend's house and sadly between several of us consumed a large bottle of Cointreau. Before the bottle was cracked open, I knew that nothing good would come from this development. Later we staggered out of our friend's home and somehow made it to the bus stop for the last ride home.

I don't remember leaving the house or taking the bus. It must have happened, as several hours later I awakened and found myself impaled in the middle of a huge rose bush the size of a small tree. My face was slashed by several thorns. Blood was running down my chin. It took me an age to untangle myself. I looked up and surmised that I had fallen straight over the wall upon exiting the bus. I had been out for several hours.

A few hours later, we played in the final. We had tied one all. Due to an earlier altercation, where we had gotten into a fight with a few kids from that school, the headmasters of both schools got together and decided that we would share the trophy.

To this day, the mere smell of Cointreau is nauseating. I think I had alcohol poisoning. For weeks after, every time I would sweat, I smelled like a bloody bag of oranges. It was unfortunately the gift that kept on giving.

Rumble in Rotherham

"Everyone needs a little Rocky in their life!"

—Me

As I turned fifteen, I was now almost six feet tall and getting stronger by the day; however, the beatings at home were relentless. Even though I was now able to fend the Darkness off easily, it was still traumatic having some deranged person attacking, knowing one miscalculation and I could be bodily harmed.

At the same time, the beatings were toughening me up and keeping me laser-focused for any attack. I became a quick study in the finer art of defense and close-quarters combat. Getting kicked in the teeth helped the learning process and the necessity. Many nights I would not catch any sleep, waiting for a sneak attack, and that vigil paid off, as many attacks came. To this day, I am able to drive twenty hours straight without the need for a break.

So that leads us to the big fight. On this night, several of my friends and I were outside a local fish-and-chips shop near Gary Macquire's home, one of my best friends at the time. We had taken to congregating there nightly. My milk round, which paid a few quid weekly, did not cover my lunches at school. The Darkness's policy for me was that if you wanted lunch, then you walked the four miles home and back to school. Quite funny, when the lunch break was less than an hour. I never attempted to make the trip and doubted there would have been anything to eat anyway. Just another opportunity for her to attack. To state that cash was tight would be an understatement. I spoke broke fluently and often. My legs were my only available mode of transportation. That's saying something, as the bus ride was only two pence but still out of reach. Yes, that broke!

We were goofing off outside the chip shop. We usually showed off for the girls, but they were elsewhere this evening. I had just gotten a portion of chips and was thoroughly enjoying myself. This constituted my dinner.

Guy and Gary Noble, two brothers several years older than I, walked up. From out of nowhere, and most certainly not invited, Gary proceeded to reach in and grab a handful of my chips. I quickly pulled back the food out of his reach and shouted for him to get his own.

Gary was an elder statesman pushing midtwenties. Gary was also a known head case, said to have a tile loose and not to be messed with. I decided it was time to test that theory. I did not think about it. I just did it. That's when Macquire, one of the best football strikers I had ever seen, immediately stepped in between us and told Gary that I was sorry. Gary had dispensed with the pleasantries and was making references to rearranging my face. *Charming*, I thought.

I handed my chips over to another friend, Daryl Ashbury, and pushed past Macquire, who was shaking his head and telling me that I was making a big mistake. Everyone except me thought I was not going to fare well and was going to get the proverbial stuffing kicked out of me; however, a calmness overcame me. I knew I was ready to deliver an alternative outcome.

Once a fight was inevitable, my policy was to throw the first punch. Even more so when a bully was involved, but I have never gone out and looked to start a fight. I have found that bullies hate being bullied. They can't handle it, so the faster you manhandle them, the better. I morphed into warrior mode. As Mike Tyson put into words many years later, everyone has a plan until they get punched in the face.

Armed with that critical knowledge, my inside trick to a near spotless fighting career was that I always waved my hands in front of a person, motioning for them to attack me, muttering, "Come on." It kicks in the instinct to mimic. That's when I'd drop the hammer.

As soon as they started to make the same hand signal, I attacked violently with as many punch combinations as possible. All delivered at warp speed and maximum power. This ploy worked beautifully with Gary. He fell right into the trap as if on cue. In less than thirty seconds, Gary was lights out and spread out on the asphalt. I then proceeded to deliver a few beautifully timed kicks, which I should not have, but I was amped up.

That is when I heard his brother release an ear-splitting primal scream. Guy was also known as a someone not to be messed with. Guy then raced toward me with fists swinging. So much for a fair fight. My thought was to make this a twofer takedown. I was now having my own Neo moment from *The Matrix*. I blocked his punches and knocked him straight on his backside. He did not attempt to get back up. That evening I became a mini local fighting celebrity. I felt a little like Rocky, minus the muscles.

This was a confusing time for me. I was a tough guy to my friends and being beaten mercilessly at home. Every night I would walk home from my friends and try and make sense of my life. It was like I lived two lives, and they could not have been more different. I would sing all the way home to try and block out reality. "Sweet Dreams" by the Eurythmics was my favorite at the time. Ironic, because it was getting harder and harder to remember the comforting arms of my mother around me.

Money's Too Tight to Mention

"The devil finds work for idle hands."
—Henry David Thoreau

Regrettably, at this time, the same group of friends and I started down the criminal path. Masterminds, kingpins we were not. I wish there had been some way to have stopped this in its tracks. Candidly, there was no adult supervision around. Not that that is any defense—more that we were incapable of managing ourselves. It was a perfect storm, and we jumped into those waters headfirst with zeal and extreme foolishness. I often wish I could go back and talk to my younger self.

Our crime spree did not start small either. It was of the "go big or go home" variety. It was genius, and I cannot take the credit for any of it. We would seek out where British Telecom was laying their cable. There were usually vast quantities of copper wiring left unguarded overnight. We would hit their stash in the early hours of the morning. We would strip the cable and sell to the local scrapyard. The scrapyard owner really knew where the wire was coming from. He chose to turn a blind eye, but let's just say the conversion rate he offered for wire was on par with the Russian ruble.

To make things work, I had gone all in and quit my milk round so I could focus on this nonsense. Again, inferior thinking at work. All it took was a few weeks of the scrapyard manager, a Fagan-like character, squeezing us further and a few near arrests for me to abandon this endeavor. My earlier dedication folded like a cheap suit. It was good timing for me, as my former crime gang were rolled up and arrested a few weeks later. The lesson is that you cannot hit the same place twice, or don't do bad shit in the first place.

I was once again without income. Sadly, for a while I "liberated" money from the pockets of the other kids' trousers hung up in the boy's locker room. That yielded little success and made me feel dirty. I knew I was stealing. Looking back, I am so ashamed, but I also know what being constantly poor can do to you. While I cringe at the memories, it was take this money or go hungry. Until you have been in this position, it is also not wise to judge. Stating you would never do this or that is pointless until you are confronted with the situation. I know this through firsthand experience.

Escalation of Desperation

"When you are in a hole, stop digging."
—A blue-collar philosopher

This led me to my first brush with the law. My not doing bad shit did not last long. I was digging myself a hole I knew was going to get real deep, real fast. I decided it was a good idea to break into the local pub. At this time my nightly fight sessions with the Darkness had changed. My father was recovering in hospital. I started picking the evil one up from Wincobank a few miles away. This happened several times weekly. I'd meet her on the last bus ride of the night and walk her home. This, in my thinking, was a better alternative than fighting in close quarters at the top of the stairs. The open space allowed me to hone my defensive skills and take the fight out of her quicker. I was learning how to defeat her.

On those walks home, we sometimes stopped in the local pub so she could have one last drink, because every drunk always needs just one more. I broke into that very same pub. I smashed the window in the back door and quickly went to the bar area and picked up the glass jar full of change and emptied the till, which had the float. For me, it was a nice haul. I should have left it there and learned from my friends not to hit the same place twice. I wished someone had dropped some Confucius wisdom on me: "A man who has committed a mistake and does not correct it is committing another mistake." But my brain at fifteen had not fully formed. I did not even know that Chinese fellow existed. Unintelligently, I hit the pub again about a month later. The great man from Qufu no doubt rolled his eyes at the lack of learning. This time the landlord was alert, and cops were called. I was driven to a cell.

It further solidified in my mind that I was destined for prison. I remember after being put in the holding cell I would not give my name up for several hours until one of the officers got a little aggressive, shall I say, and put a squeeze on my chat box and encouraged me to realize it was in my best interest. I was terrified of what the Darkness was going to do now. Thankfully, my father, who was now back home, turned up at the police station. He told me to keep this between the two of us, and he never said a word to the Darkness. He did not need to tell me twice.

Enough Is Enough—the Final Straw

"Final thoughts are so, you know, final."
—Craig Armstrong

In my final year of comprehensive school, my father was once again having surgery difficulties with his back and was getting an additional operation. Nothing new there. This saw him recovering in hospital and away from home again. One Saturday morning, the Darkness came into our bedroom as I was luckily walking out of the room. She saw me walking over, but she made a path for Damian, who was laid in bed, eyes wide open, terrified. I launched my body and landed on her, my body weight taking her down. I pushed her back toward the door as she grabbed my hair and tried to scalp me with her fingernails. The Darkness was way past drunk and again went to punch me. This time I ducked under her swinging arm, but instead of taking my usual defensive position I reached out and grabbed her by the neck and pushed her out of the room to the top of the stairs. Anger took over, and I launched her down the stairs, where she went head over heels and landed heavily at the foot of the stairs. I walked down after her, slapped her a few times hard, squeezed her neck firmly, and told her if she ever touched one of my brothers or me again that I would kill her. In that moment, I meant it. Something in her eyes told me that she got my message. She never raised a finger again after that. I hoped my mother would understand that I had to hit a female, but only because she was pure evil.

Livin' on a Prayer

> "It's your life. Live it your way."
> —Bob Hoskins

Shortly after the stairs incident, my father was released from hospital and was back home. It was less than a pleasant rainbow and sunshine homecoming. The moment reminded me of my favorite song at the time, "Cruel Summer" by Bananarama, which I blasted nightly on the same old player. While not summer, it was certainly a cruel time.

I returned home from school late after practice, and immediately upon entering the back door, my father was in my face. Incredibly, the Darkness was in the background—crying, stating I had attacked her, and playing the victim. It was an Oscar-worthy performance and would have been funny if she had not terrorized our family for over six long years. Things got bad fast. My father began to prod me in the chest, demanding to know why I had attacked his wife and my mother. That was too much for me. I pushed his finger away and angrily stated that woman was not and would never be my mother. I was not going to fight my father. I was not going to let her win, so I immediately turned around and left home to never return.

I was just shy of sixteen. I was now on my own. I was also homeless. It was terrifying, but I also felt I would somehow get through it. Even though I was now out of the house, I kept an eye on my brothers like a hawk and knew if she ever hurt them I'd follow through with my promise.

My experiences to date had instilled in me a purpose that I was meant to protect others, and I am thankful for that.

Where You Going to Run To?

"Don't let the fear of striking out hold you back."
—Babe Ruth

That first night out in the world by myself was rough, to say the least. I tried to visualize Dickens's "best of times," but all that came into focus was a very bleak outlook. Near the park where I played tennis, and just down from my school, I knew there was an abandoned house I walked past daily.

That's where I decided to sleep on my first night of freedom. It was fitting that Michael Jackson's "Thriller" was my go-to song at the time. I was simultaneously scared and excited. I have no idea why I did not go straight to one of my friends. I think at the time I needed to process things and talk things through with my mother, in heaven. I always thought she was watching me. That was odd, as by then I had no belief in God.

Anyway, I sat there in this dilapidated house. There was no flooring on the ground floor, and the stairs were bare of steps. No stairway to heaven here. Thinking I'd be safe upstairs, I carefully traversed them. I laid down in the corner of the darkened room and attempted sleep. A few hours later, upon waking up shivering, I realized there was little left of the roof. The moon was shining brightly, illuminating the room. I looked up at the beams and saw demonic symbols had been carved in them. It was terrifying. I had images in my head of being tortured and sacrificed in some kind of cult ritual. Candidly, I never liked horror films and still do not to this day. As I processed the carvings, my imagination ran amok. I do not think I have ever moved faster, and in seconds I leaped down the stairs and fled into the park. It was an age before I thought my heart was not going to pump through my chest.

I spent the next few days and nights living in the park under the bushes away from the buildings. I felt like Oscar in *The Muppet Show*. In those times, there was not a homeless problem. I was the only vagrant in the park, but why take the chance of being discovered by others? This was a new low point for me. I contemplated if anything mattered in life. I never wanted to end my life, but I questioned why I was living it. I was losing hope. These thoughts were also becoming harder and harder to push back.

I would like to say I was working up a plan, but I was not. Sadly, with no master plan in sight, I got into more mischief to feed myself. Let's just say the police would frown upon my actions. But I plead the Fifth on those. Then an idea came to me. It should have surfaced sooner, but then I was a hormonal, deranged fifteen-year-old with semiformed decision-making skills.

My eureka moment was to get a job from a family friend whom my older brother Paul had worked for. It was my last hope—really my only hope. I had no other options other than to turn to illegal methods, and I did not like the prospects of that.

Saving Myself

"Your fear is 100 percent dependent on you for its survival."
—Steve Maraboli

Before leaving home, I knew Paul worked in a fish-and-chips shop. The owner was named Malcolm. Malcolm owned a few businesses—a fish-and-chips shop and a convenience store—at the time. I also knew he passed daily a few miles away from where I was on his way to work. I also knew the red Datsun truck he drove, having seen him pick up my brother several times.

The very next morning I waited and flagged him down. Maybe there was someone looking out for me after all, as that day he hired me, and I started to learn a trade. I do not even want to think what would have happened if the meeting did not occur. Ultimately, Malcolm truly saved my life, but not without further trauma.

I was immediately put to work in the fish-and-chips shop. At the beginning, which is a trend in my life, and until I developed self-belief, I thought I would never learn how to perform the tasks and felt utterly hopeless. But there was never a thought about quitting. While not a rocket scientist, I knew I had no other options. This was my last ticket to freedom. Leaving this job, I knew, would never lead to anything positive.

After a few weeks, I began to get a grip on the tasks. Malcolm also took me in and gave me a small room in the back of his home. For the first time in a long time, I had a settled and safe environment. These experiences are really why I have made a lifelong mission of supporting the less fortunate. Everyone should have a safe place to rest their heads nightly. No exceptions!

Within several months, I had progressed from peeling five or six fifty-pound tubs of potatoes daily and cleaning the floors to working on the shop floor. Hard work and application were paying off. The business was extremely busy and, in all honesty, intimidating. Malcolm had developed a vibrant business that he built around the concept of having the "freshest cod in town." It was brought in from the coast daily. Years later I would drive over a hundred miles each way to Hull and pick up that fresh cod myself. Looking back, it was my first illustration of the power of differentiating a business. The business was generating over £4,000 per week, and at the time fish-and-chips were £0.80. In today's terms, these sales would be generating over £20,000 per week, or £1 million-plus per year—from a small fish-and-chips shop about half the size of a Subway restaurant.

We Are the Champions

After playing a pickup football game in the park, the very same one I had stayed at upon leaving home, I was approached by two gentlemen: Buster and Bob, an odd couple. Buster was in his midthirties and rail thin. Bob was built like a sumo wrestler and much older. They were coaches of an under-eighteen boys football team. Both could still play. Bob was so light on his feet it was hilarious and remarkable to watch. Imagine a hippo with the lightning-fast footwork of a ballerina.

They wanted to recruit me and asked me if I had any friends who would like to join. In the end, five of my friends joined. We immediately dominated the league and won the championship. That game was magical to me. We won 5–1. All our friends visited. It was quite the celebration.

Scouts from around the area and beyond attended our games. We were all excited and thought we were going to be playing in the big leagues very soon. Two of my teammates—Kenny Macquire and Darren Fletcher—were actually picked up by professional teams. Kenny, the best striker I had played with, was picked up by Barnsley. Darren, a midfield wizard, was picked up by Huddersfield. I thought Daryl Ashbury, my best friend, and I would also have been picked up, but it was not to be. That final ended up being my last competitive match; however, I quickly became laser-focused on my career.

A Pit Life Is Not for Me

By now the majority of my friends—and schoolmates, for that matter—were signed up as coal miners. I think I knew of one or two from the entire school year who actually went on to college. It was a completely foreign thing for anyone in our standing. Mining was the top industry by far at the time. Their facilities dotted the landscape in every direction. This was mining country. It was a very hard way to make a living. Our community and the surrounding ones were their ready-made recruitment market. The pay was decent. Darren Grey, one of my friends and newly minted miner, encouraged me to give it a try. I did for a day. I could not wait to get above ground. It took me bloody hours to get the soot out of my hair and face. It was a terrifying experience, and one I would never repeat. A pit life was not for me. I have a lot of respect for those who did choose that profession.

The Incident

"Be afraid. Be very afraid."
—Veronica Quaife in *The Fly*

Most nights after work I would join Malcolm at the Sportsman pub for after-hours drinking sessions. The landlord, Terry, would operate a kind of speakeasy. Malcolm and several of his friends would turn up for the after-hours drinking sessions. I had tired of throwing up lager and graduated to sipping Bacardi and Coke and later brandy and champagne. A couple of off-duty police officers would also be present, and they shall remain nameless. Often Malcolm's cousin Barry would join us. Barry was a huge man, easily six foot seven, and weighed in at almost three hundred pounds. Barry was also openly gay, which was strange for the times, but he was always friendly to me. On many occasions, Barry would stay overnight with us.

One night after a drinking session, I was in bed and sound asleep when my door violently opened. I was still in a daze and felt someone grabbing me and powerful hands turning me over in the bed. It took a few seconds before I realized it was Barry. *What the hell?* I thought. I tried to pull away, but I was pinned under his weight, and he landed a few painful blows to my head and grabbed the back of my head and pushed me down into the pillow. The more I tried to struggle, the more I gasped for air. At one point I thought I was going to pass out as I struggled to get air into my lungs. Thankfully, I felt the pressure come off the back of my head. The relief did not last long, as I felt my underpants being torn off and a sharp, stabbing pain as he inserted himself in me. This fat fuck was raping me. I could not believe this was happening. That I was also powerless only added to my frustration. As hard as I tried to get him off me, I could not. The pig simply collapsed on me and breathed heavily in my ear. It was disgusting. I was having an out-of-body experience and thought, *This cannot be happening to me.*

It was over quickly, but it felt like a lifetime. The physical pain I felt was like no other I had experienced, and I'd had my fair share of injuries. Barry got up eventually. He looked down at me with a smug smile on his sick face. He told me if I told anyone he'd say that I had "fucked him freely" and left the room. I laid there for several minutes in the fetal position and cried my eyes out. I could not believe this had happened. This was worse than all the beatings I had received combined. This cut deeper. It was humiliating. How could someone who was supposed to be so tough have allowed this to happen? I was consumed by shame and blamed myself. To make things worse, I thought everyone would think I was to blame. That I was somehow responsible. I should have said something, but the shame won through each time. I also knew Barry was friendly with the police officers. They would not take the word of a troubled teen over their friend. I felt utterly helpless. And worse, I felt absolutely worthless. Music, which previously lifted my spirits in times of darkness, made no impact. I stayed in my room and cried all weekend.

From that night on, I wedged a chair under the door handle, and whenever I saw Barry I would immediately bolt to my room and barricade myself inside. When I close my eyes, I still vividly recall that night. Even today it gives me the shivers.

Moving Up

"Learning is always a painful process."
—Lucy in *Lucy*

Over the next several months, I pushed the rape further into the recesses of my mind. Truth be told, I blocked it out and even started to deny it ever happened. Music was also back on the menu. Elton John's aptly named new single "I'm Still Standing" was my record of choice and helped me get through the process. The reality is, I was barely standing, but I pushed forward. I started to actually refer to the rape as "the incident," further in denial. Instead, I focused on saving money and got into the rhythm of work.

I fell into a daily routine in which I had breakfast and either biked to work, approximately eleven miles one way, or I took a lift in with Malcolm. I always enjoyed those rides, where we would spend time talking about the business. These lessons were invaluable and helped me to understand the business through his lens. Initially, I did not follow half the things he was saying, but little by little I caught on to more.

Malcolm talked about the need for great service but to not rush people out of the shop. He explained why he actually liked to allow a line to form. His reasoning was that people saw others queuing and instinctively thought the food must be worth the wait. Another lesson was Malcolm's obsession with cleaning the front windows—his logic being that people could see in the cooking area as they looked in, and he wanted the shop to be spotless. Same thinking for all posters to be mounted with no tape visible. He would often repeat, "People buy with their eyes."

I suppose the biggest lesson was the value Malcolm placed on differentiation. He often would state there are chippies all across town. What makes customers drive out to me? Along the way, I also came to learn that Malcolm, while a wealthy businessman, had also suffered his own setbacks. He had owned a very poplar nightclub that had gone bankrupt. At the time, Malcolm had been in a car accident that had left him with burns on 80 percent of his body, and somehow he managed to fight through it. When I asked how he kept going, he responded simply, "What else was I going to do?" In reality, Malcolm had put me through a master class in branding, marketing, and dealing with adversity. It was priceless.

After several weeks learning the back of the operation, I was moved to the front of the shop. Instantly the same feeling of inadequacy surfaced. *Here I go again*, I thought, just like my go-to song by Whitesnake. This place had a long line of customers out the door from the moment it opened until it closed. It was terrifying, and there were several people serving who were like synchronized swimmers moving elegantly around one another, and then there was me. All had their task, and all knew it down pat. I was slow, hesitant, and I'm sure had a full-on deer-in-the-headlights stare. The funny thing was that I was only serving up peas, beans, curry, and gravy, the lowest rung on the ladder, and could not keep pace.

Over the next year, I graduated from running the till, assisting in bringing the raw products to the "fryer," who was the quarterback of the operation, and then on to finally serving the customers. Each day I got just a little better and quicker. After a while I was moved up to assistant fryer and then finally promoted to the manager of the shop. I had just turned seventeen years old.

I learned so much in that operation—how practice makes perfect and that if you apply yourself, you can achieve things you at first think are impossible. Also, how to build a brand was ingrained in me. I also got my hands burned very badly several times when floating battered cod into the hot fryer. It underscored that you needed to always be focused and you could get hurt at any moment. That led to my first workplace violence incident and brush with death.

Night of the Three Idiots and the Sharp Knife

"Warriors, come out to play."
—Luther in *Warriors*

I was now the manager of the chippy. Malcolm would call around eight each evening and ask about the business. You have to give it to the man—he kept his finger on the pulse of the business. Malcolm was always interested in understanding the challenges of the day before he went out drinking. I remember cod quality was a big problem, as was labor and other supply challenges. Seems like the greatest hits never change.

Candidly, Malcolm's attention to detail was incredible and is a lesson I have taken to heart throughout my career. If you care about the small things, just think how you feel about the big things. This was even more impressive when I found out later he could not read or write. What he could do was make money. It taught me to never discount anyone and that all people could add value and be valuable.

On this particular night, I was taking the nightly call with Malcolm from the back of the store, when there was a commotion coming from the front. The shop was temporarily empty of customers, and the servers were having a well-deserved break in the back of the store with me. Seconds later the employee-only door was being banged on. It was a sturdy door and had a secure lock. The door handle was being violently yanked. The bolt held, but I knew it would not hold out much longer. I was still on the phone with Malcolm, wondering what the hell was happening, but I moved the phone to my right ear and leaned through the entryway to see what was going on. The next thing I knew, a young man, referred to as Idiot Number One, was jumping over the counter and charging at me. I knew he was not asking for directions. He confirmed this when he started demanding the money in the register. I momentarily dropped the phone, and as the man approached, I headbutted him hard. I thought that was a good answer. I heard bone crunch as he went flying back into the storefront. I was thankful the screaming had stopped. I hate tough guys. That's when the bolt on the employee-only door finally gave, and Idiot Number Two stormed into the back of the store. The two female servers ran to the back of the room and hugged one another and watched with hands over open mouths, clearly terrified.

Instinctively, I quickly reached the twenty-five-gallon boiling pot of mushy peas that I had been marinating on the stove. I picked it up by its metal side handles, fully knowing I would burn my hands badly in the process. I also knew I had no other options. I knew offering a cup of tea would not work. I fought through the pain but held on for dear life and threw the molten contents on Idiot Number Two, who was charging toward me and now only a few feet away. Idiot Number Two screamed and tumbled backward. In seconds, he had thankfully lost his footing and was spread-eagled on his back, jerking the hot contents off him. He looked like he was having an epileptic fit. Idiot Number Two was temporarily out of commission and posed no further problem. It would have been a funny sight if the setting was less dangerous.

Unknown to me, more trouble was ahead. Idiot Number Three had also now jumped over the counter and joined the fray. My adrenaline was stoked. I was ready.

Prior to taking the call, I had been skinning and boning cod fillets. The cod and the extremely sharp knife were still on the counter. The knife was in reach of Idiot Number Three as he moved in to confront me. Idiot Number Three picked up the knife and approached me and echoed the same demands as his would-be-attacker friends who were still in a heap, kissing the tiled floor. Clearly, they had very limited vocabulary.

The two ladies were now screaming and loudly crying out. I registered it but tried to block out all distractions. My full attention was on the knife and Idiot Three, who jabbed its sharp blade in front of me. Eventually, Idiot Number Three lunged forward. I shifted to my right, quickly squatted, and allowed the knife to sail past me over my left shoulder. Idiot Number Three had overextended and lost balance, his momentum taking him forward. I spun around, grabbed his arm, and snapped down. Idiot Number Three yelped and released the knife and fled with the other two attackers. I had survived the three idiots and the sharp knife. I was the talk of the town after. I'm not sure if I addressed that in a politically correct fashion. Again, you decide, but I do like that justice was served.

First Political Awakening

"I have been sleepwalking for too long. And now I wake up."
—Pierre Cadault in *Emily in Paris*

Ironically, at this time, the miners all over the country were striking. Arthur Scargill, the union president, was riling up his members. My brother Paul, who was working in the automobile business in a management position, was a big supporter of Arthur and the unions. So was Malcolm, who would ask me to give the local miners our leftover food each evening. We did this for years.

I was conflicted. I was a big fan of the miners. After all, I knew so many of them. I was not, however, a fan of the unions. I was not then and have never been. They were making outlandish demands from my perspective. Initially, the press was making Arthur out to be a latter-day Robin Hood. That's until the violence erupted that they had helped stoke. Sound familiar?

I actually liked the female prime minister, Margaret Thatcher, who had a different vision for the UK. In fact, I was the sole Conservative Party member in my known orbit. I always wanted to meet Mrs. Thatcher, and it is great sadness I never got to speak to the Iron Lady and tell her how she inspired me in my youth. How a daughter of a shopkeeper could go on to run the country was truly inspirational. She underscored that it did not matter where you started in life but what you made of your life. Thank you, Maggie.

One night, when I had closed the fish-and-chips shop down, there was a loud knock at the door. I went to see who it was. I saw it was a handful of men wearing their mining jackets. They asked for the scraps. I explained that we had already given the scraps away to another group moments before. The miners were not happy, and one of them pushed me back harshly and screamed a few crude words. Luckily, the shove was in the direction of the door, which I was easily able to close.

That night those miners put a brick through our window. That was the last night I fed the miners. It was also the night I took an interest in politics. I would not get active for a while, but the seed was planted. I have never seen unions to be the answer.

Expanding My Skill Set

"Sometimes you can't see what you're learning until you come out the other side."
—Diana Prince in *Wonder Woman 1984*

The following year Malcolm opened the first video shop in Rotherham. This was years before Blockbuster was even a thing. Betamax tapes were the tape of choice. No one had heard of VHS. From day one I was slotted to be the manager in addition to managing the fish-and-chips shop. It was an awesome and very busy time for me. The lessons were ridiculous. First there was the day-to-day management of the video shop business as well as overseeing the chippy and grocery store. Hard work, commitment, and getting up at silly-o-clock became my best friends. Managing the video business was totally different from my other experiences. There was managing the inventory, purchasing the films, and managing the check-in and checkout progress and early ordering.

The responsibility of picking out the films to buy, how many copies, and which ones to pass on, I found out quickly, made the difference in running a profitable business. The margin for error was slim. Additionally, the entire service experience was more like that of a hotel check-in than grabbing a quick coffee or quick meal. It needed a more polished approach. I was learning new skills on a daily basis.

I actually got to convert an old building that had been a public toilet years prior. I oversaw the layout and set up the store, shelves, and merchandise. I was a team of one, and I was working around the clock. I had also purchased a 50cc Honda motorcycle to get me to and from work. In addition to managing the businesses, I was also responsible for banking the takings daily and then later to prepare and manage the taxes for the growing business that now included a butcher's shop. Work had become all-consuming; I really had no time for friends—work was my friend. I had just turned eighteen, and like the recent McDonald's advertisement stated best, I was lovin' it.

I was all focused on my career, so much so that I had stopped going to the nightclubs on Friday nights with my brother Paul and his friends. To be honest, alcohol just did not sit right with me. After just a couple of pints, my head would be spinning around like a crashing helicopter. Without fail, I would be praying to the porcelain bowl after each session. What made it worse was that Paul and the gang could literally drink for England. We found a workable solution through trial and error. Our pub crawl comprised visiting ten pubs before we hit the club. I knew this group would never let me get away with my brandy and Babycham, so instead I would get half a pint after every two or three pubs visited. Even then the porcelain god was beckoning. What a bloody lightweight!

The upside is, I got to spend more of my money on clothes, which had become my favorite thing. Armani was my designer of choice. When I got my first Armani suit and black suede shoes, I cried. In time, I was buying *Miami Vice*-style jackets, growing my hair long like my hero at the time, Simon Le Bon, and even got my ears pierced—very edgy indeed for those times.

One day my brother told me that his friends thought I was wasting my time and that I would never get out of here. That the sooner I realized that the better. That made me more determined than ever to create something of myself. I was now ordering more aggressively new video releases for the store. Making big bets on some over others. It was a hit from day one. It was also a gold mine. It far exceeded the sales of the fish-and-chips shop. I also got to build a team. I performed all interviews and did all hiring and firing. I was evolving as a businessman, if not a person.

Risky Business

"It takes talent to make money, but it takes brains to keep it."
—Robert McCall in *The Equalizer 2*

After turning nineteen years of age, I began to experience difficulties with Malcolm. Life was not easy. He began to make it a habit to question my every decision. It seemingly did not matter that the businesses were running better and smoother than ever. My favorite song at the time was "Never Ending Story," and this felt like I was living in never-ending misery.

Malcolm had recently become serious with a new girlfriend. She did not like having me around. I was barely ever there, but I was becoming a problem. Things bubbled over one Boxing Day, which is the day after Christmas and a big British football day, for the uninitiated. Malcolm came to see me in my room and told me to go and open the fish-and-chips shop that evening. We had previously agreed this would be my night off, as the local pub, the source of the majority of our night business, which was situated around the corner from the shop, was also closed. The bottom line: there would be no business. Eventually, I agreed to open the shop, and in fact we only got a handful of customers. But that night I knew I had to move on.

A few days later, I was thinking constantly about what I could do to provide security and safety for myself. I was on pins and needles just waiting for the guillotine to drop. I had packed and unpacked my belongings several times, but in reality I was scared to leave and be on the streets again. I knew nothing good ever came from that. I had no escape path, and I hated myself for that. So I sucked it up and did what was necessary to survive.

Several weeks later I saw that the Tattoo, a large fair, was coming to Rotherham, and they were looking for food vendors. A friend's father had an old caravan I was thinking about purchasing as a stopgap and temporarily moving into if things turned pear-shaped, which looked more likely by the day. Then I would just have to solve for getting a job. No small feat. *One step at a time*, I constantly had to remind myself.

Then I had the idea of converting a caravan into a mobile food shack. That next week I went to the motor auction and brought a real beauty of a caravan for next to nothing, but it had good bones. Then I went about upgrading the cooking stove and making it workable. It was a sight for sore eyes. It would not meet any of today's standards, but it worked. I now had purchased my first car that could pull the food truck and was all set. The car was more beat up than the caravan, and that's saying something.

I quit my job and boldly set out on my own. Whitesnake's "Here I Go Again" still played in my head. I was going to follow the fair around and make a living. The reality is, this is what I always wanted to do ever since I had watched a news alert about a helicopter crash on the way to Alton Towers, a Walt Disney–like theme park, only smaller. Anyway, the crash had killed a wealthy businessman and his family. I remember being sad, but that one newsbreak solidified for me that I was going into business and would one day have my own helicopter. My future goals were set that day. It was time for me to make my play.

Leading up to the fair, I had done a few dry runs serving outside several construction works. They served the purpose of helping to ramp up my service times. For the fair, I had purchased thousands of hot dogs, hamburgers, and rolls. I was unknowingly doing all the right things, keeping the menu simple for maximum throughput. I hired Dominic for the event, and off we went. Basically, doing all the things instinctively that I would see in a more structured and formalized manner in later years; however, for all the planning, let's just say the day did not go anything as planned.

En route to the event, I was traveling up a long stretch of road that narrowed in different parts. My new favorite song, "Smalltown Boy" by Bronski Beat, blasted out through the speakers. I felt they were singing about me. The lyrics resonated. While I think I am a great driver, history may render a different verdict.

Anyway, we reached the narrow part of the road, and the back tire of my car clipped the curb. I knew nothing good was going to come from that. Instantaneously, the caravan careened from side to side, and with each passing second moved more and more out of control. Moments later the caravan started to turn sideways, and it pulled the car violently with it. In the next moment, I remember crashing into a lamppost, ripping it out of the ground, and coming to a stop in an open field. Thank God there was no one hurt or any building in the vicinity. I recall stumbling out. I was so relieved to see Dominic was also unharmed.

In that moment, the business went down the tubes—or more accurately, wrapped around a lamppost. I was distraught—in shock, even—as I struggled to catch my breath as the consequences hit home. Not only had I lost my new venture; I had also taken out a loan on the car from a loan shark that still needed to be paid off. Now I had no income, and I was forced to sell my record player (my prized possession), along with some of my clothes, but at least I avoided any unpleasant late-night visitors. What should have been the start of my new venture had ended in flames.

I remember moping around, visiting my friends, and just getting drunk—not a hard thing for me—and really doing nothing productive. I was falling back into bad habits. One morning, after spending the night at Gary's place, whose parents were awesome, I woke up and felt that my brother's friends had been right all along: I'd never amount to anything if I did not act now. The thought shocked me into action.

PART 2

YOUNG MAN IN A HURRY

Entering the Corporate World

"Curiouser and curiouser."
—Alice in *Alice in Wonderland*

As luck would have it, I saw an advertisement for a trainee manager of Wimpy Hamburgers in the papers. This was fate, as I had not read the papers in years. I applied, and to my disbelief I was hired. Clearly, they did not have high standards.

My initial thought was that I wanted to learn all the skills of a large enterprise and then apply them to my own concept that was just taking shape in my mind. The game plan was set. A quick in, learn all you can, and get out play. Sounded good at the time anyway.

Instantaneously, I loved the professionalism of the business and the employees and managers. To this day, I am thankful for the skills and opportunity they provided me. My experiences in the fish-and-chips shop served me well, but this operation was in another league. There were eight cashiers, each with a runner speeding up orders. There were two people pouring fountain drinks and two more people feeding the broiler—one for the patties and one for the buns. Then there was the chute captain and managers and supervisors at each station. There were cleanup crews for the back kitchen and the customer dining areas. There was even a team that handled the children's parties that were back-to-back every ninety minutes on weekends, with a few others sprinkled in every weekday. There was a place and procedure for everything it seemed. This machine exceeded the revenues of the fish-and-chips shop for the week in a few hours.

The sheer speed of the operation was something I had never come close to experiencing before. I watched as the orders were constantly called out and thought this time I had really outstripped my capacity to perform. For the first week, I finished my shifts more mentally than physically drained. My day off was scheduled for Sundays. For the first several months, I never took a day off, and most days I worked double shifts. There was simply too much to learn, and the stakes of failure were too grave.

When I was not in control of the shift as manager in charge, I would read manuals, watch corporate training videos, and ask endless questions of the more seasoned managers and full-time employees—who in most instances actually knew the inner workings of the operations better than most of the managers. It underscored a key lesson that you can learn from everyone and that every individual adds value. I also constantly shadowed those I was impressed with, endlessly picking up tricks of the trade.

Within half a year, I not only mastered the business; I was managing a secondary Wimpy restaurant in Sheffield. I had to pinch myself. From there I was slated to open the franchisee's latest restaurant in Wakefield. A few months later, Burger King acquired Wimpy, and I opened the first Burger King in Rotherham. It was an awesome achievement, and I was proud to do that in my "adopted" hometown. Ironically, it was a few steps away from the same police station I had visited just a few years previously.

The hits kept coming. Shortly after, I took over the Wakefield location as well. The days when I thought I would truly end up in prison were moving further into the rearview mirror. I had made my way out. Truthfully, the days were long, and I was burning the candle at both ends but loving life.

It was at the Wakefield restaurant where I was able to start helping those less fortunate than myself. As the business was growing, I was able to hire a couple of young men who had previously served prison time. To be honest, this was not a poplar move at the time, but I felt we have to give people a second chance. The irony was not lost on me that I could easily have been in their place—that I was no better than them and absolutely was not in a place to judge. I remembered how Colin, back in my youth, had tried to help me, and I was compelled to give it try. Eventually, there were several ex-convicts hired, and although my initiative had mixed results, providing a different future for even one person, in my opinion, was worth it.

Financially, things were great. I was basically working nonstop and had no opportunity to spend my salary. In no time, I had amassed £10,000 in my Halifax savings account. I thought I was a millionaire. This in itself was a haul; again, something I never thought possible—that is, unless I robbed a bank. So much so that I purchased my first home before my twentieth birthday. It was also in Kimberworth, within spitting distance of Ewers Road, and went for the princely price tag of £27,000. Just a few short years prior, I could not have imagined this would ever be possible. Cleaning or breaking into the house, yes. Owning it, hell no! This house, to me, represented more than a home. For the first time since my mother had died, over a decade earlier, it provided me with safety and security. It may as well have been a palace. It was mine. While it was so small that you could not swing a cat without hitting the walls, it was my home. In my mind, I was truly living large. I also upgraded my car and purchased a used classic BMW with a custom plate: CHERISH. I loved that car.

End of the Road

"Stop cheating on your future with your past. It's over."
—Unknown

They say things get easier with practice. I think some things should never have been done in the first place, like crashing your car—*again*. This is where I may lose you in believing I possess mad driving skills. Here goes! I was on my way to Wakefield, about a hundred miles up the M1, a busy motorway, early one Friday morning. I was exhausted from working both venues, and for the first and only time in my life, I fell asleep at the wheel. I crashed straight into the roundabout, thankfully not hurting anyone—mainly because no other idiot was on the road at four in the morning—but did I manage to total my beloved Cherish. Looking back, I believe God, with a major assist from my mother, was looking after me. Elton John's "I'm Still Standing" reemerged as my old faithful. I thought it was most fitting.

The next several months were painful, as I was forced to make the daily trip on my peashooter of a motorbike that had a top speed of about thirty-five miles per hour. Getting my next car could not come soon enough.

The Kidnapping of Ronald McDonald

On a funnier note, at this time while running the Wakefield store, I was embroiled in a fierce competition with the Wimpy Sheffield team to see who could produce the highest hourly revenue. I started off with a huge disadvantage: the population of Sheffield dwarfed that of Wakefield. It was not even close. To make things worse, in Wakefield, we operated just up the street from McDonald's, which famously walked its Ronald McDonald character in the downtown square to stir up business. At Wimpy we had the Beefeater icon. In my opinion much tougher.

One Saturday I let the competitive juices redline and decided that one way to nullify the McDonald's threat was to "kidnap" Ronald. Okay, before you get all riled up, steady down. It was not a kidnapping in the real sense of the word. Let me explain. My business was opposite a church and graveyard. I suited up and went off in search of my redheaded and spooky-looking foe. I offered the kid in the Ronald outfit five quid to sit in the graveyard for an hour in a "friendly kidnapping." It must have been comical to see the Wimpy Beefeater man walking hand in hand with Ronald. I thought we made a dashing couple; however, as hard as I tried, we could not beat our Sheffield store—but we got an A for effort.

Shattered Dreams

"Yup, flying through the air. This is not good."
—Ricky Bobby in *Talladega Nights*

At this time I was making good on learning and applying the lessons learned in the corporate world for my own enterprise. Admittedly, I was a tad delayed. I was desperate to get that helicopter and make good on my vision. I started to spend serious time and research on my idea—my very own restaurant company, Prince of Cod. I did not want a fish-and-chips shop. I wanted a restaurant and not just one. I wanted a whole chain. It would span the UK, and it would be epic. It was a homage to my fish-and-chips shop days. Malcolm had created a great half a box.

I wanted to add a seating and hospitality area to elevate the experience. The plan was to improve and replicate. I had gone as far as to buy a closing restaurant's furniture package and place it in storage in preparation for the launch.

Around that time I heard the local fish-and-chips owner in the area was not renewing his lease. After depleting my previous savings with the purchase of the house, I had by this time built up a tidy little nest egg of a few thousand pounds, so I had the funds available to make a move.

Anyway, the shop was in the perfect spot, and there was a shop next door available where I could expand the operation and provide seating. Talk about serendipity! The lease for both was something I could afford. There was no financial wiggle room, but I could live in the back and sell my home if I had to make ends meet. I was in negotiations with the owner, and everything was running smoothly.

The night before signing the leases, I went out with a few friends, and we were celebrating the venture. One of my friends somehow bumped into Malcolm outside the massage parlor—the kind with the happy endings, of all places—and told him excitedly what I was doing. To this day, I have no idea what possessed him to do that.

The next day I turned up bright and early only to see that Malcolm had purchased the lease. He never operated those businesses. The look Malcolm gave me when he walked away and the rage I felt for him, I am thankful I did not act on, or I would be doing life with absolutely no chance of parole. I added Malcolm to the list of people, along with my father and the Darkness, I would never speak to again.

There are so many lessons here, but the main ones are loose lips sink ships and to never celebrate anything until it is done. Lessons that have served me well.

Moving On Up

"The world was on fire, and no one could save me but you."
—Chris Isaak in "Wicked Game"

While I was growing at Burger King, I felt unfulfilled and very much underpaid and underappreciated. The loss of my own business to Malcolm weighed heavily on me. One of my colleagues, Colin, who ran the Huddersfield Wimpy restaurant, called me and stated he was joining another American-based pizza company, Pizza Hut. Colin was raving about the company, the management, and the opportunity.

I applied and was accepted into their management program for their new delivery business. After my experiences in the fish-and-chips, butchers, and video shops, and most recently with Burger King, I immediately found my feet. I was trained by Greg Mason, who was later my best man at my wedding, and reveled in the opportunity. I can truthfully say I loved Pizza Hut.

Upon completing my training, I was assigned the Abbeydale Road business in Sheffield—about fifteen miles from where I lived. It was perfect. The business was good but not great; however, I quickly implemented many of the local marketing campaigns I had either used before or had heard about. The business mushroomed. As luck would have it, a new corporate marketing manager had just been hired. I invited him to my store for a visit. He wanted to try out a new direct marketing strategy. I was immediately all in. It was an overnight success, and the business quickly doubled and then tripled its revenue. We were on fire.

One day I had the idea that my little store should sponsor Sheffield United, the local professional football team. I remember having no authority to do so but inked the deal anyway. The pickup in business was spectacular and probably was the only thing that saved me from getting fired. The experience taught me that you have to always be on the lookout for ways to powerfully and uniquely drive your brand. Also, better to ask for forgiveness than permission.

The sales of the restaurant had skyrocketed and again gave me the opportunity to implement what I now referred to as my Second Chance program for offenders. I have always believed that most people want to do well and will do well if given the opportunity. Within a few months, several were enrolled in the Second Chance program. This is not to say it was easily implemented. I had challenges of support not just from corporate but the actual group participants. First of all, most of the participants were twice my age. From the looks on their faces, it was clear that many thought I was just a kid. How could I relate to or help them?

Candidly, it took time to earn their trust. It helped that I openly talked about my challenges, and I explained while I was not them, I had also faced adversity and suffering. I allowed myself to be vulnerable, and it worked. It helped that they were learning a trade, and on most shifts I would spend one-on-one time talking to each of them individually and sometimes as a group. I absolutely never talked down to them. I also never pitied them and never thought I was better than them. I was trying to find a connection that would alter behavior and hopefully have a positive influence on the rest of their lives. Again, the results were mixed, but every success was worth the time and effort. I'm not saying I did not get very frustrated, but I pushed through.

My team, as Tina Turner sang, were "Simply the Best." We were like a well-oiled machine, and in no time we were the top revenue-generating unit in the country, with by far the best operating standards by any measure. We were unbeatable, and within a year we were awarded Manager of the Year. While the award was given to me, I truly received this for the team. That has always been my philosophy and has served me well. One of the things I am most proud of is my track record of developing others and helping them reach their true potential. Each of my assistant managers and supervisors went on to become managers and more from Abbeydale Road. Unknown to me then, this would be true throughout my career.

I won a trip to the States as part of the award. What an eye-opening, heart-pounding experience that was. Up until then, the biggest city I had seen was Sheffield. I had never even visited London. So imagine my excitement landing in Orlando. The airport seemed bigger than Rotherham. The giant signage that covered the roads leading into Orlando and then the hotels themselves were breathtaking. *How did they make signs that big?* I thought. I was experiencing a visual overload, as was my girlfriend at the time, who joined me. The hotel they put us up in was not five-star, but it was very nice. Better than anywhere I had ever stayed before in my life for sure. So much so that halfway through the trip I had a panic attack that the hotel was not being paid as part of the trip and that I would never be able to cover the bill. I called back to England to confirm, and the relief was palpable.

Everything about my journey was magical, from the Orlando theme parks to my restaurant of choice for the trip, Sizzler, to seeing this new concept called Blockbuster. America was the most special of countries. I loved it from my first step.

Don't get me wrong—I visited the beaches and the parks, but I also spent hours every day visiting the malls, the shopping centers, and the numerous restaurants. I was a sponge, soaking in absolutely everything. This trip was really the initial catalyst for my lifelong love of and belief to never stop learning. It was also the beginning of the end of my relationship with my girlfriend.

Big-City Lights

"Toto, I've a feeling we're not in Kansas anymore."
—Dorothy in *The Wizard of Oz*

Upon returning from my trip to the US, Sheffield was no longer big enough. I wanted and needed to do more. I had seen the light and did not want to go back. Luckily, my old area manager had been reassigned to London to work on rolling out a new computer system for the entire delivery business that by now was nearing one hundred locations. I was tapped to be one of the six SUS (single-unit system) trainers. The task was to Englishize the system that was operating in the United States.

The job was based in London. It came with a lot of firsts. I would have my own company car. My own phone, even if it was bigger than a brick. My own company apartment, also not much bigger than a brick. I was beyond speechless. My girlfriend did not want to move to London, and for the first several months, I would travel down to London at two o'clock every Monday morning so I could be first in the office. I'd then travel back late Friday and arrive back home in the wee hours of Saturday morning. It was exhausting, and we simply grew further and further apart. The writing was on the wall.

The trips became less frequent until they basically petered out. My weekdays saw me traveling for multiple hours a day. I was also a terrible map reader and would get constantly lost traveling through the maze of streets that made up London. To keep alert, I'd run through the cassette tapes of my favorite band at the time, Bon Jovi, along with my old reliables: Duran Duran, Spandau Ballet, Depeche Mode, Wham!, George Michael, Bronski Beat, Howard Jones, Adam Ant, Roxy Music, Whitesnake, ABBA, Diana Ross, and the Bee Gees. I know—some are sad. Once I ran through those, I'd switch over to the radio. Those days with just me and my car are some of my very fondest. I was growing and learning to live as a functioning adult. In a sense, I was my own boss, managing my own schedule. Something I never thought was possible.

Until recently, I had never visited London, and it did not disappoint. It was absolutely the city of lights, and I loved it. I dedicated myself to work and earned a reputation as an up-and-coming leader. Whitbread, the joint venture company with PepsiCo, was celebrating 250 years of operation, and the *Financial Times* wanted to do a piece on the business. I was chosen to be featured. The article was titled "Young Man in a Hurry." It summed me up well. It put me on the map. I have nothing but great respect and admiration for the company. I had finally escaped my childhood and teenage trauma. I knew this was the opportunity of a lifetime, and I was not going to squander it.

Climbing the Corporate Ladder

"Just put one foot in front of the other."
—Austin Peck

I was quickly promoted to managing the other SUS trainers. I learned how to manage other people. At first I found it hard to delegate. The reality was I was no longer making decisions but coaching people through their issues and helping them solve their own problems without simply making decrees. I went through an endless stream of leadership books and absorbed the key lessons like a sponge. From the outset, my expectations were high, but it was a real fun time for me. I put the hours in. To this day, I believe hard work should be everyone's best friend. I had to pinch myself most days that I was in this role, with this type of responsibility. I was leading a crack team of up-and-comers. The program was a resounding success, both for my boss, Darcy, and for me. The project was completed three months early and under budget. Individual store-level performance was now available, and the insights led to radically improved service times. Improved service led to enhanced sales and greater profitability. The project concluded, and I had my sights set on becoming an area manager, where I would be responsible for several locations. I campaigned, but the competition was fierce, and spots were limited. I lost out.

Quality Control Manager

Okay, stay with me on this one. I know what you are probably thinking right now: *Boring!* That nothing good can come from discussing the life of a quality control manager. I get it, but I'm not going to drop a book of heavy on you. There will be no mention of mind-numbing policies and procedures that make your eyes glaze over. What I will tell you is that these types of roles make companies great. To all my quality control, audit, and loss prevention colleagues, you are the true unsung heroes.

With the above stated, I was disappointed to not be promoted to area manager. Instead, I was appointed as one of two quality control managers.

It felt at the time like a consolation prize, but I now recognize it to be a great gift.

In this role, I was the auditor of the operations for the business. I learned how the sausage is made, if you like. Call me strange, but to me it was beautiful. I got to learn all the components of what made an operation tick or come off the tracks. My job was to evaluate my assigned restaurants four times yearly. This role honed my skills on what a good and bad operator looks like.

While incredibly frustrating for me, it opened my eyes fully to the fact that the talent you hire and groom are absolutely your greatest asset. At times I could not believe how some managers operated their stores. I would turn up time and time again and see the same issues identified previously go unaddressed: poor staff scheduling; an out-of-date production schedule, or no schedule at all; no bike maintenance plan; not enough third-party drivers; insufficient inventory—all the things you need to be on top of to operate a well-oiled machine. My recurring thought was that there had to be a better way.

Time to Hit the Books

"I figure life's a gift, and I don't intend on wasting it."
—Jack in *Titanic*

At this time it became increasingly evident the young man raised in Rotherham needed to up his education game if he was going to compete in the big leagues. I had left school with no qualifications. I was now working in a place and at a level where everyone else had strong credentials. I enrolled at Open University and worked nights to get myself educated. I knew I had to differentiate myself. Passion alone only gets you so far.

The courses were great and challenging. I got to interact with some seasoned professionals, and we had group sessions in Europe every semester. I traveled to Amsterdam, Brussels, and Barcelona, among other cities. The insights from the classes were exhilarating, but the real value to me was in traveling there in the first place. These trips and the previous one to the

United States gave me my lifelong passion for travel. Seeing new things equate to charging up my life battery. Knowledge is key.

Anyway, as luck would have it, the first Open University course, targeted selection, was instantly applicable to my current role. Targeted selection was basically a program that forced you to work on the biggest opportunities with a given problem—to home in and work on what was critical. In my case, how could I improve the audit scores of the business? I brainstormed with my counterpart. We were coming up with a game plan when I was provided a profound and painful lesson.

I Made It through the Rain

"I'm the guy who does his job. You must be the other guy."
—Sean Dignam in *The Departed*

While I was growing in my management abilities, I was in a relatively junior role. I was not in a place or position to understand the bigger picture. While I thought I was successful at the time, I was really but a minor cog. Humbling but true. I was also not yet familiar with two of the most dreaded words in business speak: *corporate downsizing*.

From my vantage point, I thought the business was doing great. We were opening new stores, and in my mind that equated to success. I did not understand at the time how the health of a business was driven by the financial performance more than anything else. The business was not growing as fast as it needed to in order to make plan—words I have lived by ever since. You have to know where you always are to plan.

One Friday I arrived for work early, as always. Later that morning, the entire corporate team was summoned to an impromptu meeting in the open area of the office. Like Pavlov's dogs, I have also learned that these sessions are usually never good and therefore should be avoided like the plague. The head of the delivery business, a South African, Paul van Staden, gave a brief summary of the business and the wider challenges we faced. He went on to explain we were being forced to make changes. "Good people were going to have to be let go," he said. I liked Paul. He was blunt and a straight talker. I wish he would have been a little more compassionate and caring on this day. Another lesson I tucked away for future use. The HR leader was up next and stated she would be calling people in for a one-on-one discussion. The room was eerily quiet.

The area managers, who I wanted to join the ranks of, were summoned first. They were then followed by the corporate support staff, which I was among. Many were released that day. Candidly, I felt there was no way I could be let go. I was a recent manager of the year, had just implemented a flawless IT program, and had just recently been promoted.

My confidence was justified, but my partner was not so lucky. Becky was let go that afternoon. It was an awful moment, which I made worse when trying to make Becky feel better by asking, "Are you all right?" Of course she was not all right. She had just lost her job. Think, man! I learned in that moment it is important to choose your words carefully. You have to be authentic and thoughtful.

Adapt or Die

"You can break a man's skull. You can arrest him. You can throw him into a dungeon. But how do you fight an idea?"
—Sextus in *Ben-Hur*

Adapting is critical for continuous growth and a skill every great leader needs to develop. I began to hone mine right then as I took the increased responsibility of managing the quality control program for the entire delivery business. This is where my education and job needs intersected. As I mentioned, the first course was on targeted selection. I quickly realized in my now solo position there was no way I could do the work of two auditors, even though at first I did try to meet the numbers. It would mean on average eight store audits a day. Another lesson is to know when to accept defeat. I waved the white flag on that endeavor.

I put the final touches to my plan and presented it to the director. I set the stage by outlining what we were doing and what the results were. We needed to adapt and do things differently if we expected a different outcome. I proposed that we target the bottom 20 percent of the business and audit monthly, but that instead of just giving a score, I would work out an actual game plan with the store manager to see that actual improvement measures were taken and implemented. For the rest of the business, they would still be audited once a year. After all, the well-performing stores simply needed to carry on doing what they were doing.

Along with this shift in focus, I proposed we rename the role from quality control manager to quality consultant. The shift signified I was there to consult and improve the business and not merely police. The area managers also liked this. Up until now, they had seen the role I performed as a punitive one that showed them up and ultimately affected their bonuses and ranking in the business. In essence, when the next corporate downsizing came, and it would, the ones who scored poorly were more at risk. Now I was actually helping coach their managers to improve their game and to ultimately make the area managers look better as well—a win-win. The operations began to witness a steady improvement. They had "faith" in me, which also happened to be the title of my favorite George Michael album. Boy, could that man sing.

The London Rant

During this time there was one incident that took place that would change my life, but at the time it did not feel like it. It was the London Rant.

It occurred one Friday night. I was training a Polish delegation on how to perform an evaluation on a restaurant operation. The place was slammed, and our experience was horrendous. I thought about stopping the evaluation and asking the Poles to come and help put things back on track; however, I knew that would serve no purpose. First, they would not be trained on what they came here to do, and frankly the operation was so far behind we would have made no difference. We sat painfully through the experience. I explained to the Polish delegation I would usually sit down with the manager and review the findings. I talked them through it so they would understand my logic. We left the restaurant, and I gave the manger a copy of the report and told him that I would reach out to his area manager the next day.

I did not have to wait. Roughly an hour later, my cell rang. It was Paul Clark, the area manager. He went off on me like a polite Mel Gibson. He was clearly agitated, demanding to know why I had continued with the audit when obviously the operation was being buried. I calmly stated that was the very time we should stress test the operations to find where they needed to be strengthened. That night, while still not happy, Paul developed a level of respect for me, as I held my ground and did not let him railroad me. That interaction, while almost blowing out my eardrums, would lead to something great, but I'll get to that later.

You Keep Me Hanging On

"Every window in Alcatraz has a view of San Francisco."
—Susanna Kaysen

About a year later, I finally got the role I wanted, or to be more precise, I nearly did. I was told I was going to be promoted to an area manager designate role, not a full area manager. To me, the whole experience was a letdown. For something I had been working hard for years to achieve, it was a gut punch. It was a role I have never personally placed anyone into in my entire professional career. They either got the job, or they did not. There was no in-between. The designate title in my mind screams, *"We are not sure you can do the role"* and immediately undermines the individual. In essence, you are setting people up for failure. No, thank you.

The reasoning behind the designate role was that there were not enough stores for a full-fledged area manger role, and this would allow me to grow my territory as more stores opened. I found out later the new Pizza Hut operations leader for the entire UK, whom I had spent a few days visiting stores with, and whom I had impressed, wanted me promoted. This was the first time that corporate politics visited me. There would be many more times that grim reaper visited me in the future, but in this moment I was at least ignorant to the danger I faced. My operations manager was based out of Croydon. Looking back, it was clear he did not like having me thrust on him. I can sympathize with him on that point. How he handled it, though, not so much.

Light-Switch Moment

> "Sometimes it's the very people who no one imagines anything of who do the things no one can imagine."
> —Christopher Morcom in *The Imitation Game*

In this role, I learned a valuable lesson. I'd gotten along so far by being reactive to events. Show me a problem, and I'd fix it. I was great in the heat of the moment, but not so much in thinking in bigger-picture terms. I don't know why, but I just knew I needed to be great at both.

Being in this reactive mode, one is not in control of one's actions and can't function properly as a leader. I was following the plays but not calling the plays. I had to evolve. To do so, I needed a mental reset. I had to allow myself to be vulnerable. I had to start developing plans to shape a better future. Allow my ideas to be exposed and battle-tested. At times it felt like I was on a tightrope high in the sky, with no safety net. I had learned to fight back my fears previously, and if I were to become the leader I wanted to be, I had to get comfortable in the uncomfortable.

Jumping off the proverbial ledge consciously and with intent forced me to develop my critical-thinking skills. It helped me to crystallize what vision and end state I was seeking for a particular problem. With those set, the tactics became easier to determine. Almost a paint-by-number play.

A few months later, I developed Delta Force, a program that would help managers open up their stores more systematically and methodically. I had seen several new openings go very poorly. My vision was to open operating at the highest standard from day one. Basically, think of it as a step-by-step guide that had become so public in recent times. The program was, thankfully, fully supported by the operations team. It reinforced that "thinking" was my future way to success and not merely outworking others. Over time the bigger the idea, the more alive I felt. Game on!

I spent the next six months shepherding my four stores like a doting parent. It required a little more doing than thinking, but I was still a work in progress. I visited each of the units daily, blasting my new favorite songs: "All That She Wants" by Ace of Base and Meat Loaf's "I'd Do Anything for Love," which nicely summed up my state of mind at the time. I would do anything to succeed. I was also responsible for opening a new location in Elling. The manager, Leah, was also an up-and-comer and did not disappoint. The store deployed the Delta Force plan and opened above expectations. My managers liked working for me. We were delivering the results. Time for another painful lesson. Who your boss is matters. Big-time and every time.

Huge Thorn in My Side

"No, Mr. Bond, I expect you to die!"
—Auric Goldfinger in *Goldfinger*

The leader of operations for Pizza Hut UK, Blair—no relation to Tony, but the very same one who had pushed for my promotion—resigned or was forced out. There was much speculation as to which, but no one knew the truth, at least no one who was in our orbit was a reliable source. I was sad because I knew Blair was the right person for the role and needed more time. That was another lesson—you need to move fast, with a sense of urgency. Time is the enemy. Implement your ideas quickly, or they will not take root. The life span is short at the top. Competition is fierce. Act as if your life depended on it.

A few years later, I remember being on a corporate retreat in Australia. I was accompanying my wife as her guest, who was heading up operations for PepsiCo Europe. We had taken a yacht cruise around the harbor. I looked down and stated to a few executives standing around me, "Look at the sharks in the water."

A gentleman, who will go nameless, looked at me and stated with a straight face, "I'd be more worried about the sharks on this yacht than in the bloody ocean." Too funny, but it sums up life in the fast lane rather well. It is not for the faint of heart.

Back to my sponsor's abrupt uprooting. I have always believed it is better to be lucky than good, as you always meet your match. My luck had just run dry. Bone dry. With my "supporter" now gone, I was exposed and an open target for my operations manager. He wasted no time and went to work. Suddenly everything I was doing was being questioned. It felt like Malcolm had resurfaced. My boss's store visits became wildly critical. I knew my standards, having been an auditor, better than anyone. In fact, I knew all 954 standard and critical deviations. This guy was hell-bent on finding small issues and making them appear mountainous.

Ultimately, I had not been his choice, and in no time I was being axed from my position. I was summoned to the Croydon office. On the drive over, I did my best to calm myself and prepare for what I knew was to come. It was inevitable. The discussion was one I would never want anyone to endure. There was zero respect shown. Instead, he launched into a litany of fabricated reasons why I was not area manager material. Never mentioned once were the performance of the team and the improvements being made on any metric. This was personal. I was being shown who was the boss. He spent more time waxing on about how my demotion letter would take him a few hours to craft. What a jackass. A real plonker. I turned to UB40's new hit "Red Red Wine" to get me through the moment. A few bottles of red for sure helped me that night.

Heaven Knows I'm Miserable Now

"In this world, it's just us. You know it's not the same as it was."
—Harry Styles in "As It Was"

I was reassigned to work in operations support with my former boss. My heart had been ripped out. Most mornings I could barely make it out of bed, and most evenings I was drinking way too much. I was definitely taking the UB40 hit a little too seriously. It did not help that I replayed that final conversation on loop. The shame and misery just built inside me. I could not believe after all I came through that this was how it was going to end at Pizza Hut. I did not know it at the time, but it was something I later understood to be situationally depressed. All the while I thought I was pissed off. Who knew. I had never entertained a job offer from a competitor, even though I had received a few overtures since I had arrived in London. I honestly thought I'd be with Pizza Hut for life. That was about to change.

I wish my exit would have been smoother and had played out differently, but it did not. My former boss had taken me back with no questions asked and felt betrayed when I resigned, especially when I stated I was going to work for a competitor, Domino's. I, too, felt betrayed, so in my mind we were even.

I was willing to just move on, when my boss called me back and went on to explain I was not owed any severance pay. Then he smugly told me that I actually owed them money. I consulted a lawyer that afternoon, and I was proven correct. Unfortunately, while right, I also lost any relationship with my boss. We were not talking about a fortune, but in my opinion how you handle someone's exit is a true reflection of your values. It was sad, but this also reinforced the need for not being a dick when handling stressful situations. Respect and caring needs to shine through. Dignity for all.

Supernatural Delight

"Live, baby, live, now that the day is over!"
—INXS in "New Sensation"

The next day, bright and early, after finalizing my exit the evening before, I walked into the offices to hand in my corporate stuff and drop off the company car. It was a cathartic event and allowed me to bring closure to this chapter. Like Ariana Grande sang years later, it was all about "Thank U, Next!" I was able to say my goodbyes to my now former colleagues—that is, all except my boss, who had walked into his office and purposely closed his door. Alas, there was to be no handshake and fond farewell.

As I was saying my final goodbyes, the office receptionist stated I had a call and asked if I wanted to take it. I thought, *Why not*. I took the call, and what a call! Talk about things happening for a reason. A minute and my life took a different trajectory and would never be the same. Fate is sometimes in the hands of the gods. My favorite band, Ace of Base, had just released their new hit single "The Sign." This I took as my sign.

The area manager Paul Clark, who had gone apoplectic when I had scored his London restaurant poorly the previous year, was on the other end of the line. He had just been promoted to operations manager of PepsiCo Restaurants in Poland. He must have heard through the grapevine I was leaving. He asked me to come and be his area manager. There was no job interview; there was only a job offer. I loved his style. Paul knew me and believed in me. I stood there and thought my heart was going to explode. I knew Poland was in Eastern Europe, but I could not pick out where Poland was on a map. Nevertheless, I thought for a split second and said, "Let's do it." It was one of the very best decisions I have ever made in my life. Paul and his awesome wife, Laura, have been lifelong friends. Also, at this time I was now dating someone who worked in the office. My belief has always been if it is meant to work out, we will find a way. If not, it was never meant to be. We were going to see.

Frankfurt Fracas

"Are we supposed to fly that close to the mountains?"
—Federico Aranda in *Alive*

Getting to Warsaw was by far my most uncomfortable travel experience. First, the PepsiCo offices in London made the travel arrangements. They spelled my surname on the ticket incorrectly—*Haig* instead of *Hague*. Second, it was 1994, and the UK had been rocked by IRA terror attacks, a particularly vicious one just a few days prior. Third, I had somehow misplaced my passport and had rushed to get a replacement one and was traveling on a one-day-old passport. And fourth, I was born in Belfast, the place where the terror originated. All the makings of a disaster.

In those days, there was no direct flight to Warsaw. It would connect through Frankfurt. I landed and proceeded to go through German customs and immigration. The security guard looked at my passport and checked my ticket. By his mannerisms, I knew something was amiss. I was told to move to the side for additional questioning, further reinforcing trouble.

Suddenly I heard footsteps slapping down on the corridor behind me. I turned as several fully armed police officers with assault weapons held across their chests were running directly at me. My internal alarm screamed danger. Moments later I was roughly shoved to the ground, and many weapons were pointed at me. I was just thankful I did not poop my pants. I might admit to peeing a little. I was harshly pulled to my feet and ushered into a room and interrogated. It ended up in a complete strip search. The final embarrassment was the rubber-glove treatment, which I knew meant a cavity search. I made the comment of "never on a first date," but the officers saw no humor and proceeded. I think a little more harshly than needed and with way too much professionalism for the task.

Eventually, I was released but had missed my flight and was thankfully put on the first flight out the following morning. I did not have any credit cards at the time and no German money, and I ended up having to sleep in the terminal that night. What a clusterfuck. From that day forward, I have always avoided Frankfurt.

Rocking It

"Win or lose, good or bad, the experience will change you."
—Richelle E. Goodrich

As the plane touched down in Warsaw, I hoped Paul would be there to greet me. Ever since leaving German soil, I had been singing George Michael's "Freedom," followed by Frankie Goes to Hollywood's "Relax" to help put this disaster behind me. It worked to a limiting degree. Paul thankfully was there and was equally grateful I had arrived, fearing I had gotten cold feet and bailed.

From my first breath of fresh air, I loved Poland. It was a special place. The people were the best. They were a little cold at first, but once they got to know you, they were friends for life. Almost thirty years later, I am still friends with so many. It also helped that this was the same team of managers I had spent time with in London.

I was assigned a company apartment and over the next few days got it furnished with the bare essentials from IKEA. I settled right into work. Within no time, we were transforming the business. The delivery business was still using manual guest checks, even though I had implemented the SUS system years prior in the UK. We quickly changed that. The business also had only one phone. I immediately purchased two expensive mobile phones. Our CFO had more than a few complaints about that.

I decided to let the results speak for themselves. Previously, the store was doing roughly one thousand guest checks per week. A reasonable number, and there were five people delivering the orders. Within weeks, with the new SUS system and a tripling of the phones, the orders rose to four thousand weekly. At its peak, we had twenty-seven drivers on the road. I was told this was by far the busiest delivery unit in the Pizza Hut system globally at the time. This had taken a few weeks. It ushered in a dramatic acceleration in the growth of our delivery operation. We were rocking it.

Killing a Competitor

"There is but one path. We must kill them all."
—Spartacus in *Spartacus*

Steady down, not a real killing. In Poland, if I was competitive before, I took things to a new level. Domino's, which I nearly joined in the UK, had also entered the Polish market. I could not believe their temerity and wanted to let them know the gravity of their mistake. With a frenzied focus, I wanted to know everything about their operation. I, along with members of my team, would sit outside their Warsaw locations for hours on end. We tracked hourly the number of guests entering for pickup and drivers sent out on delivery. We'd then go back with our delivery team and compare their orders to ours and estimate their sales. We were beating them badly, but they still were taking market shares.

In those days, my thoughts about competitors were they cannot be allowed to survive. It was all or nothing. In no time, we worked with our new marketing executive, Joe, who I liked very much, and we executed an all-out blitz using direct mail. This had really worked for me in Sheffield. It worked perfectly here as well. Within a few months, Domino's closed their locations. We celebrated by going over to their closed locations, playing Queen's "Another One Bites the Dust" throughout the ride, and slapping Pizza Hut posters with our telephone numbers on the vacant windows. We even saw a nice uptick in sales from that as well.

Next, we supercharged the bigger restaurant operations at Zodiak and Gruba Kaśka. These were massive boxes doing unprecedented weekly sales numbers. Zodiak was the biggest of the venues and was situated in downtown Warsaw. The building was a former animal-slaughtering facility and now housed the first four-in-one concept for PepsiCo: Pizza Hut, KFC, Taco Bell, and a Polish ice cream company I had negotiated a deal to carry.

Hundreds of people worked in this one restaurant daily. The volume was in excess of $10 million annually, and that's with an average check of less than $4.00. This would equate in today's terms to generating annually in excess of $30 million. From one operation! It was an incredible machine.

The lessons came in daily. My ability to adapt and be creative, in my humble opinion, put ten years, maybe twenty years of experience on my résumé. I learned how to be self-sufficient and solve problems I had never faced in the UK. For example, when we were opening a delivery unit in Morena, a city in northern Poland, the local governing bureaucrats stated, "Phones not possible. Come back in a few years." They were under the illusion they were still operating in the Communist era; however, under any circumstance, this was not good news. Phones are an essential need when your business relies solely on telecommunication. We could have easily thrown our hands up and moved on. But we owned the problem. Our solution was that we placed an urgent order for more mobile phones. The CFO frowned upon this move as well. Only there was a lengthy waiting list. So we pivoted again. We placed CB stations in the apartment high-rises in the surrounding area. We found a way to be successful despite the obstacles. Here it was like operating in the Wild West, and I loved it.

The managers were world class as well: Karol, Jan, Marcin, Caesar, Dorota, Margosa, Renata, and so many more. I love these guys.

Call from the Head Honcho

"Well, let me just close this conversation by saying you are one unique individual."
—Neal Page in *Planes, Trains, and Automobiles*

In late November, the president of PepsiCo Restaurants International, David Williams, called me personally. David had visited Poland several times. I had toured the market with him, along with my superiors. I was still surprised David would call me, or at least have his assistant track me down to my office in Gruba Kaśka. I tried to only go to corporate offices once a week so I could stay focused on the business and not get caught up in the office politics. David went on to explain his other regions were well below budget and asked me to optimize more profit from my operations for the next few months. David could have called anyone higher in my chain of command, but he chose to call me directly. That is something I have taken to heart and used as part of my leadership style. I was not going to fail him and ultimately did not. That led to one of my most exhilarating and terrifying experiences.

After the call with David, I sat down with Karol, the GM of Zodiak, the largest of our operations. My challenge was to take out 15 percent of the labor costs. Not to fire the employees but to reassign to stores that were opening up or stores that needed additional help. We worked through every department and made changes. We then got to the cleaning department. As I stated earlier, Zodiak was a very large facility. Each concept had a quick-service restaurant counter ordering area and its own dining room. The place was massive. You would get out of breath running to the other side—it was that big. So much so that there were almost thirty employees assigned to cleaning the business each night. I spoke with the cleaning supervisor and asked, "How can we reduce the number required?" The response was it was impossible. I like a good challenge and thought this would be a great coachable moment.

That night the cleaning crew turned up for their eight-hour shift. I had them all sit down in a long line. Karol, the GM, translated that I was going to clean the business by myself. They sat there more than shocked; many smiled and laughed. Over the next six-plus hours, I moved around like the Tasmanian Devil. I first started the cleaning of the kitchens of each of the concepts. That really broke the back of the task. I had done this many times at the fish-and-chips shop, Wimpy, Burger King, and Pizza Hut operations back in the UK. Then I moved on to cleaning the tables and vacuuming. The task was complete. I had done solo what a whole crew did each night and with almost two hours to spare. The supervisor reduced the team from the next day onwards, no questions asked. The lesson here is how I like to think I have lived my life—never ask someone to do something you would not do yourself.

Eventually, sweat soaked, I left the business at around four in the morning. I was beat and wanted to sleep for a few hours before getting after it again. Little did I know what was in store for me.

Trip to the Warsaw Sing Sing

"Unless we're parked in San Diego Bay, you're at war every time you step on this boat."
—Rear Admiral Leslie McMahon Reigart in *Behind Enemy Lines*

As I was leaving downtown Warsaw to a dusting of snow, I saw flashing lights directly behind me. I really was exhausted and was not in the mood to give out more merchandise, which was my usual way of handling being pulled over by the police. I lowered down the driver's window and knew this was not your typical stickup. The officer demanded I get out of the car and aggressively asked if I had been drinking. Clearly, that was the only possible reason he thought someone would be out at this time. He probably had a good point.

While I looked disheveled, I certainly had not been partying. The officer demanded me to hand over a million zlotys—about fifty dollars. I did not like this new game. I refused and did not have the fifty dollars, even if I wanted to pay. The officer proceeded to pull out a Breathalyzer kit, and in his haste he dropped one of the tubes into the dirt-caked snow on the side of the road. He scooped it up and shoved it into the device and demanded that I "breathe here." I told him no way; it's dirty. The officer then cleaned off the tube and shoved it back into my face again. He was not to be denied. I relented and breathed into the machine with the confidence that it would come back negative for alcohol. The officer made a show of looking at the machine and shouted, "You drink. Two million zlotys."

So much for technology, I thought, and I refused to make the payoff. The game was getting worse by the moment.

That's when it got scary. Moments later I was hauled into the back of their Scooby Doo–looking van, and I was being driven away. At that moment I could not believe what was happening.

A short time later, I was being walked into a dark prison facility. I was summarily deposited into a cell. I wondered what horrors had happened here during the Soviet era and shuddered. I began screaming and demanding to see my ambassador. Unpleasant visions of a beating took hold, and I promised that whoever came through that door for me was not going to have it easy. I was prepared to fight and at least take a few with me.

Sometime later the cell door opened, and the officer simply said, "You leave." I have no recollection of how I made it home, but I did and was thankful to have survived the ordeal. Life was not always easy, but I survived.

I Can Feel It in the Air Tonight

"If everything seems under control, you're not going fast enough."
—Mario Andretti

If ever there were a need for me to scream the immortal words of Tom Cruise in *Top Gun*, "I feel the need—the need for speed," it would be this instance. In the beginning, the plan was for Poland to open five units in 1994. With our amazing results, the global leadership team went big on Poland. It became the big play. Project ZBig: 54 in '94 was birthed, meaning we were challenged to open fifty-four units in 1994. We did not disappoint, and I was growing immeasurably. Like the greatest crooner in the world, Frank Sinatra, I was also committed to doing things "My Way" and have done so ever since. My perspective is if you win or lose, do so knowing you did what you believed in and not what you thought others would want.

It also helps when you know your boss has your back. Paul was a great leader. He told you what he wanted and then let you figure out how best to achieve the results. In Poland, I saw firsthand the true impact a brand can have. Pepsi moved people. I was extremely proud to work for this powerhouse brand.

Rocket Man, Burning Out His Fuse Up Here Alone

"Whatever happens, it happens because we choose for it.
We decide our fates."
—Spartacus in *Spartacus*

In early 1994, all previous plans were basically supersized overnight. Whatever we were doing before to build the infrastructure of the business was supercharged. Support managers were brought in from Canada, England, Europe, Australia, South America, South Africa, and the States. In total, over a hundred trainee managers were hired and placed under my leadership. Every Monday a posse of all my restaurant managers and the key trainees would storm the corporate offices. We made a racket, but we were delivering.

We were having so much fun.

In Poland, while admittedly beating to my own drum, ultimately I experienced exponential career growth. Like the business, I had my own hockey-stick experience. In my case, more like a magic carpet ride. It was here, during these crazy times, I started to experiment and develop through trial and error my blueprint for business success. It was a four-part play. First, you hire and train the right talent. Second, that same talent delivers the right service. Third, the right service drives higher sales, and fourth higher sales delivers more profit. Then you rinse and repeat for optimum results. From those early days in Poland, I would obsess about hiring, retaining, motivating, and developing talent. This was my number-one focus, and I truly believe played a determining factor in my entire career. As the saying goes, "you can go fast alone but further as a team." Sage advice.

Also, in Poland, I was introduced to an important Pepsi mantra that I am profoundly grateful for and have used in every business since: Bigger, fewer, better. I have always found that distraction is the alluring enemy. Clarity of focus, violently executed, is what we all need. Poland prepared me well. Thank you.

In July 1994, Andy Rafalette, managing director of Poland at the time, summoned us in for an update. Andy told us that due to the unprecedented growth they were looking at bringing in a seasoned operations veteran who had, in his words, been there and done that. I was instantly worried due to previous reorganization in the UK and wondered if I would still work for Paul.

First Meeting with the Future Mrs. Hague

The next week the seasoned operations leader, Carol Halsall, arrived in Poland for a briefing on the business and to see if this was someone they thought was a fit. I sat next to Carol for the session. Each department head gave Carol an assessment of the state of play under their control. Carol had barely said a word throughout the session. Later Carol would tell me that she had the trip from hell. Her luggage went missing, and she had entered the meeting after scrambling to find a fresh set of clothes. On top of that, she could hardly understand a word of what was being spoken. So many accents, and all spoken at rapid fire.

After Carol left to have dinner with Andy, I turned around and said that was the last we will see of her. Deep down, I did not want or think we needed anyone to come in and mess up the team and our game plan. How little did I know what was really ahead. Life, as Forrest Gump eloquently stated, is in fact like a box of chocolates.

Hail Caesar

"You can't handle the truth! Son, we live in a world that has walls, and those walls have to be guarded by men with guns."
—Colonel Nathan R. Jessup in *A Few Good Men*

One Monday afternoon a few months later, my team and posse arrived at our headquarters as part of our weekly scheduled trip. We were storming through the building when I saw a head pop out at the bottom of the corridor. I recognized it immediately as belonging to the woman I thought we ran off a few months previously. Talk about a deer-in-the-headlights moment. Clearly, she had come to investigate who was making all this racket.

Carol was introduced as the incoming director of operations. While taken aback, I introduced myself and stuck my hand out. I then stated if she had time, I'd love to show her my restaurants. Carol stared me down and replied, "I'd love for you to show me my restaurants." Talk about a power play. She was horrible. Only joking, Carol. It was obvious Pepsi was betting big on Poland and thought adult supervision was needed. I was most offended.

First Impression Was a Doozy

"Look, if you had one shot or one opportunity. To seize everything
you ever wanted in one moment."
—Eminem in "Lose Yourself"

Later that day Carol took me up on the offer of showing her "her restaurants."
For the trip, I asked if we could take her car, as mine was a one-person FIAT
I had to fold myself into. How the person running Poland was given this, I
have no earthly idea! Carol, being the director, had a brand-new Saab 900.
Go figure. We got into my new boss's brand-spanking-new car. The fact that
it had heated seats and electric windows did not go unnoticed. Shaking off
the slight, I drove out of the Zodiak complex and turned right to head to
old downtown. I kid you not, but we had traveled no more than a hundred
feet when a large pothole swallowed the car. Thank the Lord we had seat
belts on. It was not pretty, and I prayed Carol, my new boss's boss, did not
have whiplash. I sensed I'd never hear the last of it.

Thankfully, the car had ground to a halt. I got out to inspect and saw
that the front wheel had been torn off the axel. We were going nowhere. I
thought, *Bloody hell.* I had totaled the new boss's car in less than a minute.
What an awesome first impression, Desmond! I motioned for Carol to get
out of the car and tried to regain control of situation. I stated we were going
to leave the car here in the middle of the street. That one of my team would
come and get the car towed and that I'd flag a cab down and have another
car sent to us before we finished the tour of the old town restaurant. Well,
let me tell you that went over like a fart in church with Carol. She pulled
rank immediately and refused to move until she saw the car towed away.
Right then and there I knew this woman was not to be messed with. I'm
thankful that we were not in the military, or I fear I'd have been frog-
marched to the brig or worse.

Audit of the Heart

"You play fair with me, I'll play fair with you."
—Alex Forrest in *Fatal Attraction*

Remarkably, Carol and I developed a great working relationship. The woman was whip-smart. A couple of times a week, we would meet up at one of the restaurants and talk shop. She knew her stuff. I had tested her repeatedly and was impressed. A few months later, I was a regular guest at her home and in a totally platonic way. At this time I was engaged to my friend back in London and would travel back monthly to visit. A couple of months prior to the wedding, I had an epiphany. I liked spending time with Carol more than my soon-to-be wife. I wrestled privately with this and told no one my concern. I buried the feelings deep down.

In November 1994, I went home to the UK for one of my monthly trips. On this trip, I sat my fiancée down and said I wanted to slow things down. She did not and insisted we keep with the schedule. I could not agree to this and split. I felt awful, but I knew she was better off having the ability to find someone who really loved and worshipped her. I knew I would make her unhappy, and no matter how hard this was, I knew it would be for the best in the long run.

Crazy Little Thing Called Love

"Oh, girl, I like you, I do."
—Post Malone in "I Like You"

The following Monday I made it back to Warsaw. After a full day of work, I made it to Carol's place for our standard glass of red wine. Over drinks, Carol casually inquired about my weekend. Little did I know, Carol, over the past weekend, had mentioned to her best friend during their weekly check-ins that she loved it in Poland but was going to miss her friend (me), as he was about to marry and most likely relocate back to the UK.

Eventually, after I did not immediately respond and was playing with my wineglass, Carol inquired again how my weekend had been. I thought it was time to reveal my hidden feelings. I cavalierly stated I had called off the wedding. In reality, I was terrified to reveal my feelings and did not know what I would do if she rejected me. But I fought back the fear and leaped in. Carol was shocked and nearly spit out a mouthful of wine. "Why?" she eventually stammered.

I replied, "I have met someone who makes me a better person and someone I love and want to be with."

Carol stared on in disbelief and asked, "Who?"

I replied, "You!" I wish I could have taken a picture of Carol at that moment—the look of sheer joy on her face was priceless. I am sure it matched mine.

Carol reached over and kissed me. It was amazing, and our life's journey together began on that day. The single best decision I have ever made. A relationship that had started off as pure friends had morphed into love. I was also attracted to Carol; however, due to never revealing the intimate details of a lady, I would never admit to wearing out more than a few bed-springs. So no questions on that subject, please!

Czech Run

Every 184 days, I needed to leave Poland for tax-avoidance purposes. Carol and I decided to make a fun trip to the Czech Republic and to take Patrick, her son, with us. Late on Friday, we set out, with me at the wheel. For most of the trip, we sang songs, which has become a family tradition. You should hear our rendition of "Take On Me" from A-ha. Marvelous! I must admit I'm great, but they are a little pitchy, as Simon Cowell would say. Please keep that on the downlow. On second thought, you may want to pass on that. Save the ears and all.

Around midnight we had just crossed over the Czech border. Carol had taken over driving under the guise of giving me some rest, but I believe her nerves were shot from my lead foot.

Moments after the driver change, we saw flashing bright lights behind us.

It was a police car that appeared out of nowhere, flashing its front lights, signaling that we pull over. Carol slowed down. *We have no chance of getting a speeding ticket*, I thought. Carol was a stickler for observing all rules, speed limits in particular. This was not an exception.

Carol pulled the car over to the side of the road. This was a small road, with zero traffic and no buildings. Just empty fields in every direction. Very bleak and dark. We saw the police officer get out of his car and walk toward us. We were all on edge. Not that we had done anything wrong, but we were in a country that had just gotten out from under Communist rule. A trip to the gulag could have been in our future.

Carol rolled down her window, and the officer did the usual, asking where we were going and why so late at night. Carol smiled and said, "We are on our way to Prague." Everything was going well, and the officer asked for Carol's documents. Carol pulled out her driver's license and handed it over. The officer looked at her license and stated she was a very pretty woman. *Who on God's earth would say that?* I thought.

I turned in my seat to say something, but Carol reached out and put a hand on my knee. I could not believe he was hitting on my woman—and in front of me. The officer gave us directions to the best local hotel, as Prague was still hours away, and we needed a rest. When Carol asked a few clarifying questions, the officer simply said, "Please follow me," and took off back to his car. We did just that, but I had visions of being killed in those damn woods.

Thankfully, my fears were alleviated when the police car pulled up in front of the hotel. We got our luggage and made our way inside. The lobby was busy, and we could hear loud music was playing somewhere in the building.

We had not made any reservations, as we were hoping to make it to Prague without stopping. We walked up to the reception desk and asked if they had two rooms available and if we could pay in dollars. They answered yes to both and asked for twenty dollars. Carol had a one-hundred-dollar bill, which I handed over to the receptionist. She looked at the bill and stated she could not change it.

I was going to say I'll come back in the morning to pick up the change, and if not they could have a nice tip. But a large man who was standing opposite, strangely guarding a door, stepped forward and stated he would change it and bring money back and slapped his chest. We looked on laughing and said fine and walked off to find our rooms. I never expected to see that money again.

Remarkably, an hour later, there was a knock at our door, and the man was there with our change. I had made a bet with Carol that was the last of seeing that money. Wrong again. I handed him a twenty-dollar bill, and this huge polar bear of a man hugged me.

Later on, we found out the hotel had operated a brothel, and the large man was the bouncer. The friendliest people in the world. The rest of the trip went drama-free. Prague is a beautiful city and should be among everyone's places to see.

Hit My Ceiling

"I suspect the truth is that we are waiting, all of us, against insurmountable odds, for something extraordinary to happen to us."
—Khaled Hosseini in *And the Mountains Echoed*

While I was truly enjoying Poland, I realized I had hit my own ceiling. In Poland alone, there were three directors and a Polish national hired to take over the market. Their horsepower was truly incredible and more than adequate to quadruple the business and then some. There was simply too much talent on the board.

On the personal front, I was having an awesome time with Carol. I felt we fit like a glove, and our values and life outlook were aligned, even if our personalities differed. I was the life-of-the-party type, while Carol was more of the quiet-and-wise type but also a lot of fun. This combination has served us well and constantly gets us both out of our comfort zones.

I had more than earned my title of area manager, but now I wanted more. Also, truth be told, I had a bee in my bonnet about never making it to area manager in the UK. I wanted to right that wrong. As luck would have it, that opportunity came knocking.

Trip of a Lifetime

"I want adventure in the great wide somewhere. I want it more than I can tell!"
—Belle in *Beauty and the Beast*

We had a long weekend coming up, and we wanted to make the best of it. It was that time for a break. For this trip, Carol and I decided to hit the road—or the train, to be more precise—for a trip to Berlin. It was cold and snowing; the train ride lasted several hours. The countryside looked like a scene from *Doctor Zhivago*.

In Berlin, we headed for the large shopping center and picked up a tour book of the city. We looked up restaurants, and Nikola's came highly recommended. Their exquisite four seasons squid soup was the suggested feature. We headed to the hotel and got ready for a great evening. We had no idea how great.

Nikola's

We got in a cab later that evening and gave the taxi driver the name of the restaurant. We thought something was off when the cabbie looked perplexed and said he had never heard of it. How could this be one of the most sought-after restaurants in town and be unknown? I handed him the tour book, with the restaurant highlighted. The driver got out his map and shook his head slowly and said he would take us there. The ride was about a half hour, but for the last ten minutes or so we had been traveling down darkened, desolate roads. I looked at Carol and said, "I do not like the look of this." The taxi pulled up. There was one lone post lamp working—all the others that lined the streets were burnt out or not working. It looked ominous, foreboding. The driver pointed and said, "It's right over there." I again stated to Carol that we should go. Carol answered by quickly exiting the cab. That woman has always been fearless.

We got to the door of the restaurant. I was not receiving any positive vibes, but I pulled on the door handle. Immediately a very large German shepherd, who looked like he could eat Carol and me as a small snack, jumped to attention. It just stood there watching us, no barking or growling, as Carol pushed me inside. The floor was covered in sawdust. *What sort of place is this?* I thought as I walked to the bar. There were several other people sitting around. The place was not hopping, for sure. As I got to the bar, I asked for a table for two. The bartender looked at me like I had lost my mind. I said you were highly recommended in the tour book. He looked on, knowing now that I was crazy. The bartender asked me to show him, which I did. He started laughing and showed the same advertisement to all the people in the place, who had now joined us at the bar. The barkeep eventually said the place had been used by the senior Soviet and East German military prior to the collapse of the USSR and the demolition of the Berlin Wall.

The bartender then led us to a table. He explained they did not serve food anymore, but he had a small kitchen upstairs in his apartment, and he would cook us something. We protested and said no need, but this man would not take no for an answer. We ordered our Jack and Cokes, to which my wife had introduced me. All the people in the bar now gathered around. Finally, I had found a spirit that I liked that didn't make me want to vomit. Unbelievably, the barkeep served us steak frites. It was delicious.

In no time, we were talking, laughing, and singing. We had entered the place at around eight that evening and exited well after four in the morning. We were feeling merry and had the best night of our lives and made a lot of new friends. So much so we went back the next night. We were hugged immediately by all upon entering. Not thinking it possible, we actually left even later than the previous night and had an even better time. What special memories. Without Carol, I can assure you that I would have left that first night without entering. The tough Yorkshireman would have chickened out. Great lesson there.

Some Other Place I'd Like to Be

"Do not try to make circumstances fit your plans. Make plans that fit the circumstance."
—George S. Patton

In December 1994, Whitbread, a joint venture partner of Pepsi, came calling. Whitbread owned the Thresher drinks business and were the third-largest hospitality and leisure company in Europe at the time. Thresher, however, was struggling, and they wanted new blood to shake up the business. I met with the HR leader and head of operations. I really liked them both but pushed back when they offered me the role of area manager running thirty stores. A little over a year ago, I would have snatched their hands off. But I had evolved and grown. Most importantly, I felt I could and should do more.

After a little back-and-forth, we had agreed I would join the Thresher operations team but would also be given responsibility for some upcoming and critical strategic projects. I signed up. Now the hard part: telling Carol.

First, I should have told Carol what I was thinking before I accepted the role, and I regret that. At this point in my life, I was not good at sharing my personal feelings with others. I had, after all, relied on myself up until then. Pepsi tried hard to keep me in Poland, offering my own home and more compensation, but to me it was never about the money. It was always about the role. I knew the money would always follow and should never be the primary motivation. My mantra was "Get the experience, and the money will come later." I wanted a role that challenged me. This was now my burning desire. I wanted to run a company. I wanted to be a CEO. I also wanted to do things like Frank states best: "My way."

Sultan of Swing

> "I know your tricks."
> —Mr. Zadir in *A Night at the Roxbury*

For my farewell bash, the entire Polish operations team threw a party for me at Ground Zero, the biggest nightclub in the city. It was aptly named, as the building had housed nuclear weapons during the Cold War. After running through more vodka shots than sensible, I did the only smart thing one can do: I hit the dance floor. Techno and house music were the rage at that time, and I started dancing solo on the huge dance floor to the electro beat. I was doing my best Travolta moves, and my group and others started cheering. Right Said Fred's "I'm Too Sexy" started playing. This got me to intensify my pace to near epileptic seizure speed. The cheering became louder, and with it I commanded my body to move faster. All of a sudden, the cheering hit another level. I thought, *My God, they love my moves*, and my smile broadened. I saw the bouncers charging the dance floor. I thought, *What the hell did I do?* Then I did a quick couple of 360 spins and realized there had been a solitary man dancing behind me and mimicking my moves. The out-of-control cheering came, and the bouncers leaped into action, when my shadow dancer dropped his bloody trousers and moved up closely, gyrating behind me. Alas, the cheers were not for my breakout dance moves. Regardless, the partying continued into the very wee hours. What a great way to end my tour of duty in Eastern Europe. I have kept in touch with many of the team from Poland, and I am truly privileged to call each of them a friend.

The next weekend Carol drove me to the airport. It was a sad moment as we hugged and kissed farewell but not goodbye. To Carol's credit, she supported my career move. I can never thank her enough for understanding my motives. We promised to meet up every other weekend. We kept that promise.

Hero's Return

"Here's looking at you, kid."
—Rick Blaine in *Casablanca*

In my mind, I had a hero's return. I was listening to my new favorite, "Love Is All Around" by Wet Wet Wet as we touched down. At this moment I was truly loving life. Within a little under two years, I had gone from being told I'd never be an area manager to taking on a major area manager role and with even greater responsibility around the corner. The congratulatory notes came in from many of my former Pizza Hut colleagues. It felt like the hero's return. I had also, in my mind, righted a wrong.

I settled into the work at hand, and in no time my area was delivering superior results. I quickly handpicked a few managers who I felt certain could do more and started to train them to handle talent development and other strategic initiatives for my business. Over a three-month period, we developed a management development program, Right Start, and a new area manager orientation program named Golden Start. Both were adopted by the entire sixteen-hundred-store Thresher chain.

This was also my first role in pure retail and except for my video shop experiences was nonfood related. I quickly got to see firsthand the power of effective merchandising. The Thresher buying and marketing teams, also an awesome group of people, made a big bet on bringing Australian wines to market—in this case, Penfold Bin 23 and Penfold Bin 5. Our job was to execute at store level. We adopted a "pile 'em high" strategy. In each location, we put in place the biggest possible display that each store could handle. The displays were small buildings, as each branch manager tried to outdo their peers. You simply could not miss them. From my perspective, having fun and letting the team loose should never be underestimated. The results were astounding. We replicated this many times, bringing in new wines from various countries around the globe. I have taken these lessons with me throughout my career. Go bold or go home!

The Big Reveal

In February 1995, Carol and Patrick visited me in England. We were planning to go on vacation to Italy later in the week. I could see something was bothering Carol; she looked a little on edge. We got Patrick settled and told him that we were going for a quick trip and would be back. I remember that walk like it was yesterday. We were walking hand in hand, and Carol tensely turned to me and told me that she was pregnant. Carol did not know how I would react and was worried. I honestly did not know how I would react, but upon hearing those words I was overjoyed. I swept up Carol, and we hugged for an age. I was going to be a father. I was walking on air. I was also simultaneously scared stiff. What if I was a terrible parent and hurt my child? I did not want to repeat the same mistakes and ruin another person's, especially my own child's, life. What if I turned out to be an abuser? I pushed those fears deep down, but they would resurface.

While we were thinking about a wedding the following year, this awesome news had moved up the timetable. The next day we went into London, and I secretly picked up an engagement ring while Carol shopped Selfridges. Later that afternoon, while walking on Oxford Street, I dropped down on one knee and proposed. Some passersby had stopped, and there was some yelling and clapping all around. What a twenty-four hours!

Ticketgate

Manchester United was playing at midday. I tried to never miss a match, if possible. We had a lazy morning and then drove over to Hampstead Heath for a stroll. The grounds were always so comforting. Anyway, we headed back to the car and drove to a pub that was playing the game live. On the way into town, I traveled down a one-way street in the wrong direction by mistake. Carol had already highlighted the infraction, and very vocally. That's when, out of the corner of my eye, I saw a police officer running toward me, waving his hands, instructing me to pull over. I started to do just that. As the officer was about fifty feet behind, walking as fast as his little legs would move him, I realized he was not in fact a police officer but a traffic warden. I thought for a split second and just took off down the road. I saw in the rearview mirror the traffic warden shaking his fist in the air. Carol screamed for me to stop. I looked at Carol, laughing, and said, "It's a bloody traffic warden. He's not police." Carol slugged me and did not see the funny side of the incident.

Carol's Big Position

Around this time, Carol was being considered for a position managing PepsiCo Restaurants in Spain. We had spoken about this, and I had actually agreed, to my utter amazement, that I would leave Whitbread and move to Spain so we could be a family. I had an idea for a novel and thought I'd take a run at that. I was rather fancying a life of leisure on the beach. Plus, who does not love Spain? Bring on the tapas and sunshine!

Here Comes the Sun

"I think this is the beginning of a beautiful friendship."
—Rick Blaine in *Casablanca*

Carol worked with friends and family back in New Orleans, her hometown, and the wedding was set for April 1995. We had purposely arranged this around Patrick's spring break at school. Patrick was now fourteen, and from day one I loved him and thought of him as my own. In my mind, he was not my stepson. There could be no half measures. He was my son. I was also going to show him the love and encouragement I had so lacked in my childhood. I was not going to be a bad parent. If truth be known, I was worried if I would be a good father to both Patrick and my yet-to-arrive child. Had the Darkness damaged me in ways I could not see or realize? What if I ruined my child's life? What if I turned out to be an abuser? I was scared senseless. What if they grew to hate me? That I had been through too much. Suffered too much. The questions were endless. The answers were not comforting, but I knew Carol would never tolerate abuse of her children. At times I thought I was going to have a panic attack. Eventually, I pushed these thoughts away and realized I would not only survive but thrive. That poor, scared shitless little boy was no more. Desmond 2.0 had surfaced.

Sooner or Later, It Comes Down to Fate

> "I tell any girl I'm going with to assume that all plans are soft until she receives confirmation from me thirty minutes beforehand."
> —Lewis Rothschild in *The American President*

Just before we headed off for the wedding, Carol was called to a last-minute meeting with the president of PepsiCo International, who was based out of London. I met Carol at Heathrow Airport and drove her to the dinner meeting. We both thought we were Spain bound.

Later that evening Carol came out beaming. "Spain is off," she told me. "I am being promoted to run operations and training for all of continental Europe." I was thrilled for her, and then she stated the best part: "And it's based out of London," she concluded. Talk about serendipity. I was speechless, as in less than two weeks I was prepared to give my notice and head off to Spain. Now that was off the table. We both had our careers, and most importantly we would live together as a family. Talk about the stars aligning perfectly. I had to say, though, a small part of me was a little disappointed, as I had already purchased tubs of sunscreen and a rather fetching pair of snug Speedos for the beach. But it's all about how you roll with the punches.

Good Times Never Seemed So Good

Our wedding was set for April in New Orleans. I had not met any of Carol's family up to this point. Her best friend, Linda, made a trip to Poland, and after several hours of interrogation about my intentions and a few days of putting on the charm, I had won her over.

Carol had been working with her sister-in-law, Karen, to arrange the wedding specifics. Her sister Bonnie was making the dress. These ladies are special. All this had been done remotely and without FaceTime or Zoom. Old school on the phone with the poor connection and all that. We landed in New Orleans, and I got to meet the family for the first time. And what a family! There were hundreds of them in the extended family, and they all were in each other's lives. It was a foreign experience to me, but I have come to love them all.

I remember meeting Carol's father, Tildon, a French Cajun who to me spoke an entirely different language. We shared a bottle of red wine on his porch that first evening. Just him and me talking to one another. I climbed in bed later that night, and Carol asked what we had talked about. I stated we talked, but I honestly did not understand a word he said but enjoyed the company and the wine. Ironically, the next morning, Carol asked the same question to her father. He replied the same as I had: he did not understand me. We bonded over French wine from day one.

Meeting Carol's family was in itself an amazing experience. Their regular get-togethers, seeing one hundred of their clan under the same roof, were unbelievable. They all welcomed me with open arms. In fact, we have visited every Easter since our marriage. We have perfect attendance, only missing in the recent COVID era. We have had so much fun, events, parties, and cookouts to fill several lifetimes. Those Cajun folk are truly scary. I love every one of them.

Along with all the countless sporting events and the actual Super Bowl of 2010, my father-in-law's seventy-fifth birthday ranks right up there with the best of them. We had several hundred in attendance, and I was introduced to line dancing. It was not pretty. It ended up with me moving in the wrong direction and causing complete gridlock. More than a few times entire sections of the dance group ended on their behinds on the dance floor due to my less than graceful exertions. As Frankie Valli states best, "Oh, What a Night." The video review still brings howls of laughter.

Dancing on the Ceiling

After the wedding, which was perfect, I headed back to London with Patrick. Carol headed back to Warsaw to pack. I was living at the time in a one-bedroom apartment, which cost an arm and a leg. I would leave Patrick home alone and come back as early as possible each evening. I remember one day coming home and Patrick was sitting in total darkness. The electricity needed to be fed constantly. I didn't keep up. Anyway, Patrick decided that unless he got a new jacket from Planet Hollywood, he would have to tell his mother. I told him that he would never be able to blackmail me. Strangely, the next day he had his jacket—Carol was none the wiser. Well, maybe after reading this.

The next week we toured homes and settled on a place in Penn, near Beaconsfield. It was an awesome home, and to Carol's delight it came with its own gardener, who would grow whatever vegetables she requested. At the center of the village was a small pond, and across the grass-covered square was a wine shop and a butcher's shop. This was quintessential old-country England.

We had settled into life in Penn. Patrick enrolled at the American School in London and started playing rugby, much to his mother's dismay. Carol was becoming more pregnant by the day. Every opportunity I got I would listen to the baby growing in her stomach. I was so happy I could burst. Seal's "Kiss from a Rose" was appropriately my go-to tune.

Put Me In, Coach

My superiors at Thresher quickly made good on their word and called on me to be part of a cross-functional team to provide the operations team with better reporting capability and eliminate paper from the business. It was a major effort. Our team got to work and within a year we had developed a program called SURF, which stood for Searching Under Real Figures. It made a profound impact on the business and also enabled for wider spans of control and instant visibility to the key financial metrics of the business. In essence, it was of the first interactive business dashboard. This project went on to become the UK Project of the Year, beating out the likes of Pfizer and Microsoft.

The project also provided significant, if not frustrating, development. I had to learn to present and present well. I was very confident in speaking, but when it came to public speaking I'd rather have a root canal. So there laid the challenge. I had to present the project to many different groups. I would take home the overhead projector and practice for countless hours with my wife patiently providing encouragement and feedback. I have to tell you, that projector survived being thrown through the window on many occasion.

My issue was that I wrote out a script, and when I veered off it, it threw me off-kilter. After countless suggestions by my wife to ditch the script and instead look at each slide and communicate the main point, I found my cadence. Over time I was able to expand on that and bring in other points that provided deeper color and context. Those sessions lasted for several hours and were monthslong exercises. I was honing my craft.

After the SURF initiative was completed, I was solely responsible for rolling out a labor program across the Thresher business. Quite the feat. This too was a resounding success and also won the UK Project of the Year award, meaning I had won back-to-back countrywide awards. This led to me being promoted to one of six team leaders overseeing six area managers.

Fly Me to the Moon

"Miracles happen every day. Some people don't think so, but they do."
—Forrest Gump in *Forrest Gump*

On Friday, October 13, 1995, our baby was born at 6:44 p.m. Like my favorite Michael Jackson song, "We Are the World," this bundle of joy was truly my world. Previously, I had avoided the number thirteen like the plague. Now it was my lucky number, as I was married and my son was born on the thirteenth. We knew it was a boy, as when we were in New Orleans for the wedding, we had had some tests due to some previous complications that my wife had. Those tests were terrifying. You usually have a million-to-one chance of having this or that illness. We were in the hundreds-to-one chance of a serious illness; however, we held firm together, and when asked if we wanted to keep the baby, there really was no questioning. "Of course!" We both empathetically stated. We were always together.

My wife insisted on calling our son Desmond Junior. I was not thrilled with the idea, as in England this was a standard used for royalty—and royalty I am not. I remember once when my sister-in-law introduced DJ to her friends, she whispered in their ears, "Carol is American, you know." I have come to love my son taking my name. Yes, my wife was right again.

Dramatic Entrance

DJ's arrival was nothing less than an ordeal. After severe cramps, I had, under doctor's orders, driven Carol to the local hospital. Upon checking in, the nurse checked my wife's dilation and informed her it would be a while and suggested a good old soak in the tub. Translation: take a bath. So, to my great surprise, about ten minutes later, while soaking in the tub, my wife urgently asked me to get the nurse. She said the baby was coming. I helped Carol, between bouts of heavy breathing, out of the tub and got her into her robe before going in search of the nurse. The nurse, upon hearing the news from Carol, stated that was not possible. My wife, who has never been a shrinking violet, got agitated. I tried to defuse the tension and asked the nurse to check. Moments later the nurse examined my wife and was screaming, "It's crowning!" I did not know what that meant, but by then I knew it was not good, as the nurse grabbed a nearby wheelchair and rushed my wife to the elevators, with me in hot pursuit.

We took the elevator down, and the nurse was wheeling Carol into a delivery room. The nurse was clearly flustered, and that was not doing anything for my nerves. She then stated, "This is really dangerous," which shocked me. And incredulously to me, she said she would be back and needed to find the doctor. That did it for me. I stood in her way and told her that she was not leaving my wife and to use the phone to call for help.

Luckily, she did as I had asked, because I was not going to let her leave my wife after stating it was dangerous.

Thankfully, several nurses and doctors quickly stormed into the room. I was not planning to be at the business end of this little procedure. If truth be known, I'm not good with the sight of blood, and I was worried I would faint. I know—I'm a lightweight. My wife had elected for an epidural, but due to our son already making a quick entrance, there was no time, and Carol was doing this naturally.

Within an hour, Desmond Junior was born. I cut the umbilical cord and was in the thick of things. While I had not liked seeing my son's veiny bald head pop out between my wife's legs, this moment was one of the most special in my entire life. Winning honors and accolades paled in comparison. Within another hour, my wife had had a bath and was enjoying crumpets and tea. That's how we do things in England.

DJ was the greatest gift and responsibility anyone could have given me. When I held him in my arms, I just could not have been happier. He was small, weighing in at six pounds seven ounces, but to me, from that day on, he was the world. Candidly, until I met Carol, I did not want to have children. I was scared after all my experiences that I would be a terrible parent. I had no role model and did not know if I was capable of being a good parent. I was terrified that I could have the potential to carry on the cycle of abuse or the ambivalence that my father had demonstrated. Holding that young boy in my arms melted away my worries. I focused on being the best parent on the planet.

I thought all the drama for the day had ended, but I was wrong. I left to go check on Patrick. I made my way to the hospital car park. As I got to my wife's car, I noticed the driver's side window had been smashed in. The music system was one where you removed the front plate so thieves would not break in. In my rush to the hospital, I had forgotten to do just that. Even that could not put a damper on my mood.

In the Middle of the Night

A few months later, under doctor's orders again, we took DJ back to the hospital. He had a bad case of croup. The little man was immediately admitted, and Carol stayed with him overnight. I headed back home to take care of Patrick. The next morning I got Patrick prepared for school before heading back to the hospital. I entered the room and could not see DJ in the oxygen-assisted unit next to my wife. Alarmed, I asked where he was, and Carol smiled and pointed down to her chest. DJ was not much bigger than a bag of flour and was scrunched up on his mother's chest. The nurse came in and cavalierly stated, "We nearly lost him last night! It took us forever to find a vein." I processed this and candidly have never been more fearful and scared of anything in my entire life. I knew this boy and this family were special—the most important thing in my life. My only troubles in life have come when I allowed myself to forget that.

Upon being released from hospital, Carol and I would spend a lot of time walking around the pond with DJ, trying to lull him to sleep. Eventually, we had hired an Irish nanny, Kathleen, to take care of DJ so Carol could go back to work.

Dancing in the Streets

From the first year of our marriage, Carol and I have hosted countless parties and events. We have held too many to count. Family, friends, and business associates from all over the world were always welcome at our home.

During our time in England, we tried to travel as much as possible. Our thinking: to see as much of Europe and Asia as possible while in Europe. Our plan was to eventually move to the States. We took this opportunity seriously, and most weekends we would head off to the Chunnel or an airport on Friday afternoons, eager to hit a European city. We took in France, Norway, Sweden, Holland, Germany, Belgium, and Switzerland, among others. We traveled to Hong Kong, Thailand, Australia, New Zealand, and Egypt. We liked to tour as many castles as we could find. I had a passion for history, and we would do pop quizzes with Patrick on every city we visited.

Our favorite place to tour was the UK, especially Scotland and Ireland. The fun we have had and memories created underscore our commitment to live our lives to the very fullest.

My advice to all parents is to try to get away with just your significant other annually. Kids can take over your world if you are not careful. Case in point coming up.

Our First Solo Trip

After the birth of DJ, we wanted to have a break. That little guy kept us up every night. To be clear, Carol took the night work burden much more than I did, but while an unbelievably happy time, like all new parents know, it's exhausting. Patrick was now fourteen, so we fled out of town and left him to look after DJ. We thought it would toughen him up. Only kidding. Our delightful Irish nanny, Kathleen, looked after our boys beautifully while we hit the Maldives.

We mainly choose the Maldives because the climate brigade said they would be disappearing imminently, so we wanted to catch them while we could. Spoiler alert: they are still there almost thirty years later. Before you scream disinformation, please don't. We know because we visited them again. We have eyeballed them.

Anyway, we had an awesome time. For someone who used to think Blackpool Beach was spectacular, this was truly out-of-this-world amazing. Being in the ocean with sharks and stingrays was special, but actually swimming over an almost forty-foot whale shark is up there as one of my most special moments. So happy I got to do this with Carol.

One night over drinks, we met another couple. After a few drinks, the husband kept asking his wife if he could tell us something. I hoped he was not going to ask me anything awkward. Well, we are British. The wife nodded, and he blurted out they had won one million pounds in the first lottery in the UK. Ironically, Carol and I also won that first lottery as well. Ours, though, was for ten quid. We told them that and had a good old night. It's awesome to celebrate someone else's success. We should all do that more often.

Terror Attack

Back in England, the fun times were shattered one afternoon—violently. I was traveling up the M1 motorway, the same one I had traveled back and forth on for my first assignment in London years before. I was headed to a meeting. That never happened. What happened was sheer terror.

As I mentioned at the beginning of this story, the IRA and the English had been engaged in a several decades' long battle. My family fled, so we knew the stakes were high and not to be messed around with.

Over time, though, you got used to living with the fear and the possibility of an attack. You let your guard down to a degree. You have to, or you can never get on with your life. It does not mean you take reckless chances. I suppose you just factor the possibility of danger into the life decisions you make.

As I traveled northbound on the M1, I saw a massive plume of smoke on the horizon. All traffic northbound ground quickly to a halt. After a few moments, I saw passengers getting out of their vehicles to investigate. In minutes there were ambulances, fire engines, and police vehicles swarming around with their lights flashing and sirens blazing. It truly felt like a war zone.

The bridge just a little bit ahead of me had been attacked and partially blown up by the IRA. I was no more than a minute or so from being directly impacted. It sent shivers down my spine and reminded me that evil was still around and unfortunately thriving. I remember getting home several hours later and hugging my entire family. Unfortunately, this would not be the last time I saw this fight up close and personal.

Brush with Death

The fortunate thing this time was that I was not in danger, but I was heavily involved. While visiting Ashford Castle in Ireland one weekend, things started off bizarre and got stranger. Upon leaving the airport, we were greeted by a pair of horses running down the motorway. They were traveling in the opposite direction of traffic. Could you imagine calling that one in to the police? "Hello, officer, I am being chased down the motorway by a horse."

As we got closer to the castle, the wildlife was not done entertaining us.

We were then greeted by a whole flock of sheep that had decided to stop and chat on the only one-lane road to the castle. We looked on and had a right old laugh. That exhibition took a good hour to conclude. We even got DJ out of his bulky car seat and showed him off to his new furry friends.

Carol, DJ, and I were on this trip. Patrick was back in the States visiting family. We had arranged a babysitter and were enjoying an intimate dinner at the castle's wonderful restaurant. Our sitter called down about thirty minutes in, stating DJ would not stop crying. I headed back to the room. It took a few minutes, but I got him settled down and then headed back to dinner.

As I was walking through the dining room, I noticed an elderly gentleman clutch his throat. His face had turned a deathly white, drawn of all color, as he slumped heavily face first on the table in front of him. Everyone around him seemed to freeze, and no one made a move to assist. I jumped around a few chairs and positioned myself behind the man as I prepared to give the Heimlich maneuver. After applying pressure around his midsection, and a few motions, a fairly large food item popped out of the man's mouth and flew across the table into a woman's lap. In moments, he came around, and I sat him down.

I returned to my table to a round of applause from many of the diners. I received so many thank-you drinks I nearly could not make it back to our room that night. When I came to pay my bill, the waiter told me the gentleman I had aided had taken care of it. Good guys can win!

Speaking Words of Wisdom

"There is no failure except in no longer trying."
—Chris Bradford in *The Way of the Sword*

In late 1995, Carol was back at work after maternity leave and traveling to Germany for a meeting. She was on the plane enjoying a fabulous breakfast. Those were the days when traveling was actually a real pleasure. I was on the M25, a major motorway circling London, but most times operated as one large parking lot. Anyway, on this day, I had received word my MBA application had been rejected from the American College in London. After my wife's term in the UK, we were talking about going back to the States. My wife also said that to be taken seriously in the States, having an MBA was essential.

So, with that backdrop, I called Carol and told her about my rejection note. Her response was infuriating but drove me to immediate action. Carol told me that I had more talent and brains than most people—to stop whining and go and do something about it. I pulled off the M25 and took the side roads to get me into the city. I screamed a few choice words at Carol, but I plead the Fifth on those as well. Love you, baby cakes!

I drove my car and pulled up outside the American College in London, situated on High Marylebone Street. I briskly walked into the administration offices, demanded to see the dean, and barged into his office. Today you'd be arrested, but this was 1995, and it was England.

The person behind the desk looked up and introduced himself as the dean. Amazingly, he did not have me escorted out. Rather, he patiently listened while I explained my predicament. Mainly that while I had no formal education, my current role was quite senior and should be taken into consideration. The dean calmly explained that an MBA is not for everyone and can be far too challenging for those with a lack of formal education. He made a point, but I swatted it away and asked to take the aptitude test and let the chips fall where they may. That afternoon I had my test. I aced it. The dean shortly afterward welcomed me to the MBA class of 1996. Without Carol's stern reply, that would never have happened. Plus, in truth, I did not want to tell Carol I had failed in getting enrolled. It would not go down well.

Threading the Needle

As the saying goes, be careful what you wish for. The euphoria of being enrolled in the MBA program quickly wore off when the realization set in that I had a very, very full plate. I already had a demanding job, a family to take care of, and a new son who was not a great sleeper, meaning a lot of broken sleep. Luckily, Carol stepped up her game and shouldered much of the family demands.

The MBA added four nights a week of classwork, for three hours per night. Then I would head off for home. Thank God the traffic was lighter by then, so the twenty-mile trip could be done in about an hour or so. Then each class had homework. So my days were known as dark days. I got up in the dark and went home in the dark.

The MBA, in reality, supercharged my lifelong passion for learning and applying new skills. Barely a course went by without me being able to apply something to my job. Some of the courses were easier than others, and some not so much, especially the ones involving calculus. That's when my leaving school at fifteen hurt the most. Throughout it all, however, I sucked up the tough times and muscled my way through. I was learning and evolving and adapting on the fly. I think the experience of building self-reliance in Poland and the teachings from my MBA were two of the seminal events in my professional life. My passion for personal growth was limitless. Since this time, there has not been a week where I have not read one to three books. Knowledge truly is power.

Two years after storming into the dean's office and making a case for enrollment, I graduated top of my class, magna cum laude. I was also featured in the MBA journal as the spotlighted student for the entire American College system. That's why I have made it a point to measure a person by much more than their formal education. We all have greatness. Some just need a little coaxing to reveal theirs. Be patient.

I also need to acknowledge that Carol, for all intents and purposes, graduated with me as well. Every week she would spend time into the wee hours of the morning helping pull together the various presentations. Truly that woman is one of a kind.

Alive and Kicking

Carol was big on celebrating birthdays. For my twenty-ninth birthday, she arranged an awesome trip to Greece. For my thirtieth birthday, she went all out. First, Carol, with the help of Patrick, had rented out Warwick Castle.

Also, we had people from all over the world coming in for the celebration. They arrived at our house and were ushered upstairs, where they changed into medieval costumes that Patrick and Carol had painstakingly selected for each couple. I was decked out as a thin Henry VIII in a tight white outfit with an outrageous hat and codpiece. Seeing me helped anyone not wanting to look foolish overcome their fears. That night two coaches set off for the event. And what an event! One of our good friends, Roman, dressed as a cardinal, walked around blessing everyone the entire evening. What a ham. Paul Clark, my former boss in Poland, had taken to throwing his codpiece around, and my brother Paul was dancing with the wrenches, much to the displeasure of his long-suffering wife. Poor Shirley! I was constantly being dragged up on stage for a dance-off and was fondly being referred to as the bride. Cheeky devils! We had so much fun that night that even today that is the first thing many talk about. Even back then life was always much more than what you did for a living and more about how you lived your life to the fullest.

Each year's celebration outdid the last, it seemed. For my thirtieth-birthday gift, in addition to the party of a lifetime, Carol also arranged a trip on the Concord, followed by a journey on the QE2 and a train ride on the Orient Express to bring it home. It was spectacular. Other years we would travel to Thailand, Egypt, the Maldives, and other faraway places. One of my favorite trips was to Scotland, where we stayed at Cameron House and in the exact suite Winston Churchill used as his Scottish retreat. That's when I took to smoking cigars à la Winston. Victory, baby!

Second Terror Attack

This time it was even scarier. Along with my team, we were attending a two-day strategy session in London. We had finished day one's agenda and enjoyed a great dinner in Central London and had returned back to our hotel. We were enjoying a nightcap or maybe two when we heard an explosion that shook the building. This was followed by all kinds of alarms going off in the distance. My party and all fellow drinkers were unharmed;

however, we all knew something horrible had happened and very nearby. It did not get lost on any of us that we had dodged a bullet and were very lucky. We were quickly moved away from the windows that had thankfully not shattered and made our way to the courtyard.

In moments, the police and emergency services were swarming all over the place. A little later we were told a bus had been blown up as it was traveling around Central London. It was a constant reminder that we were living in dangerous times.

Opportunity Knocks

"Today's horizon is tomorrow's history."
—Abhijit Naskar

I thoroughly enjoyed my time at Whitbread. The people I got to work with were the best. I got to test and grow my skills. The biggest lesson I took away, however, was the importance of evolving and adapting to the ever-changing times. The projects and people I had the pleasure to lead I am truly humbled by. I learned so much from this organization. Thank you, Whitbread. You certainly played a big role in my life.

We thoroughly enjoyed our time together in England. Things on the home front and at work were going great. Carol was being recalled to Dallas to head up refranchising for Pizza Hut. We always knew this was going to happen, so it was not a stressful time. In fact, timing could not have been better, as I had just completed my MBA. We had a great goodbye celebration with people from both Whitbread and Pepsi and family and friends. I was pleased to have met up with my former boss at Pizza Hut, who ironically was now working for my wife, and we made up. That was special for me. I had always liked and had great admiration for him. I wish we had kept in touch, but sometimes life just gets in the way. But it was time for our next adventure.

PART 3

COMING TO AMERICA

I had my own Eddie Murphy *Coming to America* moment, but not before I had one final scare. We had hired an immigration lawyer to help process my green card application to the States. I had my appointment at the American embassy, and we had booked our plane tickets for the next day. I waited in the embassy all day with DJ huddled across my chest. Carol was busy with Patrick making last-minute arrangements. I ended up being the last appointment of the day. I walked up to the window and handed over my papers. The official came back and told me my application was rejected and asked me if I wanted to know the consequences. I curtly said no and left.

I informed Carol and then went straight to my lawyer's office, who was equally perplexed. Apparently, there had been a typo of some kind. It was a tense night. Carol and Patrick flew back to the States, as they had school and housing appointments lined up. At nine o'clock the next morning I entered the US embassy full of trepidation and handed over my papers. To my relief, the official came back a few moments later and handed me an envelope with "Approved" stamped on it.

The next day DJ and I were headed to America to begin a new chapter. It did not disappoint. Just like my favorite Spice Girls hit at the time, it was time for me to "Spice Up Your Life." Let's keep that on the downlow. No need to judge.

New Horizons Calling

"Here you leave today and enter the world of yesterday, tomorrow, and fantasy."
—Walt Disney

Only four years after my first trip to the States, I was now landing in Dallas and calling America my new home. I was unbelievably excited. My favorite song at the time was R. Kelly's "I Believe I Can Fly," and right then I thought I truly could. As part of the immigration process, Carol had to sign that she was financially responsible for me for two years and that I would be no burden on the United States. I wish we still had that practice. It is an honor to come to America, and those who do, unless through political asylum, should not pose a burden and should immediately contribute.

Texas was an amazing state. We had the privilege to call it home for the next six years. We embraced everything the Lone Star State had to offer. We boated in lakes, spent time at the Gulf Shore, and took in every conceivable sports game. I have to admit I was not a big fan initially of the NFL, but my wife was a big-time New Orleans Saints fan. Growing up, I watched the Cowboys, and I stated they were my team. Carol put me straight, and in no time, I was cheering on the Saints. My loving wife did not mention at the time that the Saints seemingly relished losing games. For the first seven years, until head coach Sean Payton and star quarterback Drew Brees turned up, I had cold sweats every Saturday night thinking what was in store for me on Sunday. The punishment was not contained to just watching the game on TV, oh no, my wife wanted to take in live games. The misery then was a glorious two-day affair. My boys were face-painted up for the games, and even the opposing team's fans used to look at me with sympathy. I just quietly nodded and acknowledged them. I remember a Packers game when we were beaten to a pulp, 47–3, and that was after we scored the first three points.

We also went to rodeos and many a road trip down to New Orleans to spend time with Carol's family. I was amazed how bloody big Texas was. Back in the UK, you could travel from top to bottom of the country in six or seven hours. Just to get out of Texas took me half a day. That state is as impressive as it is massive.

They had this place called Medieval Times. We took every family member who came to visit to enjoy this event. I was in touch with my roots. On one occasion I was a little bit too much in character, screaming at the top of my lungs and insisting on the red knight's demise. "Off with his head" was my mantra, in fact. I remember the red knight actually pointing his sword at me and then pointing to his horse's rear. I could not believe he was insinuating I was a horse's arse. What a cheeky fellow indeed.

Carol had settled in at work, and I began my job search. Luckily, I had been hired as a consultant by my former boss at Thresher to implement the labor program I had helped develop the previous year. So I, too, was busy and actually found out how lucrative consulting can be. I earned in a month what I earned in salary in a year. It was a good feeling, but I wanted to be in a company, shaping things up and not coasting.

During this time I also made good on my threat to write my first novel. I was successful in the endeavor but unsuccessful in getting *Outmaneuvered* published, even though I had managed to secure an agent. I have not given up that dream of writing fiction and will one day make another run at it. Brad Thor, watch out! I have a few ideas taking shape as I peck out this book.

Early the next year, Carol again came up big. Weeks previously she had joined a ladies bunko group. Ginger, one of the group, also an executive headhunter, stated she had someone I should meet. Talk about behind every man is a great woman. That meeting led to my first executive position in the States with a company named TurboChef. It also paid me triple my UK salary. Somebody slap me.

I had a quick meeting with the founder and CEO, Phil McKee, and was hired. I was going to be the VP of TurboChef. TurboChef was a one-of-a-kind rapid-cook oven technology. It was extremely versatile. It could bake a pizza in ninety seconds, a hamburger in a couple of minutes, and raw chicken to crispier than KFC. You get the drift. It was also ventless, so it did not require an expensive extraction system.

It had two major operational barriers and then an industry barrier. Operationally, it was huge, weighing in at almost half a ton, and it was pricey at $15,000. But the far bigger barrier to entry was that major restaurant chains had already invested multiple millions and decades of time in perfecting their operating box. TurboChef was a threat to the status quo. I learned through this period that was by far the biggest barrier to success. At this time there were less than a handful of the current models in operation.

Over the next several months, our crack R and D squad also shrunk the box down to a little bigger than a commercial microwave and the cost more than halved. We hired the guy who created the first microwave. It was nonstop learning and breakthroughs. We had solved for the operational barriers. This team was simply brilliant.

I had responsibility over three sales leaders, and we quickly got to work developing a target list. All the major hotels, established restaurants, and the up-and-coming brands in general. Through my wife's connections, we arranged a meeting with the SVP operations and R and D at Pizza Hut. They liked the technology but not enough to change their long-deployed cooking platform. We approached Starbucks, only to be told they were not interested in food. Rejection was to become a daily event. Although we persevered at times, it felt like we were Neo and Trinity in *The Matrix* getting chased by the sentinels. It was exhausting, but I took comfort in a most appropriate Churchill quote: "Success is the ability to go from one failure to another without loss of enthusiasm." I channeled the great man daily.

In time, our perseverance paid off, and we started to get a few buyers. First from Hilton. Then Hyatt. This was followed by several smaller chains, and then we got a major yes from Subway. It was for hundreds of locations. We were finally gaining traction. I cannot thank Churchill enough for the encouragement. *V* for *victory* indeed.

Enter the Dragon

"The devil does a lot of commercials."
—William Peter Blatty in *The Exorcist*

I vividly remember the first time I met the company's key investor. I will simply refer to him as Bad Boy (BB). BB was a smug, arrogant, and wealthy guy. He was in the conference room with his feet up on the table as the new TurboChef CEO and entire leadership team were presenting the materials we had been developing for the upcoming Maytag visit. BB would randomly stop the presentation and make unrelated observations that candidly made no sense. He gave the impression he had all the answers, even though I later found out he had no comprehensive understanding of the technology beyond a few word-salad phrases. I learned this was a theme with BB.

Mad Hatter Moment

"I never dreamed I'd work in a place like this."
—Cecil Gaines in *The Butler*

We have all been at corporate meals we wished we had not, but my one and only lunch with BB was one for the ages. BB turned up an hour late, after we had already placed our orders and were enjoying our food. In he walks, hand in hand with a beautiful twentysomething woman. BB got straight to his point, ranting about the poor positioning of our materials. The young lady was disinterested, and we later found out she was his personal friend. Widespread speculation was "very" personal, but I'll leave it at that. Thankfully, after another rant, he got up and he and his "friend" left. We were stunned. That was another lesson well delivered. BB carried this pattern of disruptive behavior throughout my time there and ultimately destroyed the technology's value. He just simply could not help himself.

Enter Maytag

"I'm not in the big leagues just because I'm cute."
—Pedro Martinez

Maytag came calling intrigued by the technology, and ultimately their new CEO made an investment and acquired the go-to-market rights for the commercial and residential markets of TurboChef. I embraced the move, as the tension between the majority investor based out of New York and the management team was palpable, making it chaotic at best. So much so, as the Maytag deal was being consummated the major investor had the founder and CEO of TurboChef removed. In came a new leader who brought in his own team. Luckily for me they were more focused on the residential opportunity, which had a far larger addressable market. I was left alone to drive the smaller commercial business.

Maytag hired an executive to oversee the commercial business. I was anxious, but this hire proved to be awesome. Jeff Cook, in his own words, was a metal bender, but he was great to work for. We quickly established a terrific working relationship. When he visited, he would stay at my home, and I cannot tell you how many nights we'd just sit up and talk strategy, scratching out what the future platforms of TurboChef would look like while my wife just rolled her eyes. Who could blame her? We did like to repeat ourselves.

During this time I kept my penchant for reading. Knowledge is key and separates the good from the great. I believed it then and even more so now. As fate would have it, I had just read Clay Christensen's *The Innovator's Dilemma*, outlining the law of disruption. I quickly put Moore's and Metcalfe's laws to good use. In the tech space, processing power doubles every three years and costs half. While not a perfect fit for my business, the concept that prices were driven down by volume worked for me. We shrank the size of the cooking platform by two-thirds and reduced the cost by two-thirds. Now we had something to sell.

The personal growth was incredible. I was learning how to manage a sales team and how to sell technology—and commercialize a disruptive one at that. I also experienced for the first time what it was like working in a start-up and the negative impact that oversized investor egos had on the business.

Plantgate

By this time I had patched things up with my father on the condition he would not talk about the Darkness. He would visit yearly. This was one of those times. While I was disappointed in my childhood, I did want to somehow have a relationship with him. More importantly, I wanted DJ to have a granddad. It was funny to see my dad being kind and considerate with both our boys.

One evening I arrived home late from an out-of-town sales meeting. It was past midnight. The cab dropped me off at the front door. As I walked up the front path to the darkened house, I saw a motion inside. Like there was a ghost in the rocking chair. I thought that was strange. I opened the front door and looked to where I saw the motion. We had been burgled previously, and I went into full kung fu mode. I turned the light on and realized immediately we were not being robbed. I got it half right. There was a rocking chair but no ghost. Instead, it was Carol, sitting in the rocking chair in the dark and crying angry tears.

I immediately went over to comfort her and asked what was wrong. Carol said, "It's your father." I thought had something happened to him. Dad had just had his leg amputated below his knee the previous year and was not in the best of health.

Carol assured me that Dad was okay healthwise. She then went on to explain that while she was at work my father had pulled up all the plants in the garden that she had planted. He had redone her entire garden that she had spent years cultivating. Clearly, my dad may have been okay healthwise, but not in the head.

Anyway, we had a chat, and my dad did not pull that stunt again. It took a while for Carol to laugh about that incident.

Losing McDonald's but Ultimately Winning

"Learn as though you would never be able to master it."
—Confucius

Enter the Golden Arches. We targeted McDonald's, and over a two-year period we worked to secure their business. Winning their business would put us on the map. I visited their Oakbrook offices weekly for almost a year. Our relationship manager, Jay, was a rock star. We were one of the bidders for their dual-cavity platform, which is basically—for the uninitiated—a double oven. Our team again did stellar work, and it ultimately came down to price. Their current supplier sharpened their pencil, and we simply could not match it. We lost the bid, but in my opinion we saved the technology. If we had moved forward, we would have placed all our resources to build a product that made us little to no money. This experience underscored the importance of how to value your worth and when it's good to walk away—lessons I have used repeatedly.

Move to the Mother Ship

As our commercialization plans developed, Maytag moved the commercial business under their control. We were now part of the Blodgett organization, which led their efforts. The lessons came fast and heavy. There were so many lessons and pitfalls to watch out for. Initially, Jeff and I thought this move would be terrific, but in the end we realized we were spending more time managing politics and ego than actually driving the business agenda.

First, the host organization, due to internal practices and focus, will inflict organ rejection on the smaller business and ultimately try and kill it if it resides inside it. We made that mistake.

Second, trying to force the TurboChef sales team into the host's current hierarchy, usually for political reasons, also suboptimizes the opportunity. Without assigning blame you needlessly and subconsciously set up competing fractions and enemies when you handle this wrong. Again, shame on us!

Third, the leadership team needed to be aligned and share the same vision.

This was not the case. Guilty as charged.

My learning from this experience was that one must own their mistakes to evolve. With Jeff, I spent several weeks documenting how we would do things differently if the opportunity ever presented itself. Committing to paper also solidified my thinking and seared in the teachings. Ultimately, TurboChef had the potential to be a very powerful breakthrough technology. Possibly equal in size to the Blodgett business. It was never there to destroy Blodgett. They were not competitive but complementary and should have been positioned as such. TurboChef should have been a stand-alone brand in the Maytag commercial portfolio. Alas, that never happened. But TurboChef did eventually roll out in many food-service establishments across the world. I was proud to be part of that effort.

In spite of the challenges, I was continuing to make a name for myself in the Maytag organization. After the integration of TurboChef into Blodgett, I was promoted to the GVP of advanced technologies and GM of TurboChef. The plan was that I was to oversee all advanced technologies across the portfolio, which spanned more than a dozen brands. I was now a peer of my awesome boss, Jeff Cook, who was overseeing corporate strategy. To me, this was business as usual, and as we got to work hand in hand, we kept our relationship and many initiatives.

The Shame Train

"R-E-S-P-E-C-T."
—Aretha Franklin in "Respect"

One of the funniest memories I have from this time was when we launched Accelis, the new brand name for TurboChef, at the Culinary Institute of America facility in Greystone, California. Due to event conflicts, the only dates available were in mid-October. These dates also conflicted with our son DJ's birthday of October 13. It was the only time we ever allowed a business event to supersede any of our children's birthdays. We overcompensated by throwing him a pre- and postbirthday bash.

This launch was a big deal. We had all the Maytag executives in attendance, including Lloyd Ward, the CEO. An executive bus had been arranged. I was waiting for our boss and president of the commercial business and his wife to show up when his secretary walked up and told me that "our boss" was taking a private limo. I got on our bus and informed the group. We had a great experience, but our trip was forever known as the "shame train." Mark Garth, the CFO at the time, recently called me, and we laughed at the recollection. To me, this was a major lesson: to love your people is to be with them. I always traveled with the team. More times than I can remember, I have given my first-class seat and taken their coach seat if they were not upgraded.

Over the next year, I got to work on several high-profile go-to-market campaigns for Maytag—the Coca-Cola glass front vendor and the Kodak vending machines being the biggest. Now I was leading up the marketing, R and D, and commercialization efforts.

Sydney Open

In early 2000, we headed off to vacation in Australia. My brother Paul, his wife, Shirley, and son Thomas joined us. For the next twenty years, we vacationed somewhere together, never missing a year until the COVID pandemic. On this particular trip, we had an awesome time traveling around the Gold Coast and trying to play the didgeridoo, which by the way, Carol was the only one to extract a note from. Our ocean fishing expedition went down the tubes when our entire party, except Carol, heaved our lunches over the side. We all kissed the ground when we made it back to shore. Every moment was a blast.

This trip also ushered in the revival of the Hague brothers' notorious rivalry. This time we turned to golf. It was rigged from the beginning. My brother had been quite the player in his youth and still played often. I was extremely confident, as I had been secretly undertaking some serious lessons in the mastery of golf. More accurately, I'd been watching Tiger Woods destroy the field most weekends. I channeled my inner Tiger and had even worn the golfer's signature red T-shirt for the competition. The first hole was a par three. I took eight shots. Sadly, my armchair game did not translate to the course. The gods were against me, as on one hole I actually hit a bird in midflight. The bird eventually flew away, and with it my pride. It was a pitiful exhibition, and I suffered a rousing defeat. I exited the course on the fifteenth hole after hitting the grass so hard with my club I thought I'd pulled my back out. Our kids were watching and all rolled around laughing hysterically.

That evening at dinner, in the middle of a packed restaurant, my brother made a celebratory speech by standing up and thanking all those who had supported him in his pursuit of becoming a golf champion. I sat there stone-faced, in disbelief as he waxed on, not so eloquently, for a good five minutes. We have had so many such nights, and I am so thankful for all.

The King Is Dead

"I know that I'm falling, and I don't know what to say."
—Fleetwood Mac in "Everywhere"

In early 2001, I awoke to the news that our Maytag CEO, Lloyd Ward, had been removed in true palace-style intrigue. Even worse, there was a major corporate downsizing effort in the works. I knew the writing was on the wall and that I was immediately at risk. TurboChef was one of the big bets that Lloyd had made, and I was leading that, at least on the commercial side. Second, I was heading up innovation for commercial brands, whose leadership and ownership had previously resided solely with the brand presidents. Third, the former CEO was brought back in to steady the ship. I had never met the man. All this was code for "go back to the old way of doing things." Maytag eventually was swallowed up by Whirlpool, so their independence did not last long. At the time, however, when reading the scoreboard, I was zero-for-three, and no time was left on the clock.

On a personal note, I was saddened by the news. Lloyd was just what the business needed. He had great vision; however, he made a fatal mistake. He openly stated he was going to move the headquarters from Newton, Iowa, where they had been based since Moses was a baby, to Dallas. There were a lot of unhappy employees. They became the resistance. Then the market started to turn on him. Remember the dot-com bust of the late 1990s and early 2000s? It was a difficult period. Lloyd never did make the corporate move, but others instead moved against him. There were so many rich lessons from this chapter, but the biggest being don't signal what you are going to do. As Nike put it best: "Just Do It."

This time I did not wait for the axe to fall. I was buoyed on by my favorite song at the time, "Survivor" by Destiny's Child. I moved quickly and got word out that I was looking for a change. A preemptive strike was needed. I grew immensely with Maytag, but the biggest gift I was given was a twenty-year-plus friendship with Jeff Cook. You are the best, Jeff.

I believe if you are lucky, you are blessed to have no more than a dozen people enter your life who are truly consequential. Yes, you can meet a lot of people and have a lot of fond memories, but only a few will stand by you no matter what. Gerri Kies entered my life and has been one of those consequential friends. Gerri recruited me out of Maytag and for the last twenty-plus years has helped recruit dozens of executives for me. Gerri also stood by and supported me through my difficulties and never judged, just supported. Thank you, Gerri. You truly are an amazing lady, and I am so fortunate to call you my friend.

Simply Irresistible

I almost rejoined PepsiCo but instead signed on to 7-Eleven as VP of Fresh Food. While I enjoyed being on the sales side of the business with Maytag, I truly felt at home being on the retailer side. The business spanned over six thousand stores in North America at the time and thirty-two thousand globally. The size and pace of the business was on a scale I had never experienced before—ten divisions and thousands of personnel demanding time and attention. It was so easy to see why so many others before me had failed or simply quit. At times I felt like I was in the Colosseum. Move over, Russell Crowe. There was a new gladiator in town.

I did my due diligence and went in with eyes wide open. I also knew this was like going from the frying pan into the fire. In the last seven years, there had been eight Fresh Food leaders. It was a high-profile role, and clearly failure was not tolerated or forgiven. Expectations were high, and what success looked like was different with everyone you asked. My song of the day was "I Hope You Dance" by Lee Ann Womack. I hoped I could.

Good Times Never Seemed So Good

Married life and being a father was turning out better than I could have ever hoped for or, to be honest, thought possible. Carol was busy at Pizza Hut leading a refranchising effort that kept her busy. Patrick was now in high school doing well, and DJ was in childcare. I especially liked the summers and most evenings I would get home from work with a huge smile on my face. Our backyard pool, which had become the neighbors' gathering ground, was full of kids and parents. We had commandeered a few Slurpee machines and converted one to peach Bellinis, which were a hit with the parents. And yes, I paid for those machines. There was no misappropriation of funds. Often, after getting out of the car, I would jump straight in the pool fully clothed to the delight of the kids. To me, you can be serious, but you don't have to always take yourself seriously. I wanted to show my family it was okay to have fun, and fun we had.

One of my favorite memories in Dallas was buying Carol her dream car, a red Mustang convertible. I tried to steer her to the new BMW convertible that James Bond was driving, in secret hopes I'd also get to drive it. But when Carol has made up her mind, she has made up her mind. Anyway, the thought of driving around on the 635 singing Billy Joel's "We Didn't Start the Fire" at the top of our lungs still makes me smile.

We had also joined a bowling league, playing twice weekly. World champions we were not, but we loved spending time with our friends, who we would host most weekends. For me, a person who had never really known any family happiness since the death of my mother, this was like having an out-of-body experience. Was this really happening? Was I capable of having and seeing such happiness? I used to fear this was a dream and one day I would wake up and feel foolish.

Also, by this time DJ was five, and with me being a soccer fanatic, I wanted him to learn and hopefully love the sport. I saw the best way for me to achieve this was to sign him up a soccer team and be the coach. My wife and I co-opted a few of the neighbor parents to sign up their kids. Our first year was brutal. Our team was more interested in the birds that flew by, or a butterfly or ladybug that landed on or near them than the actual game. The odd kid would kick the ball in the totally wrong direction, and a few would simply sit down in the middle of the game and stare into the sky for inspiration. Talk about a practice in patience. It was like being handed the Dirty Dozen, but I loved every minute of it. This team went on to be great in the seasons to come. It just shows you what a great coach can do. You're welcome. Truthfully, the parents were awesome, and three ended up being assistant coaches.

The Late-Night Drama

It was around one in the morning. We were fast asleep. We were awakened by every parent's worst fear—a ringing phone. Our son Patrick was seventeen at the time. He was upset on the other end of the line. Patrick told me that he had been almost driven off the road by a pickup truck that had rammed him. He told me that he was hiding near our club as the pickup was roaming around looking for him. I dashed out and found him hiding in the bushes behind the clubhouse.

Patrick told me in more detail what had happened—that a blue pickup had rammed him initially about two hundred feet before the bridge and then again on the bridge and that he had escaped. I asked if he was racing, and he absolutely denied it. After calming him down, I called the police, who dispatched a state trooper.

The trooper arrived and asked Patrick to take him to where the incident happened. I thought that would be the end of that. Not so fast. Around fifteen minutes later, the state trooper who had been friendly and concerned got out of the vehicle, and I could tell by his body language that things had changed. The trooper went into monologue mode, stating he saw no evidence that my son was telling the truth and that in fact he was going to write him up for reckless driving and that would forfeit our insurance. I immediately went into Des mode, as is the case when being barked at, and demanded the trooper take me to the crash scene. If Patrick was lying, which I did not think he was, I was still going to defend him. I was also worried about the car going up in smoke.

Minutes later we were at the bridge. The trooper stopped the vehicle and turned to me and said, "If your son was hit by a pickup truck, where is all the debris?" I said follow me and jumped out of the vehicle. I stated that Patrick told me that he was hit way before the bridge. We began to walk. To my relief, we saw up ahead the plastic from the broken taillights of my wife's beloved Mustang convertible and most likely from the pickup truck too.

We walked back to the vehicle, when I saw tire track marks on the side of the bridge. I went into full Columbo mode now, pointing out that there were red paint markings on the barrier from my wife's convertible and then pointed at blue marks that hit the barrier as well. The very same color of the pickup truck that my son stated had attacked him. I looked at the state trooper, who thankfully was not too prideful to realize his error but still managed to state that if my son had said this in the beginning then there would have been no issue. Now I left it to Patrick to tell his mother her Mustang was a write-off. Even I did not have the cajones for that.

Time to Grow

It was exciting to be responsible for a billion-dollar-revenue-generating business. It was another powerful reminder to never let anyone limit your potential or tell you what you can do. At 7-Eleven, I immediately ran two parallel paths. First and foremost, I had to manage the core business and make immediate improvements where possible. The second focus was to create the future Fresh Food business, something we could become famous for. It was hard to balance the two. Candidly, at times it was like trying to peddle your bike up a hill while changing your tire, and at others it was like herding cats. It was extremely time-consuming and equal parts infuriating and exhilarating.

With my team, we quickly implemented the Plan on a Page template for each part of the business for both today's and tomorrow's business for each category of the business. I really had four major stakeholders to satisfy and bring together. First there were the Japanese, who were the principal shareholders. Then there was the 7-Eleven CEO; third was my boss and the operations team; and finally, and just as importantly, the franchisee community.

Each category plan was built on the Bigger, Fewer, Better mantra I had picked up in my Pepsi days. Thank you, Pepsi. I would challenge all that we could not boil the ocean. We needed to boil the saucepan. Focus was required. Fanatical focus, even. You have to define what you stand for and just as importantly what you don't stand for. This thinking immediately bore fruit and delivered significant improvements in the business. Barely a day went by without double-digit increases being posted. The team was starting to believe in themselves. Success begets success. Remember: they had seen eight people in my seat previously. I'm sure at first my team had pegged my shelf life at less than a gallon of milk. Who can blame them?

The all-company meetings consumed Monday and most of Tuesday. If you were not careful, you could easily let those sessions grind you to a halt. Those sessions were intense and at times crazy. I decided from the first week I was actually going to win by creating some crazy of my own. Weekly competitions became the norm, and our merchandising team was up to the task. We dialed up the crazy, and with that came success.

9/11

I remember Joe Weldon, one of my category managers, walking into my office and letting me know the Twin Towers had been attacked and had collapsed. Within an hour, helicopters were circling our building, which was one of the highest in Dallas at the time, and we were evacuated.

7-Eleven is a franchisee-driven business. We have individual store owners who span many nationalities. We were fearful that some of our Middle Eastern franchisee locations would suffer the backlash from the horrific attacks. The entire leadership team worked hard to make sure this did not happen. Thankfully, it did not. During this time I developed a close, personal relationship with the chairman of the franchise system. That relationship also helped gain the buy-in for some of my proposed programs.

In New York, we set up an around-the-clock operation to serve the first responders and government officials. My team worked out of Shea Stadium and distributed truckload after truckload of food, water, and first aid we brought in. It was the least we could do. In the coming days, we found out painfully that many of the extended family of 7-Eleven employees perished on that infamous day. I was so proud of our efforts and our unquenchable commitment to do good.

Go Big or Go Home

"I feel nobody has limits. It's all in your head. If you have a big dream, go after it and go get it."
—Romeo Miller

The attacks took the wind out of everyone's sails, and mine in particular. Jeff Hamill, my counterpart, running all of nonfoods, took me aside one day and said, "Des, you can't let the attacks get to you. You need to be the positive person I know!" I respect Jeff for telling me this hard truth. That snapped me out of my funk. I'm glad Jeff will never know how close I came to headbutting him. You were lucky, my friend.

The end result of Jeff's timely intervention was that I got back into my stride. Ultimately, we settled in on several transformational programs: Big Eats, Big Grill, and the Dream Donut for the base business and the relaunch of Fresh Food in the Austin market, where ironically we would deploy TurboChef ovens to launch our own pizza program. These initiatives would make or break us. We were all in. Go big or go home time.

Be Careful What You Ask For

Things were getting crazy busy for me, and equally so for Carol. Her organization was making a major push to refranchise the business, and Carol had been tasked with making that happen. One evening Carol mentioned in passing we needed to get some help. I jokingly stated we should get a Swedish nanny. I dropped it, and we did not discuss it again. I knew Carol would do what was needed, and a long time ago I knew there could only be one CEO of the house. I also knew that was not me. I did try a few coups over the years, but all failed.

A few weeks later, Carol called me at work and stated she had honored my request and hired a Swedish nanny. Later that night I pull into the driveway. The local kids and parents were in the pool as normal.

As I got out of the car, I saw this Adonis of a young man talking with Carol and our neighbors. This guy was blond, tall, and well-toned. Imagine Brad Pitt in *Troy*. Yes, that bloody good. Carol turned when she saw me, a massive smile plastered across her face, and shouted, "Come say hello to Kurt, our Swedish nanny."

All I could do was laugh and welcome Kurt to the family. He turned out to be a great nanny for DJ and a big help to us. I made a note for future reference that I needed to be a little more descriptive with my funny wife.

Big Eats

I realize a sandwich program is not the most riveting thing to discuss. I promise I am not going to get all foodie on you. I do think you will find the thinking behind the program and the "why" and "what" of it interesting. Right off the bat, I made sure we incorporated many of the lessons painfully learned at Maytag—the most important being to set up a separate innovation team. Equally important was to station them outside the mother ship in their very own facility.

I hired the best and brightest food innovators and set them free. Sarah Palisi Chapin and her team drove this from day one. What an A team! My thinking was to hire the best and then let them create. This was all foreign to the larger corporation, but it paid off big-time. A great learning from my TurboChef and Maytag days.

One of my biggest challenges was in finding products that could survive our delivery process. At Pizza Hut, you would bake a pie and serve it or deliver it. At 7-Eleven, our products had to hold their quality not for an hour but for days. A product that had tasted great initially oftentimes did not fare so well by the end of its journey. I cannot tell you the thousands upon thousands of promising products that never made it to our shelves.

Back to Big Eats. It was a uniform sandwich program and was going to replace the existing hodgepodge program. It comprised a national program but also accommodated regional and local tastes. Basically, it was like twenty flavors of ice cream, with something for everyone. We went big on the promotion, the in-store merchandising, and national and local radio and TV campaigns. We threw everything but the kitchen sink at this.

The business grew fivefold overnight. For those not big into math, that's a big deal. Also, it's no easy feat for a business that had been around seventy-odd years. More importantly, it showed the entire 7-Eleven system we were developing programs that made a difference. Every morning I'd get to work early. I'd get a coffee and play "Beautiful Day" by U2, because that's exactly how I felt. Also, Big Eats was introduced in many other markets internationally. Fresh Food had gone global, baby!

At this time, Jeff, the one who had narrowly missed a good old headbutt, and I scheduled a weekly check-in meeting. Jeff was so supportive he even agreed to place certain nonfood items in our deals to drive our success. Talk about a true servant-leader. I am immensely thankful and appreciative of Jeff. More so, I am proud to be in close contact with Jeff to this day. Jeff is a rock star and on my list of consequential friends. And of course, I would have never headbutted you, my friend. But I must state I am disappointed I never got to work with Jeff again. It was not for lack of trying on my behalf. I tried to coax him not once but twice to join forces; however, I will not hold a grudge. Instead, I'll give him a free promo. If you get the opportunity, check out his book, *Taking Responsibility: Heart, Mind, and Soul*. You will not be disappointed.

The Slap Heard around the Ship

Steady down, this was not the Will Smith type. Around this time I had been asked to join both the Sara Lee and Heinz innovation councils. This helped put 7-Eleven Fresh Food further on the map. Until my arrival, we had never been seen as a food-service company. We were quickly changing that. Heinz, Sara Lee, and Kraft, among others, were starting to see that we could drive their sales as well. This further intensified their own efforts to support 7-Eleven.

Heinz invited Carol and me on a cruise. We got legal to sign off, and away we went. The trip saw us travel around Italy. It was our first time visiting the Amalfi Coast. It did not disappoint. One of my favorite client nights happened on this trip. Our Heinz host, Brent Hansen, and his delightful wife, Joann, who became lifelong friends, were dining with Carol and me. After dinner, they had arranged for us to go to a comedy-cum-magician show. We sat in the audience, and the magician asked for those with a hundred-dollar bill to put their hands up. My hand went up. I always carry emergency cash. As the saying goes, better to be prepared.

I was not prepared for what happened next. The magician called me onstage; then he did a trick and disappeared with my hundred-dollar bill. The audience lapped this up. The magician shooed me away back to my seat. I thought, *Not so fast.* The magician patted me on the head. I instinctively give him a slap across the face. The audience roared, and I took off running around the stage. This went on for a few minutes, and then he recovered my C-note, and I returned to my seat. The audience thought this was rehearsed. It was not. At the after-party, the magician came up and stated I'd made this performance the best so far. Fun times. To Brent, Ken McGettigan, and the Heinz team, thank you for an awesome partnership and the memories.

Ultimately, the cruise was cool, but the connections and the thought-provoking discussions were the real highlight. It was a twenty-four-hour, weeklong learning opportunity, having breakfast, lunch, and dinner with the industry leaders. The brainpower in any given room was tremendous, and if I was being candid, humbling. Sitting down over dinner with the Heinz CEO and hearing his wide perspective on business, politics, and life in general is something I cherish. Making every discussion memorable and impactful is a key lesson I have tried to incorporate into my daily life.

Big Grill

This category was by far the biggest revenue generator in 7-Eleven's Fresh Food North American business. The powerhouse, if you like. Unfortunately, it was also the least liked by our Japanese owners. Their model in Japan is predominantly based around their fresh products, and they felt we should do the same. The lesson here was to not simply expect what works in one area of the world to work in another. Oftentimes they work, but having the ability to adapt and think on your feet to cater to unique needs is paramount.

I could not simply appease our owners and ignore our biggest business. If I did, I knew the business would suffer, and my own candle would be snuffed out. There is a reason so many had failed before me. Strategically, that is why I chose to launch the sandwich program first. Win over some hearts and minds and in the process make them a little bit more accepting so then I could launch a program they were not so keen on. Throughout my tenure, managing expectations of the different stakeholders was my number-one challenge. And talk about a program that started from humble beginnings.

Kraft was also an unbelievable partner. Mike Murnane and Randy Watkins were phenomenal partners. In fact, one of my fondest moments is when the Wienermobile turned up at my home early one morning and took DJ for a ride around town, finally dropping him off at school. It was priceless.

Cayman Open

It had been a few years since my defeat at the Sydney Open. Our next vacation with Paul and our families was in the Cayman Islands. By this time we had agreed to pivot and start up our tennis rivalry once more. Apparently, Paul wanted to retain his sporting dominance and had secretly hired a tennis coach. My spy caught wind of this. Really, Shirley, my sister-in-law and Paul's wife, had called my wife and spilled the beans. Anyway, I appreciated the intelligence.

The day of the open, I inspected the court. It was a clay court, and like McEnroe, my hero, this was not my favorite surface. In fact, I'm still looking for my favorite surface. Anyway, I digress. Due to the magnitude of the moment, I had expanded my support group and hired the club pro as my personal coach for the morning. I thought this would be a pregame intimidation move to play with my brother's head.

Patrick was the umpire and took the official chair. Our younger boys were the ball boys. The wives were spectators. The pro was my one fan on the sidelines. We played one set—winner took all matches. These were hours-long affairs, with a lot of unnecessary showmanship. All from my brother, I might add. While we talk a big game and are fiercely competitive, our skill levels could be best classified as questionable.

Paul won the coin toss, which I even disputed, and served first. I was a few feet back behind the service line. We had not played each other for a few decades, but I remembered he could serve well. That clearly was a long time ago. Paul served, if it could be even called a serve. The ball floated over the net so slow I thought it defied gravity. The result was that the serve created no speed. During that first game, everyone—including the club pro and even those playing on other courts—stopped to watch. The laughter could be heard around the entire resort, especially from the umpires and ball boys, who were physically rolling around the court. At one point I remember demanding to know if the serves were legal and calling on the pro to render a verdict. Our wives have photographic evidence of the entire spectacle.

Anyway, the set came down to a tiebreaker. I begrudgingly admit Paul had upped his game, but in fairness that was not hard to do. The tiebreak ended up being a nail-biter. My brother was up 7-6. He served for the match. I returned his serve crosscourt and celebrated saving the match. Immediately, Patrick called my play "out." My boy had gone to the dark side like a wayward Jedi. I was up in arms, full-blown McEnroe tantrum, screaming, "You can't be serious!" and demanding justice. It was sheer mayhem. Finally, my own coach walked over to where my return had marked the clay. It had missed the line by an inch. I demanded a second opinion, to no avail. My own coach gave the match to my brother, who dropped to his knees like Borg used to do and rolled around for an age. It was an awful moment. Truly soul-crushing.

That night we went for dinner. The place was spectacular. The setup and views were breathtaking, the conversation less so. My brother again took to his feet in the middle of this crowded restaurant and began his ten-minute celebratory speech. Everyone was belly laughing. I made a mental note to hit the courts as soon as I got back home. The rivalry had just kicked up a gear. From this moment on, there would be no prisoners taken.

Reinforcing my desire to destroy my brother at tennis occurred a few weeks later. I returned home and saw a package had been delivered. It was from my brother. I opened it up, wondering what it could be. My brother had framed the front page of what appeared to be a newspaper. Upon further scrutiny, I saw he had the temerity to use the photo of us all and the tennis pro inspecting the disputed line call. The headline blazed "Ice Man (that's what he calls himself; I know, ridiculous) Rolls the Hit Man" (what I rightly call myself). He even wrote a summary of his epic victory and how he had taken me apart play by play. That same framed article is hanging in my office as a daily reminder of true disinformation.

Go-Go Taquitos

I liked to visit the 7-Eleven stores on unannounced trips as often as possible. While taking on such a visit to Philadelphia, very late one night or early one morning, I came across a solitarily product spinning around on the roller grill. It had no signage or price and looked truly, truly sad. I questioned why it was there and then tasted the product, picking up a napkin, which I thought I'd spit the product back out on. That never happened. This pitiful-looking product was delicious. Talk about a hidden gem. To me, it was a true diamond in the rough. We had something here. I knew it was big but did not know how big it would become.

Over the next several months, we worked with the producer (Ruiz Foods, based out of Southern California—a third-generation authentic Mexican food company) to dial up the taste profile and develop a multiple product-line extension. From Fred Ruiz down, this company was a class act. Mark Hannay was also a rock star! I'm proud to have worked with him. Anyway, I wanted a three-year lineup of limited-time-offer products to keep it fresh. This was not going to be a flash in the pan. We also tested multiple price points and bundling strategies. And equally important, we wanted a brand name that would be memorable and fun, just like the brand. Finally, we took the lessons from the Big Eats launch and incorporated those into the pending taquitos launch.

I remember the launch day of Go-Go Taquitos well. The playbook we developed was the blueprint for all future launches. Over the years, we rinsed and repeated that playbook. We toured the Dallas business in the morning and then rushed back to the office. We were like proud parents. The grill was big business for us, and we were messing around with it. While in the various tests we had not cannibalized our hot dog business, we wanted to see what would happen nationally. We held our breath for the daily report.

My entire senior leadership team, grill category manager, and product innovation leader were gathered in my office for our 7:00 a.m. flash meeting the following day. I remember Rod, our finance leader, storming into my office with the sales flash from the day before in his hand. I had purposely not looked at my own dashboard, wanting to hear this at the same time as the team. After all, we lived and died as a team. Rod read out the results: we had doubled the grill business overnight. This was epic. Fresh Food was now on an unbelievable growth trajectory.

To keep the momentum going, part of the playbook was to build and sustain the hype for our launches. For this, we created Taquito Tuesdays. We had some stores actually sell over one thousand taquitos a day.

One of the biggest lessons from this program was to never assume anything and challenge everything. The previous Fresh Food leaders had fallen into the fast-food trap of offering a cheap menu deal. They favored $1.99— meaning the total transaction was less than two dollars.

As part of our research, we found the majority of consumers purchased a beverage. So, while humbling that Fresh Food was not their number-one reason for going to 7-Eleven, we choose to use that valuable data. Working closely with Jeff, we developed a "Leverage the Beverage" strategy.

For Go-Go Taquitos, we purposely, for the first time, did not offer a meal deal. This was questioned by more than a few, but we held firm. In our research, we found that only 17 percent of customers purchased three taquitos at a time. Our objective was to drive that number up, so we offered three Go-Go Taquitos for $2.49—we knew the customer would most likely buy a beverage anyway, and sure enough they did. The average transaction, which previously was $1.99, moved to $4.14 overnight. It was a win-win for not just the grill business but the drinks business as well. A quick $200 million in additional revenue.

Meeting a Legend

We were pursuing a sponsorship deal with Indy. We met with Michael Andretti, son of Mario, the legendary racing family. They were a true class act. Over dinner, hosted by our CMO, Russ Klein, with several of our executives and our wives, we came to an agreement that we were going to have both the seven and eleven cars, representing 7-Eleven. I was thrilled because we got to feature Go-Go Taquitos and Big Eats on the cars. With greater exposure came greater sales.

Finding Nemo (Or Really Our Future CEO)

"I'd rather be lucky than good."
—Lefty Gomez

As I was building out my team, we were in full-blown recruitment mode for top talent. One day Gerri Kies, one of my favorite recruiters, called up and said she had someone special for me to see. I was looking for a director of strategy. In walked Joe DePinto. It took me about two minutes to realize Joe was a baller. I immediately called up the COO and CEO and said I had someone they needed to see. I knew they were looking for a president of the Texas market. They hired Joe the next week. Joe is now chairman and CEO of 7-Eleven and has been for the last fifteen years. I am honored and privileged to call him friend.

The Dreamettes

After back-to-back wins, we turned our attention to the bakery category. Fran Mullin was the captain of bakery and a pleasure to work with. Fran was a no-nonsense guy, hailing from the Northeast, and one who could be counted on when the going got tough. That stated, our bakery business was not firing on all cylinders—and not through lack of effort or quality. The company had set up bakeries all over North America to exclusively bake fresh items that were delivered daily to our stores. The system was a true machine to behold, but still we were not delivering the results we were capable of. My thought was that we had not yet created a craveable product that we were famous for. That was the mandate.

I met with a few of our bakery partners. They were a little upset that other parts of Fresh Food were getting all the attention and all the hype. Why were they the last to go, they questioned. I told them flat out they were next and to be careful what you wished for because it was going to be epic.

In comes the Dreammm Donut. We carefully created the launch playbook, adding many additional elements. My thinking was that each launch had to be better than the last, or we were going backward. My entire Fresh Food team—the CMO, PR, and others—all traveled to Norfolk, Virginia, for the Dreammm Donut launch. We had an awesome time with the division leadership and even launched the Dreammm with the Dreamettes, a singing and dancing group. I wish I never participated in the eat-off, but the product was delicious.

Glazed donut sales increased twentyfold. We sold more six-packs than we had previously sold singles. The bakers scrambled to keep up, and I had a lot of fun reminding them they had been forewarned.

The above were the Bigger, Fewer, Better plays, but that did not mean all parts of the business were improved. We undertook a massive SKU rationalization program. Products that did not hit a certain hurdle for their category were eliminated. Saying no to products meant we were really helping the final products selected have a better chance to stand out and be successful. It drove cost out of the system but never at the expense of upsetting customers. We also had a fanatical focus dialing up the favor profile of all products that made the menu. Taste was the number-one reason for purchase, and we took that seriously.

During this time I was part of many conference speeches, and we won numerous awards. I loved the brand, but the desire to run my own business was building. There were also so many wonderful lessons. Recognizing that you have to drive a multibillion-dollar enterprise with the sense of urgency of a start-up being top of the list. Closely followed by acknowledging it's okay to be wrong. You don't have to be right all the time, and if you are, you are not pushing your capabilities far enough. And finally, you need a well-motivated and committed team to create something great. Anything less and you are limiting your chances of success.

The Big Bash

We were bound for New York City to celebrate 7-Eleven's seventy-fifth birthday. I actually got to present to ten thousand franchisees and licensees from around the globe. I am very proud to state I have rocked Madison Square Garden. This celebration led to an interesting meeting. My wife and I were walking around Ellis Island, which 7-Eleven had rented out for the day, when we encountered a large Japanese group. I quickly realized this was the actual ownership group, and the principal owner, Mr. Itayokodo, was among them. I was introducing my wife and myself to the group when Mr. Itayokodo stepped forward and bowed and said, "Ah, Des San. Head of Fresh Food." He looked at my wife and pointed at me said, "He has the hardest job in the company," and continued walking.

My God, he recognized me. And damn straight I have the hardest job in the company. You don't need to tell me that, I thought.

For the celebration, Judd Chapin, the husband of my good friend Sarah Palisi Chapin, who was also heading up our innovation, came up with a brilliant idea. Judd had been part of the team that developed the original 7-Eleven jingle. He wanted to bring that back for the big finale and have a massive choir sing "Oh, Thank Heaven for 7-Eleven." That night, like Macklemore sang, the thousands of franchisees and licensees in attendance put their hands up like the ceiling couldn't hold them as they sang along. Then Nelly performed "Hot in Here" live. What a way to cap off the event.

It Ain't What You Do; It's the Way That You Do It

While our results had improved immeasurably, the CEO was still under pressure for Fresh Food to grow faster; therefore I was always under the microscope. I felt I was built for the pressure and thrived. In fact, in one board meeting I attended in Japan, where I thought we were going to be thanked for our performance, the Japanese CEO of SEI turned to my CEO and demanded to know when we were going to fix Fresh Food. You could have knocked me down with a feather. I just shrugged that off and kept ticking, though, more determined than ever.

Then it got much worse. I was called into an executive session with the senior leadership. This was a meeting that still gives me the shivers. Our leader at the time, in front of the entire group, stated we were under increasing pressure from ownership to drive Fresh Food and should fire Des. The group let out an audible gasp but all rallied to my support. From that day forward, I was looking for my next move. It amazes me that people believe this is the way to motivate. The CEO called, and we talked it through. He insisted it was a joke, and he was looking for a reaction. He was thrilled the team rallied to support me, but the light extinguished in me that day. I knew it would never be the same.

Big Decision

"When a defining moment comes along, you define the moment, or the moment defines you."
—Roy "Tin Cup" McAvoy in *Tin Cup*

Kohlberg, a New York–based private equity company, came calling. Yes, that one, the very same spin-off outfit of the *Barbarians at the Gate* variety. The world works in mysterious ways. My life has taken many turns and twists. Doors have opened, and doors have closed. But when opportunity came knocking, I always opened the door. This was one of those times. The chairman of TurboChef was a gentleman named Marion Antonini. Marion, unlike the principal investor, BB, was a class act. He also fully supported the actions we were taking to commercialize TurboChef and knew the liability the primary investor posed. Marion was also the operating partner of Kohlberg. Kohlberg had recently made an almost $100 million investment in a turnkey food franchise business predominantly operating in the convenience store channel. Their same-store sales were down almost twenty points, while ours at 7-Eleven were up the same period thirty to fifty points. They were looking for a CEO to turn things around. I was built for this. I was excited about the prospect, but it did not come without its challenges.

We had in front of us a critical and really life-changing decision—not the "this wine will change your life" claim but truly life-altering. This was no game of Monopoly. The stakes here were real and consequential. The elephant in the room was that the position was to be based out of Sioux Falls, South Dakota. It might has well have been a million miles from Dallas. First, we were a two-executive family. My wife was still in an executive position at Pizza Hut. She was very career-oriented. It did not define her, but it was important to her, and she was up for a promotion. If we made the move, Carol would have to resign and leave her career. Remote work was not a thing. This was not an easy decision, and candidly it was not one I could push for.

We had some thinking ahead of us. So we did what anyone would do and headed to the mountains in Colorado to decompress, enjoy the slopes, and think things through. While on the slopes, we weighed the pros and cons. The list was stacked high on both sides of the equation. On the plus side, the package would cover the loss of Carol's annual income, so from a monetary standpoint, we would not be worse off on a day-to-day basis. On the minus side, Carol had worked her entire career, and money alone could not put a value on her professional life.

In addition, the potential move would free up Carol to focus on the family. The woman was daily juggling work-home issues with the dexterity of a Cirque du Soleil artist. This move would allow a reset and for Carol to focus more on our youngest, DJ—who had just turned six at the time—as well as other things she cared deeply about and simply did not have the hours in the day to pursue. This was a major plus.

On the negative side, and of great consideration, was that Carol was close to completing twenty years of service and was eligible to collect her pension—a seven-figure payout. Again, this was no small consideration. Carol was a year short, but if we made the move, living apart was off the table. This payout was going up in smoke. It gave us a lot to think about. If things did not turn out as planned, this would result in a major financial hit.

With all these considerations swirling in our heads, our schedules fell into a routine. Get up, breakfast, head out to the slopes, dinner, then relax. Every night after putting DJ to bed, the relaxing was done in the hot tub with a drink in hand while looking up at a sky full of the most magnificent stars.

While wanting to be CEO, I had privately formed the opinion I could not ask Carol to make this kind of sacrifice. I knew what her career meant to her, and the loss of her pension weighed heavily. Saying goodbye to over a million dollars was too big an ask. I was about to state that when Carol said simply, "We should do this, Des." I looked on, speechless, as she continued.

"You deserve this, and most importantly, it is just the beginning for you. We have to do it." I welled up with tears as we hugged tightly. We had made the big decision—or rather, Carol had made it all possible.

I called Kohlberg the next evening after traveling home, and we quickly agreed on terms. I was going to be a CEO and fulfill my life's ambition. Like my favorite song by 50 Cent at the time, I was "In Da Club." I was just shy of thirty-three years old. Only eight years ago I had been told I would never make area manager. Let that be a lesson to all. You are the only one who can ever define or impose limits on yourself. It is a lesson I misremembered later and had to painfully relearn.

Dances with Wolves

I would not call my introduction to Orion Food Systems a friendly one, but I took it in stride. After all, I had operated in many places and seen many bad actors and actions by then. This was not my first rodeo. Demonstrating confidence was critical. I doubled down on that. On the day of my arrival, it was snowing hard and was colder than a witch's tit. I thought I had experienced cold in Eastern Europe, but this was on another level. I remember calling home in the afternoon, and Carol asked me what the weather was like. I simply muttered bright. I was not lying; there was bright snow everywhere. This was true *Dances with Wolves* territory.

The business had been a part of the Schwan's portfolio since its inception. Schwan's was family-owned. Jeff, the son-in-law of the owner, had been running the business. Jeff was universally liked, but the business had peaked and then stagnated under his leadership. Upon my arrival, Jeff made no effort to relocate from his office and let me move in as the new CEO. It was a passive-aggressive play, but I simply moved into the conference room and eventually would build that out.

The leadership team were competent but not fully focused. It had the vibe of a party atmosphere. Most summer afternoons the executive team would cut out of the office for a round of golf. We immediately shook things up. During my Maytag days, I learned you have to implement your changes quickly and keep them to yourself until finalized. I'm proud to say the majority of the original team were a part of the successful transformation of the company in the years ahead. Sadly, Jeff passed away a few years ago, and I never got the opportunity to meet up and talk about the old days. Let that be a lesson to us all—reach out to your friends now while you can.

Forty-Two-Tornado Welcome

"Now I'm four, five seconds from wildin.'"
—Rihanna in "FourFiveSeconds"

My wife stayed behind in Dallas to handle the move and allow our kids to complete their school term. Actually, Patrick was a young man at this time. Patrick had gone off to college and left to run a Blockbuster. Small world indeed. Patrick asked to join us in South Dakota. The band was back together, and they moved several months after me.

Their welcome was, shall we say, less than hospitable. I picked them up at the airport and got them settled into the long-stay hotel. I had the operating partner from Kohlberg in for a business review and stated I'd be back later that day. They were right next to the mall, and DJ had his mind set on a long trip to Toys "R" Us. That afternoon the heavens opened, along with heavy rain and winds. As I left the office, the air raid–like warnings were raging; forty-two tornadoes had touched down that afternoon.

I made it back to the hotel and was greeted by my family all chilling out in the corridor, well away from the windows. My wife just took it all in stride, like she did with everything else. We were a team.

Within three months, I had visited every district in the company and saw every one of the twenty-plus concepts we operated in person for myself. We operated six hundred locations and had that many brands. It was clear that Bigger, Fewer, Better was a foreign concept. But not for long. We solved this by rebranding to Hot Stuff Foods, placing the signature items of all brands into this primary concept. Eventually, we pared down to four brands. The shift was rewarded, and sales quickly reversed and in fact doubled over the next three years. In the words of my go-to song at the time from Pink, it was time to "Get the Party Started."

Next we developed the same playbook for the different brands that had been effective at 7-Eleven. A few strategic hires helped to smooth that process and accelerate learning.

This was a period of great personal development. It was a rude awakening. Being at Hot Stuff Foods was a humbling experience. I was working in a small, relatively unknown company for the first time since a teenager. With

Pepsi, Pizza Hut, and 7-Eleven, people flock to you. They court you. At Hot Stuff Foods, that was no longer the case. Now we had to chase talent. We had to get creative. I also did not have an army of people to help get the job done. I recall going to numerous trade shows, where Carol and I would actually put our booth together. This was a sleeves-rolled-up experience from the first day. I was in a true "you eat what you kill" environment.

New Thinking

"Insanity is doing the same thing over and over and expecting different results."
—Albert Einstein

Being a constant student is central to how I operate. Coming into Hot Stuff Foods, we created a threat matrix on the business. By this time Bob Merz, who was the CMO at 7-Eleven, had joined me. As did Roman Stone, who had dressed up as the cardinal from my thirtieth-birthday bash. I had worked for Roman in Europe, and he had then worked for me at both Maytag and 7-Eleven, making this our fourth tour of duty together. A few key veteran category managers, including Joe Horres, joined the mission. Joe is a giant among giants.

Between a few of us, we realized the Hot Stuff Foods' core model was based on baking a pizza from scratch. We were misaligned. We would get steady growth opening fifty of these more complex operations annually, but our model was not for 90 percent of convenience stores. Also, the cost of opening a location was prohibitive at almost $100,000. If we wanted to tap into that market, we would need to think and do things differently.

I Want Some Hot Stuff, Baby, This Evening

Running Hot Stuff Foods was my very first opportunity to run a company. Sometimes it is easier to want something than to have something. I did not want to be like the dog who caught the car. This was what I had been working toward all my life. A key learning for me, which may appear counterintuitive, is that it is easier, in a sense, to manage a larger business than a smaller business. If you make a million-dollar bad decision in a billion-dollar business, it is a rounding error, but in a smaller enterprise, it is business-ending. Ultimately, while the business was smaller, the stakes were higher. My thought process was to get the box right once and then replicate. I took the responsibility seriously but wanted to run the company my way. I wanted to have fun. If people were happy and felt appreciated, they would freely give more than anyone could demand.

We set up a fun committee and worked on ways to celebrate the team. Every weekly update was delivered by a voice message from me. Every week for those three years I started off with Donna Summer singing her iconic song "Hot Stuff," which I would duet with full conviction, if not off-key. I believe that being relatable and self-deprecating as well as offering high doses of passion and courage can take you places. Having fun and making work fun is also up there in my formula for delivering sustainable long-term success.

I vividly remember our first conference as Carol and DJ walked into the conference at the end of day one and proudly showed off our new addition. A boxer puppy strolled across the stage and was adored by the whole audience. She was named Cassius, after the boxer, and she was an awesome member of the family.

The Law of Disruption

Enter Hot Stuff Express. The backbone of the concept was offering parbaked products that needed limited, if any, preparation time. This allowed the concept to be executed with a lower skill level. Ironically, it was solely powered by the TurboChef oven. Within three years, we opened up almost one thousand of these units. Each had a price tag of less than $10,000, a tenth of the cost of the more labor-intensive concept and a fraction of the space requirement to operate. This was our very own industry disruptor.

Ten-Year Anniversary

As 2005 rolled around, Carol and I were celebrating our ten-year anniversary. For me, it seemed we had just met yesterday, but at the same time it felt like I had known Carol all my life. Anyway, I wanted to make it a special occasion, and we decided on Bora-Bora. I think Carol chose this island because it was totally off the grid. There were no telephones at the resort, Hotel Bora-Bora. It was a place frequented by movie stars, so I thought we would fit in.

As luck would have it, or not, we were refinancing the company as we headed out. There would be some paperwork for me to handle. As I stated, there were no phones in the rooms. They took relaxation very seriously. Not as serious as Carol, who took no chances and confiscated my phone and held it hostage in the room safe in case I got tempted. Cheek of the woman!

Thankfully, there was a small business center, which was no more than a closet off the game room, with a fax machine and a sole computer from the 1960s, it seemed. This place truly frowned upon work. The computer was still of the dial-up variety. On this occasion, I had been booted off several times and was becoming agitated. Out of nowhere there was screaming and laughing from outside the room. This went on for a good ten minutes. I finally had enough and pulled the door open and was face-to-face with a scruffy-looking man and two kids. The man asked if they were bothering me. I snapped yes. The man apologized, and I slammed the door. Later I found out that was Sean Penn and his kids. Fun times.

Here We Grow Again

Around this time, we also developed a very compelling proposition for none other than the US military. Within a few short years, we were operating on twenty-plus international bases and even more stateside. We had gone global. We actually deployed TurboChef at the Pentagon, of all places. On one particular visit to the Pentagon, I walked right past the office of secretary of defense, William Cohen. He was right there behind his desk. We were living in different times then and did not know what a threat level was.

Lightning in a Bottle

The launch of Palm Pizza is the program I am most proud of in my career by far. It was not the most successful, but to me it was the most innovative launch I have ever led. Again, Hot Stuff Foods was a small company. I did not have the luxury of a multimillion-dollar launch budget. Our executive chef, JJ, was one of the best in the business. We had lucked out talentwise with him. Chef JJ and I spent early mornings, late nights, and weekends in our innovation center.

Pizza was our core product, but at the time our proposition was built around bake from scratch. I wanted a par-bake alternative for our Xpress concept. But for years everything we attempted fell short of the mark, at least in the pizza department. That is, until Chef JJ reformulated a recipe and created a small boat-shaped product we could sauce, cheese, top, and cook in either a conventional pizza oven or TurboChef. This was a breakthrough. We had developed a product that was best in class. We finally landed on the Palm Pizza—the pizza that fits in the palm of your hand. Easy concept to communicate. For our franchisees, it was also far easier for them to execute at store level. This product instantaneously became our biggest hit. If I would have had this at 7-Eleven, it would have been a billion-dollar business.

Packing on the Pounds

"The greatest wealth is health."
—Virgil

One morning, walking out of the kitchen, I looked down at a photo on the counter. I asked Carol when we took this of my father. Carol laughed and said that's you. I looked again at the picture and was horrified. There was no easy way to say it, but my dad was a little on the heavy side. Truthfully, more than a little—a lot. Not to mince any words, I looked like the Pillsbury Doughboy. I had packed on some pounds. Little of the extra baggage, if any, was muscle, but mostly good food. Even my chins had chins. It's funny, as in my own eye I was in gladiator-type shape. Denial!

The reality is, I had fallen into the business-obsessed trap that many suffer. I was not placing enough focus on my own health and wellness. Only bad things come out of that.

That very same afternoon Carol and I went to the gym and signed up. Patrick joined us. I weighed in at almost 230 pounds—a good 50 or 60 over my fighting weight. The constant dinners out with clients, which included my favorites—red wine, bread, cheese, chocolates, and, of course, pizza— along with zero exercise, had caught up. It did not help that I was a regular also at all our daily food tastings.

We got into the gym regimen hard. For the next couple of years, we would be there four to five times a week at the crazy time of 5:00 a.m. I liked to be in the office by 7:00 a.m., so my days just got longer by a couple of hours. My nephew Tre came to work with us. He tells the story best of me waking him up at 4:45 a.m. when he was in town to "Physical" by Olivia Newton-John. I think I may have been taking this exercise thing a little seriously. To this day, he states he has PTSD from the ordeal. Charming!

Carol signed DJ up for karate. Several times a week we'd go to his practice sessions. The next thing I know, Patrick, Carol, and I are also signed up. The sessions were three nights a week. The fitness regimen kicked up a further notch. Over the next few years, we all advanced. Patrick excelled and got his black belt and then second-degree black belt. We progressed and all got to red belt when Carol tore her meniscus. I sat out and waited for Carol to recover so we could get our black belt together.

Making a Difference

"The highest tribute to the dead is not grief but gratitude."
—Thornton Wilder in *Our Town*

Hot Stuff Foods was one of the biggest employers in the city of Sioux Falls. As such, nothing we did went unnoticed. It was also the first time I got to think about how I can drive a company to be a force for good in the community.

Of course, the companies I had worked for previously supported many causes, but they did not have my fingerprints on those efforts. Even my Second Chance program back in the UK had been limited. This opportunity was on another scale.

Hot Stuff Foods, ironically, had been heavily involved with helping support battered women and children. After my life experiences, how could I not love those programs? We quickly doubled down on our commitment. Next up was supporting the Children's Home Initiative, which also helped disadvantaged children. The following year we made a half-million-dollar pledge to the Stanford Children's Hospital. I remember bursting into tears as I made this public announcement. I just could not control my emotions. Thankfully, the CEO of the hospital joined me at the podium, gave me a hug, and joined me in crying openly. These moments truly supercharged my passion to be a force for good and to make a difference in the community. Here I learned what it was like to do good and do well. The millions we raised annually gave me an adrenaline boost to do more.

In a little less than four years, we had doubled the top line and more than doubled the enterprise value. Kohlberg sold the business to another PE group. At the time, it was the firm's second-best return in history. I wanted the top spot and would later correct that error. Ultimately, my first CEO role was in the books and a success. The transaction made me a multimillionaire. The boy from Rotherham, who was slated to do no good and be no good. I had just turned thirty-seven. I was living the life. I had swapped out equity partners and would see very quickly if that was going to be a good move.

(I Just) Died in Your Arms Tonight

Even though this was a very successful time, misery visited painfully and profoundly so. Cutting Crew's classic song "(I Just) Died in Your Arms" could not have been more accurately titled to describe the situation. Luckily, it was not me dying, but it was someone very special.

Carol and I were in New York City and had just checked into the Waldorf

Astoria, our favorite at the time. The trip was a double celebration for us. First to celebrate the deal, and second it was my birthday. Room service had just delivered a chilled bottle of champagne to get the festivities started. No sooner had I popped the bottle than my cell phone rang.

I saw that it was my brother-in-law Jay on the phone. I answered, thinking it was to wish me a happy birthday. Jay asked to also speak to Carol, so I hit the speakerphone. At the time I was still expecting Jay and Ginny Sue to break out into song. Things took a turn when Jay stated that Tildon, their father, my father-in-law, had just been rushed to hospital moments before and had died en route. Our celebration ground to an immediate halt. We made arrangements and immediately flew to New Orleans.

Later that night we were told that Tildon had actually passed away while dancing with a nurse friend. While dancing, the nurse, sensing something was wrong, had asked if he was all right. Tildon stated no and collapsed into her breast. Initially, the nurse thought he was just having fun, then realized it was serious. But what an amazing way to go. I always imagine Tildon singing, "I just died in your arms tonight," as he checked out. Right up until the end, the man lived his life fully. Dancing and bowling four to five times a week. A true inspiration to us all.

Major-League Call-Up

"Some beautiful paths can't be discovered without getting lost."
—Erol Ozan

New equity owners came into Hot Stuff Foods and wanted to move the business forward their way. I had been around the block and knew I could either bend or be broken. Like Kenny Rogers sang, "you have to know when to hold them and know when to fold them." I decided to work for a negotiated settlement. Ironically, within a week of starting these conversations, Safeway came calling. Within the span of a week, I had exited one business and joined another. I took the weekend off and reported for duty in Pleasanton the following Monday. The executive recruiter was Melanie

Steinbach, who handled the senior searches for the retail space at the time. Melanie was more vigorous than the IRS and took me through my paces. It was a brutal process, to say the least. Melanie throughout was the consummate professional and in my eyes a giant in the space. It is no surprise that Melanie ascended to significant roles in the corporate world, serving as chief people officer at McDonald's and Cameo. The woman is brilliant. Think Wonder Woman. I am also pleased to call her a consequential friend to this day.

This was to be my third retail company, and I was hoping for the third time to be a charm. It almost was. Melanie briefed me that the current CMO, Brian Cornell, was going to ascend to president and CEO. The missing element he needed was a president of perishables. The perishables business was a $20 billion-plus machine and the growth engine of the company. Earlier in his career, Brian had worked for Pepsi and managed their Tropicana business. I knew of him but never had met him in person. We immediately clicked.

Bend the Knee

Prior to my sign-off, I was told the current chairman and CEO wanted to interview me. I thought this was a strange move, as Brian would be taking over shortly. I agreed to fly out that Saturday. I had a family engagement on Sunday and did not want to miss it, so I had arranged to meet the CEO at his golf club and then travel directly to the airport for the last flight home, which arrived late after connecting in Minneapolis.

I arrived at the Blackhawk County Club for our noon meeting. I watched the hours slowly roll by until the CEO, Steve Burd, arrived almost three hours later. I should have taken this as an omen, and I would have done so if I did not think he was shortly going to be leaving. We spoke for an hour. I thought I had done enough to have gained his approval, but I never felt good about the man. To make things worse, I now had missed my flight home and would miss the family celebration. In spite of the encounter, I was excited about the opportunity.

Settling In

I got to work quickly understanding the key levers of the business. It was similar but with a twist to my previous experiences, just on a bigger scale. There was a lot of institutional knowledge in Safeway, and if truth be told a little too much not-invented-here attitude. But the perishables team had some real talent. Jewel Hunt and Geoff White were the initial standouts. Over time, Matt Gutermuth, Kelly Griffiths, Tom Schwilke, and Scott Grimmett, among others, came to mind. Over my career, I can confidently say I have never worked with a more conscientious, buttoned-up, detail-orientated leader than Jewel. Jewel could and would get things done. Sorry we did not get to work together for longer.

On the family front, we found a home in Pleasanton, California, which was almost triple the cost and half the size of our previous home—typical California. We made several friends in the neighborhood and actually hosted *Pleasanton Idol* at our house weekly, where a local neighborhood girl with special needs, Amber Ortizi, was crowned our idol. I will never forget the look of joy on that young girl's face. It was sheer happiness. She is a special girl. The rightful idol.

Uncle Sam Wants You!

While in Pleasanton, I also proudly became an American. Although I had lived in the U.S. for over a decade, we thought the time was right for me to officially become a citizen. After all, I loved the country and wanted to remove any future complications of not being allowed to stay and live here. My wife got things moving, as she always did, and worked with the attorneys.

I remember sitting in the hot tub enjoying a cigar the night before the ceremony. I heard a car stop, followed by distinctive Yorkshire voices. Paul and Shirley had arrived. As always, my wife had planned a party for my swearing-in and invited my family. Colleagues and friends arrived the next day. True to form, Carol had me dressed up as Uncle Sam. It was a day to remember. I also have it on good authority that same day the country's IQ took a major leap forward. A coincidence, I think not!

Supercharging Safeway

> "Once the mind has been expanded by a big idea, it will never go back to its original state."
> —Thomas Carlyle

After spending weeks performing a SWOT analysis on the Safeway business, I was ready to begin the work on supercharging it. I channeled my inner Sinatra and put a bold "My Way" plan together. We used the same Plan on a Page and Bigger, Fewer, Better processes and thinking. Consistency is key to success. Keep it simple! When you overcomplicate things, that's when you screw up. So don't.

Working with my department leaders, they had all boiled down their big priorities to no more than three. This was obviously in addition to running the day-to-day program. During this time I worked with several of our leaders and realized we had a great opportunity to leverage our scale that had previously been overlooked. The result was a $10 million check being handed over to us. It was by far the biggest received.

Over the coming weeks, we went to work to define the Big Three initiatives that would help transform the perishables business. Operation Dinner Out, Operation Sideshow, and Big Café were launched. One of my favorite movies is *Spy Game*, starring Brad Pitt and Robert Redford. Their big projects in the film were Dinner Out and Sideshow. I thought, *If it's good enough for Pitt and Redford, its good enough for Safeway and me.*

All Hands on Deck

> "To say my fate is not tied to your fate is like saying, 'Your end of the boat is sinking.'"
> —Hugh Downs

With Jewel Hunt, my VP at the time, we launched a very ambitious program. We wanted to launch the first restaurant-quality entrée and sides program in the grocery world a good fifteen years before Blue Apron and others came to market. We wanted this to be fresh, with minimal to no preservatives and a short shelf life of a few days. We called in all senior executives from the Safeway organizations and enlisted their feedback and support. Roger Glenn, SVP HR at the time, said he knew this was going to be special. Roger later wrote a note to me that he had never seen such leadership and that he, from that day forward, compared every aspiring leader to me. Shucks, Roger, you make me blush, but keep the compliments coming, my friend.

For this, Jewel and I, along with many others, called in the major and minor suppliers across the country. We laid out our plans and invited them to participate. And participate they did. Within a few months, we had over a dozen entrées and the same amount of side dishes ready to pilot. Operation Dinner Out (entrées) and Operation Sideshow (sides) were ready to launch.

I knew launching the program needed something else. It needed to get the media and the investor community's attention. For this, we selected the Wente Winery and invited all investors who followed Safeway. We decked the big hall like you would a high-profile gala. The table centerpieces were from our floral department and were eye-popping. Tracy and Cheryl, the leaders from floral, never failed to impress. That night we launched our restaurant-ready meal program by feeding over a hundred guests the very same food program we were about to launch in our Safeway stores. If I say so myself, that night was a raving success. Looking back, I think candidly that was the night when the outgoing CEO saw the reaction of the audience and decided he was not leaving without being a part of this major hit.

Sponsor's Departure

"Give me the grace to accept the things I cannot change, the courage to change the things I can, and the wisdom to know the difference."
—the Serenity Prayer

A few days after the Wente Winery gala event, Brian, my boss and heir apparent to the CEO position, walked into my office. He sat down and congratulated me again for a great event and then rocked my world. He told me that he was leaving. The current CEO was in fact absolutely not leaving. I heard the words and for the life of me could not process them. I was in shock. I'd made this move expecting I would assume Brian's role upon his promotion. That was my reason for coming. I thought that was still possible. How little did I know!

Old Guard Attack

After Brian's sad departure, I sat down with the CEO and CPO, and they said the right things; however, I knew Steve had no intention of stepping back. After all, he was the chairman, CEO, and president of Safeway and CEO of Blackhawk. Steve needed control and more titles, apparently.

At the time, the company was in the process of setting up a leadership summit for the up-and-comers as well as executives. I was asked to present innovation. All executives were run through the summit. I went all out, and the feedback was a hit. Many division presidents felt I should have been appointed to CMO on the spot, but that was not to be. There were some good guys there.

Unfortunately, one of the issues I was confronted with I had not experienced at 7-Eleven. At 7-Eleven, I had someone on the other side of the business who wanted to partner and saw the bigger picture. At Safeway, that was not the case; we set up the business in such a way that the perishable and nonperishable teams were competitors. We were misaligned, and we could not break the cycle no matter how hard we tried. Category managers were not rewarded for total growth of the business. They were rewarded by their category's growth, even if it came at the expense of missing a bigger opportunity. It resulted in constant turf wars and totally unnecessary infighting. Really sad!

I suppose I had big aspirations for Safeway. My close friends said I could run any company after this. It was all good, until it wasn't. Brian leaving out of the blue was a development that could not be overcome. I had been operating as a change agent bringing hope. I spoke with the CEO and tried to impress upon him that there was a better way. He did not budge, so I made the painful decision that it was sadly time to move on. Change and hope had morphed into hope for change. Mine! While disappointed about the outcome, I will always have fond memories of the people at Safeway and truly wished it had ended up differently. But like my favorite song of the year, by Lady Gaga, I left with my own "Poker Face," having done things "My Way" to the end.

Family Coup

"I could have been a contender."
—Terry Malloy in *On the Waterfront*

The day after my resignation from Safeway, I decided it was time for me to get things organized to my liking around the house. I called a family meeting, which meant we ate breakfast together. Patrick had joined the coast guard by this time and was no longer living at home. We all missed him, but we were also very proud he wanted to protect and serve. While Carol and DJ were eating, I started by saying to DJ that I was going to be spending more time at home, and that while I was home, I was going to set up a few tasks I'd like to get done and needed his help around the house. I was no more than thirty seconds into my rousing monologue when DJ piped up, "Dad, we love you, but Mom runs the house. That's what you have always said." With those few words, my attempt at taking over the house was quashed. I quickly shifted to focusing on what I was going to do next. It was actually a much more productive use of my time.

Santa Barbara Open

I knew I should have pulled out from this tournament. I was in the middle of negotiating my next role, and we were in the house-hunting process. But Paul was itching to consolidate his number-one ranking and demanded we play.

The Four Seasons at Santa Barbara offered to host our tournament. Actually, they had a court available, like they do for any guest, but that's beside the point. I was racing through the set and to victory. I was quickly up 5-3 and serving at 30-0. Sweet vengeance and victory were a few short points away. I served down the *T* and turned to collect my thoughts to close out the match. Paul then muttered that the serve was out. I knew the serve was good. He knew the serve was good. Tempers flared. Our wives were making the calls. We verbally attacked both of them. They solved that and immediately resigned and ventured off to the spa. I decided to give him the point and close it out. I did not close it out. I choked like a chicken. I lost 7-5 and walked off the court with no handshake or press interviews!

I was hoping that would be the end of that miserable experience, but oh no. At dinner, Paul again milked the occasion for all he could muster and then some. He began to regale us with the story of the epic comeback, narrating it point-by-point. What a riot this guy is. The family was lapping it up, as usual. Even though I was still furious, I could not help but join in at times, especially when my brother informed us that he had it on good authority I was being fined $100 for unsportsmanlike conduct for not congratulating the victor and still number-one tennis player in the world. Where's an alarm clock when I needed one? After that defeat, I went back home committed to some old-school Rocky training but just ended up watching more tennis on the TV or at live events.

Career Mistake

> "Breakdown? Breakthrough."
> —Jerry Maguire in *Jerry Maguire*

I interviewed for several president positions. I did not rush into my next gig, but even with the benefit of time I still made a mistake. Flo Rida's "Low" was the current hit and very fitting. IHOP is a world-renowned brand and was the largest family dining brand in the world, which I am honored to state I led for a short period of time. The mistake was that the current CEO wanted to be more hands-on than I wanted. After the micromanaging of Safeway, I wanted to control my own destiny. That's not to say the CEO was not extremely talented. Julia was all that and more. I personally liked her and her husband, Tim, very much. We were simply misaligned. I should have probed harder in the interview process. That was my mistake. That's on me.

But the franchisees were the best in the business, and I quickly got to work partnering with Mike Archer, the president of the sister brand, Applebee's. While my tenure was short with the world's largest family dining brand, we increased the bottom line by 20 percent from supply chain management savings alone. We also changed out the national marketing program and focused on the top ten markets to drive sales. This was an immediate success. Sales outpaced our primary competitor by over 400 bps. The brand was in a far stronger position than when I arrived for sure.

I also got to work with Keith King, who was assistant general counsel. I saw his work ethic and his ability to manage complex issues. For me, Keith was the best thing to come out of my tenure at IHOP.

Another highlight from my time at IHOP was sponsoring the 2010 Olympic Trials. Keith again deserves the full credit for making this happen, but I am proud to have helped our athletes pursue their dreams. It was an honor that I later got to witness the games live, but I'll get to that later.

Kohlberg Calling Again

I remember the call well. Who wouldn't? That call led to Kohlberg acquiring Centerplate. This is a company we had gone after several years prior, but we had been outbid by a consortium. Centerplate was in the event hospitality business and managed the food-service programs for about one hundred sports and convention businesses across North America. They had just lost the New York Yankees and were reeling.

The initial thinking was for me to take the chairman role and continue at IHOP; however, the more I dug into the business (and after several key client calls), the more I realized this company needed immediate leadership—or the investment would be suboptimum and my role as chairman would ultimately be feckless.

Ticket to the Moon

"Not knowing when the dawn will come, I open every door."
—Emily Dickinson in "Not Knowing When the Dawn Will Come"

Tragically, over the holidays my brother-in-law Tommy passed away unexpectedly. Tommy was fifty years old. Way too young to be taken. It was a very sad time. Carol was devastated, but we carried on. After the Christmas holidays, I gave IHOP my notice and headed to Stamford, Connecticut. I was sad to be leaving, as I knew we could make IHOP great, but at the same time happy for the opportunity in front of me. I had a conversation with the current Centerplate CEO and notified her that we were making a change. Janet took it well but remained in her office to the end. I took the conference room again. It felt just like old times.

Baptism by Fire

"Do not be afraid / Our fate cannot be taken from us / It is a gift."
—Dante Alighieri's *Inferno*

What a baptism by fire it was. Certainly not for the faint of heart. My favorite song was "Boom Boom Pow" by the Black Eyed Peas, which was most appropriate. Unbelievably within the first thirty days of taking over we had received early termination notices from two major NFL teams: the Arizona Cardinals followed by the Kansas City Chiefs. There was no honeymoon period. I knew I needed help, and quickly, so I recruited Keith King to join the team. One of the best hires I have ever made.

Making a Stand

> "A hero is no braver than an ordinary man, but he is braver five minutes longer."
> —Ralph Waldo Emerson

The two termination notices could have been a death knell for the company. In business, it gets rough at times. Elbows can be thrown and often are. It's a full-contact sport. I had a choice to make: Do I take a stand and fight back or meekly acquiesce? Really, there was no choice. We went into full defense mode. I quickly learned my new company was scared to lose a contract and would do anything to keep business. My philosophy is that all business needs to be profitable. Pro bono work is done for charity and not for business.

Sometimes in life you are a little lucky—you turn up at the right time and what you have to offer is exactly what is needed. You also need ability and hard work. That's how I look back at Centerplate. The planets were aligned. And what a spectacular run!

Centerplate was your classic tale of a good company poorly financed and managed. The very model that got terrific returns for their PE owners also ushered in the destruction of the company. Management did not help, but PE short term-ism did them in.

Centerplate was also a company shell-shocked after many losses. The company had recently lost its number-one client, one that they had let define them, and others were bailing. It was like rats fleeing a sinking ship. The company had lost its swagger, it's edge. I knew I had to instill a sense of belief, a sense of invincibility and quickly. I needed to bring the "it" factor.

The company had exceptional leaders dotted around the organization. But brilliance was not illuminated throughout. That's what I had to change. To be great, you need to excel across the board.

The Right Way to Lose

> "Be strong. Live honorably and with dignity."
> —James Frey in *A Million Little Pieces*

I used the loss of the two NFL contracts as a rallying cry for domination and not a sign of defeat or desperation. Obviously, their exit was not my preference, but I used this to signal to the organization that one win does not make you and one account does not break you. That was the message I delivered from the first week. What defines you is how you go to work every day and commit to delivering greatness. In the long run, that will separate the great from the also-rans.

Keith and I got quickly to work. The impact was immediate. We reviewed the two contracts and realized there were penalty fees in the form of undepreciated funds that were owed if the clubs exercised an early termination clause. Apparently, both ownership groups stated they would gladly give us a letter of commendation if we agreed to an early release and that we would just walk away friends. I asked both to forget the "friend letter" and that I had a better idea, or like in *The Godfather*, "An offer they could not refuse"—that they cut checks for monies owned. Cash talks, baby. Our local teams managing both accounts at the time felt this was overly aggressive. I thought this was the least we should do and candidly felt the local teams had gone native. The teams and Centerplate reached amicable resolutions, and I signed the settlement agreements while listening to Kayne's "Heartless."

For the Kansas City Chiefs, it was the same as the Arizona Cardinals; however, they tried to play hardball. I like hardball. Without going into detail let's just state I was very pleased with the settlement results. Even funnier, in their haste to exit our contract, their ownership did not have the appropriate alcohol systems ready in place. Fortuitously for them, as I am no saint, Manchester United, my soccer team, were playing a friendly at Arrowhead Stadium in three days' time. While it would have been what they deserved to leave them stranded unable to service the seventy thousand fans for the upcoming match, we took the high road and helped them out. I sent the ownership a note stating something along those lines. No thank-you came our way. Some people are simply classless.

One Hundred Venues in One Hundred Days

I have always liked to get out and visit the company operations as soon as possible. You can fake you care, but you cannot fake that you are there. Showing up is half the battle. Mix in some passion, energy, commitment, and vision, and in my experience you can make positive things happen quickly.

For Centerplate, it was imperative. They needed to see there was a future and that I was going to fight hard for them. I set off at a blistering pace and planned to visit 100 venues in the first hundred days. I smashed this record by forty days but did not rest. I pushed on to see more than 150 venues. This was in spite of also negotiating with two NFL teams. From those visits, I knew we had the raw talent in place to become a dominant player in the space. In fact, on my first venue visit to the Rose Bowl Stadium in Pasadena, I got to meet Scott Marshall, the SVP of sports at the time. Scott had a professionalism second to none and is a close personal friend to this day. Scott simply is Mr. Hospitality.

Sun Tzu once famously stated victory comes from finding opportunities in problems. Let's just say that at Centerplate the great warrior himself would have had his hands full. My biggest threats were not the ones I never saw but the ones I could see but failed to recognize fast enough. At times it felt like bobbing for hand grenades. Yes, that good. There were bad actors everywhere you turned. One of the consultants, a dinosaur from another time, was helping the industry sadly chase to the bottom. The stark reality was in order to make money, the winning company immediately lost and would have to cut corners from day one to make a dime. The fans ultimately were the biggest losers. I wanted nothing to do with that and never signed a deal that did not generate profit and deliver superior hospitality. Certainly this created some initial headwinds, especially with the dinosaur, who was thin-skinned and did not like the change in the rules. Over a few months, we passed on several hundred-dollar deals, as the returns were subpar. Actually, they would have generated less than a 1 percent return. Who would want to do that? It was a head-scratcher. It reminded me of the line "cheap is cheap" from one of my wife's and my favorite films, *Midnight in Paris*. We kept our powder dry and did not chase ego deals. I was thrilled to see our competition fight over these "duds," happy they were deploying hundreds of their talent in the process. It was a hard and valuable lesson for our sales team to initially take, but within a short time the message hit home. Winning is important, but you have to win right. Winning by the checkbook is never the right way.

Just like the Navy SEALs state, the only easy day was yesterday. On the heels of the two NFL battles, we had back-to-back dustups with a facility operator who acted with no shame or regard. I enjoyed taking them to task, as they presented another opportunity for everyone to see we were not to be messed with. I could not have scripted a better coachable moment. The silver lining is, we ultimately ended up more profitable for their bad actions. Our first order of business was done. The message was out. Centerplate was no longer an easy mark. We were back in the game. The pieces were on the board. Now we had to make the right moves. Game time.

Being a student of history is also never a bad thing. I took this more seriously than ever when I arrived at Centerplate. For the past few decades, I could count on one hand the number of weeks I have not read at least one book. I recalled how Patton had read Rommel's *Battlefield Papers*, which subsequently went on to help him defeat the Nazi's best. I wanted to use the same strategy, but instead of just reading, I also took to visiting my competitors' venues and seeing how they operated firsthand.

After the whistle-stop tour and seeing the limitations of our competitors, I was confident that with the likes of Scott and many others, we had the talent we needed to not just survive but actually dominate. I had also built a direct communications channel to the frontline leaders who would make that possible. They execute, and we provide the tools, investment, programs, unwavering support, and belief.

Ratgate

"A lie can travel halfway around the world before the truth can put its shoes on."

—Mark Twain

Unfortunately, you read that headline right: "Ratgate." It sounds ominous, and it was. It also tested our nerve and fortitude. The media did not help, but I never expected them to be so dishonest to do anything for ratings.

I arrived home in the early hours one morning after visiting clients. Even before I could get out of the car, my phone rang. It was our PR expert. I was informed that ESPN, as part of their sweeps week and in an attempt to gin up viewership, planned to do a hit job on Centerplate. I was told the next day they would run with a piece that we had rats running around the Indianapolis Colts stadium.

I knew this was bullshit, but we know a lie travels the globe twice as fast as the truth. I knew we had to get ahead of this. Several hours later, with zero sleep, the entire Centerplate executive team was en route to Indianapolis. We were not going to be ESPN's piñata. We were going to change the narrative. We were going to hit back hard.

One reporter tried to ambush us in an interview. We had escorted a group of reporters on to the field and shown them the world-class hospitality procedures we had in place. The reporter had actually knelt down on the pitch and scooped up a handful of the Astroturf pellets. The reporter tried to claim the pellets in his outstretched hand were rat droppings. A team member stepped up, stating he had witnessed the reporter scooping up the pellets from the field. That line of questioning came to an abrupt stop. The look on the reporter's crestfallen face was priceless. His gotcha moment had flamed out.

We also stood behind our client and took all press coverage and managed the PR efforts. Winning back this narrative also did wonders for inspiring confidence across the entire company. It was an early defining moment for our company. We had used the potential disaster to our advantage. We had found our mojo.

Creating Event Hospitality

"When life gives you someone very special, you don't have to dream anymore."
—M. F. Moonzajer

It took several months, but we finally galvanized around our go-forward strategy and vision for the company. Then we set about bringing it violently to life. We embarked on a powerful marketing campaign. Positioning was critical. We were creating a new category for the concessions business. First, we ditched the awful name *concessions* and redefined our category as *event hospitality*. I remember the old dinosaur consultants laughing at our move. They were more used to serving caveman dogs on sticks at carnivals. We had the last laugh though.

It was very gratifying to see all the other competitors weave in *event hospitality* and phrases like *one-of-a-kind-hospitality* and *locally inspired* as if their lives depended on it. I suppose imitation is flattery, but I was not feeling flattered.

The reality is, we were in a David-and-Goliath battle. At the time, Center-plate was a half-billion-dollar enterprise going up against companies that were ten to thirty times larger. Our initial win rate on new bids hovered around 8 percent, which reflected our challenge. But we went forward fearlessly, and our courage and conviction paid off. In less than three years, our win rate exceeded over 50 percent on bids entered.

We used our competitors' size against them and worked our nimbleness to our advantage, employing fanatical focus on executing extraordinary experiences we defined as "E3" to differentiate. We quickly implemented programs that focused on the core fans and not just the premium fans. Our belief was every fan wants a tasty hamburger or pizza. We set about elevating every single food item on the menu. If it was not special, it did not make the cut. We switched things up by the game or event and marketed it aggressively.

Within a season, our average sales by revenue were up almost double digits. We attained that growth rate for the next five years. Our competition, on average, was flat to 2 percent. We were crushing them. This played a large role in increasing our new-deal win rates.

Setting the Culture

"You travel faster alone but further together."
—Michael Benanav

From day one, it was important to be transparent. Upon arriving, it was clear the team was feeling afraid and not informed. It was like dead men walking. For years my habit was to provide the company I was leading with a weekly update. At Centerplate, this was more important than ever. In fact, on my very first day in charge, we had an all-company conference call. I was not going to be talking about corporate downsizing; I was going to be giving a message of hope and set off from day one to run the company "My Way."

From that first call, I emphasized the importance of playing to win but also to have fun in the process. Shortly after, we launched E3, "Executing Extraordinary Experience," our corporate initiative for delivering event hospitality excellence. This program was the bedrock for how we were to have brilliance illuminated throughout the organization. I stated we would feature exemplary execution in the weekly updates. At the time I was not sure if we'd get enough stories in to feature weekly. We ended up publishing several every week and could have easily done more. This set the tone and culture of the company. We celebrated success and worked to eliminate the unsuccessful moments. Every day we simply aspired to get better, and we did.

It Takes a Village

"Many hands make light work."
—John Heywood

In those early days, we knew it was important to also bring in the right supporting leadership. As the saying goes, it takes a village to raise a child. I felt the same about growing and transforming a company. I wanted real movers and shakers to help reposition the company. We added three stellar board members, not industry retreads. We needed new thinking, and we needed names that brought star power. We did that and more. First came David Robinson, the former NBA all-star with the San Antonio Spurs. Then Michael Strahan, former NFL player for the New York Giants. Finally, I also was delighted to recruit my former Safeway boss and then president of PepsiCo Foodservice, Brian Cornell. Our PE sponsor and I rounded out the board. It was world class and truly one of the best I have ever worked with. In addition to the board, we also brought in John Sergi, a well-known consultant in the industry, and set up our separate innovation and design practice that we called STIR.

Another standout was Bonnie Siegel, CEO of ASE. Bonnie and her team came on board and oversaw our communications strategy. Mainly, Bonnie and the team developed and implemented our regional and national meetings. Bonnie and her team knocked them out of the park. Every day we were getting more and more into our groove. Bonnie joined my list of consequential friends.

You Are Either Growing or Dying

> "Immortal mortals, mortal immortals, one living the other's death and dying the other's life."
> —Heraclitus

Our competitors were much bigger than us. We needed to change this dynamic and quickly. I knew we needed to grow to compete, and slick marketing and new products can only get you so far. It's great to grow organically, if you have time on your side. We did not. I wanted dynamic growth. Growth would inspire confidence in our brand and usher in even more growth. Enter Boston Culinary Group (BCG).

BCG had been on my acquisition list from the beginning. Over a twenty-year period, BCG built up a very strong regional presence, predominantly in the Northeast, along with a few marquee venues like those of the Miami Dolphins and Florida Panthers. They also had a strong foothold in the ski resort business. We made our play and finalized the deal. Within a year, we had doubled our venues being served. In the process, I had also gained an invaluable ally: Joe O'Donnell, the founder of BCG. I liked Joe from the very beginning. He was a plain talker and knew the business and how cutthroat it could be. Unlike the equity guys, who were more like princelings and who thought they had the answers until they got into the arena and got the shit kicked out of them, Joe approached things smartly but also like a street fighter.

Diamond in the Rough

At that first dinner with Joe, I drew up on a napkin our five-year growth plan. We called it our growth diamond. The reality is, the company had a real opportunity to expand its services into different sectors that served the hospitality world—managing venues, offering merchandise, and premium sales. Ultimately, we became a significant partner for all clients we served and were responsible for generating the majority of their in-venue sales and profitability. If we achieved this, we would have a true seat at the table and be in the room when big things got done. Joe and I each signed the napkin, and I still have mine to this day. I wanted to paint the corporate vision for Joe. It felt like I was sitting with Jeff Cook again. We knew there were many ways to downtown, but we had to prioritize the plays for maximum effect. We were aligned on day one. While others may have been overwhelmed by the recent losses, I moved forward, looking for the bigger plays that would catapult the company and change the narrative. I was still that young man in a hurry. Okay, youngish man in a hurry.

My Boston Tea Party

"It's always a wake-up call to get beaten."
—Usain Bolt

We were on a tear. We were picking up accounts and further cementing that we were more than just back—we were ready for prime time. Quick wins at

Detroit, Notre Dame, Baltimore, Niagara Falls, and New Orleans helped carry that message. We committed to developing powerful minority partners who were making a difference in their communities. These efforts paid off big-time.

As we were finalizing the BCG merger, the Boston convention center bid came out. I wanted that account. It was a top ten account in the convention center business, and I was obsessed with taking another competitor's scalp. Sorry, I mean account. It was also a problematic account, as BCG were currently partnered with Aramark, the incumbent provider. This was not a clean deal by any stretch of the imagination.

The day before the presentation, I was at the Saints playoff game against the Vikings. I had to leave early and head off to Boston, but my presence underscored the importance of this account. I caught the end of the nail-biting game while airborne. There were a lot of happy travelers on that flight, me included.

While this incident did not result in tea being dumped in the harbor or a war, it did end with our defeat. We were not successful on the Boston bid. I remember getting the client feedback. It was late one Friday afternoon, and I was traveling with Carol to watch DJ play basketball. They liked our offering but did not feel the GM candidate was strong enough. I knew that going in but also recognized you have to go to war with what you have and not what you want. It still did not make it less painful to hear. That loss, however, was a blessing. From that moment on, I made it my mission to take on the role of chief recruiting officer and to scour the land seeking out the best talent. The mission was threefold: hire the best and brightest, groom our internal talent, and take all to another level. It underscored what I already knew: Talent is your number-one differentiator. Those with the most win.

When the Saints Come Marching Home

"Magic is believing in yourself. If you can do that, you can make anything happen."
—Johann Wolfgang von Goethe

My wife is a diehard Saints fan. In fact, by comparison, she would make John McClane, of *Die Hard* fame, look a little soft on protecting his wife. But it is not surprising to know that like McClaine, Carol would run through glass to see her team play. In fact, she was at their first-ever NFL game and has watched every game since. No excuses. If you recall, I had also endured many of these games.

To see her team in our first year of picking up their hospitality rights go all the way and actually win the Super Bowl was indescribable. The best part is that we were at the game. The two teams in the final game and the hosting venues were all proudly served by Centerplate. I will never forget how my wife and sister-in-law, Ginny Sue, were crying tears of joy after the victory. DJ came up to me and naively said, "Dad, when you buy businesses, do you help them win?" I looked at him and said, "Of course, son." Patrick was on leave and also joined us for the big game. It was a true family event to remember. That night we played "I Gotta Feeling" by the Black Eyed Peas at maximum volume all the way back across town to our hotel. What a night!

That same year we hosted, and our team won, the BCS, and then unbelievably the San Francisco Giants won their first of three World Series titles in the 2010s. A winning team meant more fans attending games and provided us an opportunity to take our business to new heights. I was unrelenting. I modified the famous words of Rahm Emanuel, Obama's chief of staff and former mayor of Chicago, making sure we did not let this opportunity pass us by.

Shining Bright on the Global Stage

Vancouver was the host city for the 2010 Winter Olympics. Centerplate managed many of the marquee venues in Canada. Vancouver was no exception. We had the hospitality rights for the world-renowned Vancouver Convention Center, BC Place, the home of the Whitecaps soccer team and BC Lions of the CFL. We also serviced Whistler. We basically had a lock on the lion's share of the venues where the games would be held.

Carol and I were guests of Coca-Cola for the opening ceremony at BC Place. It was a spectacular event. The atmosphere easily matched the Super Bowl experience we had just attended a few weeks prior. The stadium came to life like no other I had seen to the song "I Believe" by Nikki Yanofsky. I believed Centerplate was going to dominate more so than ever.

In a few short weeks, Centerplate had hosted back-to-back-to-back epic events on the world's biggest stage, with the Olympic Games, the Super Bowl, and the BCS Championships. Our confidence was at an all-time high; however, the most special memory of the Olympic Games, to me, was being able to be the exclusive hospitality provider to the US Ski and Snowboard teams at the Spyder House. Our chief legal and talent officer, Keith King, was also a former member of the US Speedskating team himself. Keith was the driving force behind ensuring Centerplate stepped up and supported our country. There was not a sports event or concert event across on entire company where our military and frontline forces were not invited. We saluted their efforts not with platitudes but with invites.

Wall of Learning

"The days that break you are the days that make you."
—The Mindset Journey

As a leader, it is vital that you constantly learn from your mistakes and at times roll with the punches. My belief is, if handled appropriately, your failures can have a more profound impact than even your victories. That's how I approached the everyday business.

In my office, I would showcase our winning proposals, but I created a pile of losing proposals and stacked them up on the wall right next to my desk. I wanted the daily painful reminder that while we were doing well, we were not there yet. We had more work to do. It was a constant reminder of the power to never stop learning. Failure is good, if you learn from it.

At this time we also started to have material issues with the NBA's Detroit Pistons. We ultimately had to pursue action in federal court for the reinforcement of our contract. While ultimately I was very pleased with the results of the settlement, these things take a toll. I like to think it took more out of their ownership team though.

How Lucky Can One Guy Be?

"Everything comes in time to him who knows how to wait."
—Leo Tolstoy

While I was grinding it out at work, I was also enjoying life. Kanye's "All of the Lights" fittingly was my go-to song for the moment. Life was bright indeed. My friends included high-profile politicians, CEO titans, big-name celebrity actors and singers, sport stars, and more. In Rihanna's parlance, I was shining bright like a diamond.

I've never been a big believer in trying to separate work from your private life. From my perspective, it's not about balance but more about harmony. Being CEO, I felt I was always on. The trick was to ensure that one side of my life did not constantly get more attention than the other. You cannot always obtain balance, but you can provide harmony. You have to work on it constantly.

Having fun has been an effective way to recharge and combine my personal life and my professional life. In every company I have managed, we have used my mountain retreat for executive team-building sessions; strategy sessions; key client summits; skiing in the cold seasons; and hiking, mountain biking, and whitewater rafting in the summers. We lived life to the fullest.

During this time Carol and I supported DJ in all his sports. I am proud to say we only missed one game in all four of his years at King Low Heywood Thomas School, and even then we arranged for supporters to attend in our stead. I even turned up for his practice sessions. I wanted to demonstrate what it means to be a good parent.

Consequential Meeting

"The happiest moments we ever know are when we entirely forget ourselves."
—Swani Vivekanada

I got a random call from Dr. Marc Spencer. I had no idea the impact that call would have on my life. Marc was leading a nonprofit, JUMA ventures. I liked Marc from the first handshake. He was humble but was on a mission to help at-risk youth to find a better future. Marc was struggling to get a foothold for his venture. His plan was to secure employment for his "workers" in a main sports venue. To date, he had not gotten real traction.

Marc's commitment and passion touched me. It ignited a passion in me to do something meaningful. I said we would get involved, but we needed to supercharge the effort. It needed to be a go-big-or-go-home play. We had to make a meaningful difference, and my organization needed to see this was not a feel-good play. I was not doing this for favorable press. We had a chance to be a force for good. It needed to be supported. I assigned an executive, Tre Lucas, to work with Marc. Over each of the previous five years, Tre had been instrumental in enabling our not-for-profit program, raising $25 million per year for their causes. Tre quickly got to work and launched in our New Orleans operation. It was a success. We quickly followed that up and launched in Seattle, San Francisco, San Diego, Kentucky, Orlando, and Tampa. We were helping thousands of our youth to gain valuable work experience, and more importantly to help provide them with a future. It was personally enriching to see our efforts impact so many people in real need of a boost. Seeing this program take shape was a major accomplishment that I am so very proud to have been part of.

Lifting Others Up

"Work for a cause, not for applause."
—A bright person

Around this time, I challenged every one of our venues to be a significant contributor to their communities. If you are doing good, then you are seen as valuable. It was a great strategy for retaining and winning business. Good begets good. The team stepped up to the task beautifully. Our businesses across North America were recipients of local impact awards—Baltimore, Bridgeport, Portland, Seattle, Dallas, San Diego, Vancouver, Washington, DC, Denver, New Orleans, Toronto, and Kentucky, among others.

During this time I developed a deep appreciation for our military, front-line emergency workers, and especially our veterans—our true "heroes." So much so that I wanted to step up our efforts, and I asked Tre and Keith to lead our initiatives. The goal was to show our appreciation and invite as many of our "heroes" to our sports and other events. On one occasion, at a playoff hockey game, I was presented by a group from the air force with the Base Honor Guard coin. From that day on, I have had that coin take center stage on my desk. It is a daily reminder of the sacrifice these brave people make so we can live our lives.

During this time I also had the opportunity to implement the Second Chance program—this time in a bigger and more impactful way. Our client in DC, Greg O'Dell, a true friend, helped launch the program across his DC-based venues, where Centerplate also served as the hospitality partner: the Walter E. Washington Convention Center, RFK Park, Carnegie Library, and the home of the then Washington Football Team. Several former offenders were placed in each facility. The program was a success. We rapidly expanded the initiative across many more venues. The Second Chance program was, from my perspective, a project of love. It had been thirty years in the making, so hardly an overnight success, but it was a major source of joy to me. Even years later I smile every time I think of where it had all started: one little restaurant in northern England.

The Journey Home was another initiative I was very proud to get off the ground. The mayor of Baltimore wanted to eliminate child homelessness.

Now that's a worthy cause and something I wanted to be all over. Sickeningly, I found out there were thousands of children living on the streets. This should not be happening in the richest country in the world. We hosted the inaugural event and brought in Jewel to be the headliner. The next year we brought in Jennifer Hudson, and my final year featured John Legend. We helped raise millions. Every dollar helped those homeless children most in need; however, there is so much more work that needs to be done.

In Denver, we helped support the mayor's SEEDS campaign. We set up a small farm in downtown Denver outside the convention center. We were committed to doing good and giving back to the communities we served.

I suppose the award I am most proud of receiving was the Flame of Friendship from our San Diego client, Carol Wallace—not really for the award but for what it represented. At that time, we were the only outside organization to be bestowed that honor. John Vingas, the leader of our convention center business, was the driving force behind our efforts. Thank you, John. Not only are you a great business executive; you are a great human being. I'm proud to call you friend, and a consequential one at that. We look forward to visiting you in sunny Costa Rica one day soon.

Wake-Up Call

Work was intense at this time. We were on a roll, but it took a lot of energy and commitment. I was pressing the pedal down quite hard and was in full "on mode." I took this a little too seriously and was a little bit too attached to my BlackBerry at the time. Yes, I was one of the last holdouts from switching to Apple. I had actually been part of the initial pilot group of BlackBerry while at 7-Eleven, when the device was a "BlueBerry."

Anyway, I was driving to Mount Kisco for my weekly business review with Kohlberg, where I also served as an operating partner. I ridiculously was trying to reply to a text while going down one of the winding back-country lanes from Stamford. I took my eye off the road for a split second, and my car veered into the very small shoulder area. Suddenly my car's autobreak system engaged as both tires hit the curb hard. Moments later I was sitting catching my breath, realizing I had nearly killed myself answering a text that had no real significance. Both passenger tires had been shredded, but I was alive. Until this point, I had been a serial text-while-driving offender. From that moment on, I learned my lesson. The phone is now put away in the driver's console, where it belongs—much to my family's relief.

Falling to Earth

"Your money can't save you any more than it can save me."
—First Officer William McMaster Murdoch in *Titanic*

The business was going from strength to strength, but that came crashing down. I went from feeling like Aloe Blacc's "The Man," which for some strange reason I had taken to singing at the top of my lungs, to in the blink of eye feeling like I'd had a painful encounter with Miley Cyrus's "Wrecking Ball." One Friday night, Carol and I were getting ready to go to some gala in the city when my wife felt a lump under her right arm. I was concerned, but luckily she had a checkup due on Tuesday of the following week. Somehow, and don't ask me how, I knew there was a problem, even though I tried to play it down. I joined my wife for the checkup. The doctor was immediately concerned and performed a biopsy. Then we waited for a few days. Carol's mother had died of breast cancer. This was her biggest fear. Sadly, it was realized. We were told she had breast cancer and that a lumpectomy might be a solution. My wife did not hesitate a second and stated, "Take them both off." There was zero debate.

A week later the doctor did just that. It was a dark time for the family. On the surface, we had everything, but underneath—not so much. DJ took the news badly. We did everything to alleviate his fears, but we were fearful as well. I could not believe we had created something special, and it was going to be taken away. I feared Carol would be taken from us; the fear burned deep in me.

Immediately, I dialed back my travel schedule and made sure I was present for every single one of Carol's doctor appointments and chemo treatments. I remember taking a lot of red-eye trips so I could be home as much as possible. Over the course of the next six months, Carol completed nine exhausting and difficult treatments. The treatments took a day to administer the medicine. I sat by her side for every single second. The treatments were bad, but the next week was always by far the worst. By this time I'd well and truly overcome my squeamishness and actually changed out the various plastic bottles attached to my wife's sides every morning and night. I willed her to beat this, but deep down I battled with my own fears that this awful disease was going to steal her from us, like it had my mother. Carol was truly the glue that kept our family together. I may provide the entertainment and the fun, but Carol kept the trains running on time.

One night we shaved my wife's head. It was a team effort—Tre, my nephew, and his girlfriend, Carly, DJ, and myself all took turns with the electric shaver. In fairness, Tre did the lion's share. Carol's hair had been falling out, and we wanted to signify this act as part of her recovery. That night I saw my wife cry, and I had the same vivid flashback of my mother doing the same thing. I quickly wrapped my arms around her, and she cried herself to sleep. Talk about feeling powerless. In that moment, I was truly terrified.

Trip to Africa

"My home is heaven. I'm just traveling through this world."
—Billy Graham

While we have traveled all over the world, Carol, in spite of the treatments, wanted to go on a safari. In truth, we were not sure if she was well enough to go. The chemo treatments had ravaged and weakened her heart. The doctors were concerned, intensifying my own fears. Even while ill, my wife planned the entire safari to celebrate the end of chemotherapy. I think it helped her to be busy, and most importantly to have something to look forward to. We were a party of seven: Carol and I, Patrick and his wife, Debra, DJ, and Tre and Carly.

The night before the trip we watched *The Ghost and the Darkness* to get us in the mood, as if witnessing a couple of lions with uncanny intelligence kill dozens of humans would be uplifting.

The trip was magical. It goes down as our best ever. All others do not even come close. If you ever get the chance to go on a safari, take it. You will not be disappointed. My favorite memory is from our last day, when we visited the elephant sanctuary. We had pulled up on a ridge, high above the savannah, for the best view and to enjoy an early breakfast. A flock of black kites the size of giant eagles was flying above. I had just picked up a piece of bacon and was about to eat it when a bloody black kite swooped down and stole it when it was inches away from my mouth. The talons on that thing were huge. After that, I may or may not have gone screaming back to our Jeep, but I'll never tell.

Not for the Faint of Heart

"We all end up dead; it's just a question of how and why."
—William Wallace in *Braveheart*

Make no mistake, this business is also not for the faint of heart. At times it humbles the toughest. There are so many competing priorities it can make you dizzy just keeping up. At other times it is akin to juggling a chain saw while blindfolded. The problem is, someone always wants what you have. We were faced with a couple of back-to-back incidents that helped bring that point home.

MLB Mayhem

"The worst thing we can do, the absolute worst, is to do nothing."
—Fritz Gerlich in *Hitler: The Rise of Evil*

Centerplate had the pleasure of being the hospitality partner to some of the largest sports venues. Many of our facilities had unionized. As you know from my miners' strike days, I'm not a fan. I'm not saying I believe unions no longer serve a purpose—no, wait, I suppose I am stating just that.

Anyway, our client, the San Francisco Giants, made it to the World Series and were hosting a home game. The unions, I had on good authority, were going to walk out midway through the upcoming game if we did not cave to their outlandish demands—namely, that we work pro bono or at a loss. President Reagan knew it was never good to have a strike over the holidays. I knew a strike during a World Series game was also not a good look.

For this particular home World Series game, we had over seven hundred employees working the ballpark operation. Secretly, we had arranged for seven hundred additional employees to be bussed in just after the first pitch and staged in the car park. It was at great expense, but we were not going to let the union break us; however, if they did walk out, we would be ready. They were true to their word and walked out. One of the more outlandish union bosses organized a sit-in. I was happy to see the cops remove him for disturbing the peace.

That game the reserve team we bussed in actually generated $100,000 more in revenue, and they did not know the place. The union settled shortly afterward for more reasonable terms.

Before we got to a negotiated peace, the union leader also put pressure on the club ownership. This was done by making it a story that the local media ran with. That's their standard tactic, so the ownership group in turn placed pressure on us. It was straight out of Saul Alinsky's *Rules for Radicals* playbook.

It resulted in several unpleasant calls with the Giants CEO at the time. I vividly remember one occasion, when he was screaming into the phone that he would destroy me if I did not settle this and quickly. When I asked for him to chip in, he immediately stated it was my problem. I thanked the CEO and told him that we would handle this ourselves.

In time, we consummated the union agreement, and the venue continued to be recognized as the best in baseball from a hospitality perspective. Their CEO and I enjoyed drinks and dinner together. It was all water under the bridge.

Devil of a Time

"Lookin' for a soul to steal."

—Charlie Daniels in "The Devil Went Down to Georgia"

This next incident occurred with the aptly named New Jersey Devils. In spite of providing stellar hospitality, we were constantly nickel-and-dimed by their ownership. It had become a standing joke.

We have all experienced working with someone who is never satisfied. These guys took it to new and excruciating levels. They were bad actors from day one. About a year after I had taken over, while on a trip to Portland checking out our new soccer stadium, I received a call from the new CEO. The call was cordial, and the new CEO stated, "Why don't we just shake hands and part ways as friends." I think these guys all went to the same business school.

I again channeled my inner Marlon Brando from *The Godfather* and stated, "Lets part friends, but with each party simply owing the other what was due." That did not go down well, but it was better than saying, "I have an offer you can't refuse." For the next two years, we went back and forth. I had actually resigned prior to this being settled, but the fact that my former company was able to settle this amicably certainly gave me satisfaction that justice had been served in greenbacks that day.

Champagne Supernova in the Sky

"To the stars away from here."

—Steppenwolf in "Magic Carpet Ride"

While things were traumatic on the personal front, the business, in spite of the odd spat, was thriving. Our win rates were consistently rising, along with our same-venue sales. Our new strategy was picking up steam, and our venues were being rewarded. We were winning awards in the major channels we served. In just a few years, we had been recognized for the best NFL stadium, best MLB ballpark, best college arena, best college football experience, best convention center, and best ski resort. You pick a business segment, and we were leading. We were now well and truly on the map.

It was also time to take our brand global. We did this by acquiring the Lindley and Heritage brands in the UK. They operated over a hundred venues across the UK, serving marquee clients like Tottenham Hotspur, Manchester City, Brighton and Hove Albion, and also Rotherham United, my hometown. Talk about a blast from the past. With Heritage, we acquired the Royal Seal to serve HMS *Queen Elizabeth* venues. It was a big deal. In less than three years, we had tripled in size. It felt like a homecoming for me, and I remember flying over to the UK to ink the deal listening to the England soccer song "I'm Coming Home." It was a special moment.

Winning Atletićo Madrid in early 2014 was sweet. Not only did we win the hospitality rights but also the merchandise and premium seat operation. This provided so many future opportunities to grow. The potential was endless. We were well and truly making good on building out the growth diamond I had drawn up on a napkin not that long ago.

The signing dinner with the club owner and the Atletićo Madrid leadership team was special. We signed the contract and posed for pictures in the late afternoon. We then broke for a little R and R and regrouped for dinner at ten. We partied until the wee hours, and then Carol and I returned to our hotel elated and exhausted. We were a chip shot away from dominating the industry. Little did I know, but this would be the last contract I would sign for Centerplate.

PART 4

CRASH AND BURN!

Didn't We Almost Have It All?

> "The battles that count aren't the ones for the gold medals.
> The struggles within yourself . . . that's where it's at."
> —Jesse Owens

As a wise man once said, there is always a war coming. Knowing and happening are vastly different. Sadly, my war came unwanted but with full vengeance—all-consuming and overpowering. If you like battles, magnificent. It was relentless and unforgiving, at least to me. It was also avoidable. That is the saddest part. Let's begin.

Full disclosure, if there is one year in my life that I could take Taylor Swift's advice and "Shake It Off," it would be 2014. Self-sabotage would be an understatement for what unfolded. It's ironic, as the year had started so well. We had just returned from an awesome family trip to China. Glad I went but never going there again. We were featured as a company on the move, redefining event hospitality in numerous publications. The new wins had been stacking up. Winning the New Orleans convention center and Atletićo Madrid were a terrific way to kick off the year. Now we were growing in Europe and were the hospitality partner for six of the top ten convention centers in North America. Eleven of the top twenty, but who's counting? Maybe me, just a little.

The Hits Keep Coming

"We burn a hot fire here. It melts down all concealment."
—Judge Danforth in *The Crucible*

Life was not a bed of roses. In fact, far from it. My personal life was like the worst of times and the winter of our discontent, all rolled into one. A sick collaboration between Steinbeck and Dickens. Depeche Mode's "Policy of Truth" perfectly set the stage. As they sang, "It's time to face the consequences," regardless of whether I was ready or not. This was no trick-or-treat moment. My nerves were fraying, and my family was praying. I was officially formerly lucky. I just did not know it at the time. My wife was battling through her illness. To compound matters, DJ had also recently had a concussion while playing football. We didn't even know anything was amiss, at least not initially, until his usual stellar grades slipped precipitously overnight.

DJ was the captain of his football team and knew he had a concussion but did not want to be pulled from the team. We had been there on the sidelines and did not suspect a thing. So what did my smart teenager do? He told no one, including his parents. Anyone with children knows well how teenagers can drive you mad.

But he could not hide the second concussion. A few weeks later, at one of his home basketball games, we were in the stands, as always, watching. DJ at this time was well over six feet tall and played forward. He jumped for the ball at tip-off, and when coming down with it he was viciously elbowed in the face by the opposing player. He landed hard on his back, hitting his head with full force on the wooden court. Immediately, we rushed him to the hospital, and he was given an MRI. DJ had suffered back-to-back concussions. The doctors called this a second-impact concussion and were very concerned.

We were allowed to take our son home, but under the doctor's advice we blackened his room. For the next several weeks, he stayed in the darkness, allowing his brain to heal. We did not know much about concussions, to be candid, but we learned quickly. I can tell you concussions are no laughing matter. We were terrified. His mother would sleep with him at night just to make sure he was okay. Irrationally, I was terrified he would leap from the balcony. The fear of losing my son was soul-crushing and debilitating. In truth, I think this broke me. DJ had done nothing wrong. I was allowing my deepest, darkest, and most desperate fears to take over.

Sadly, our newly acquired knowledge on concussions did not help and was little comfort. Growing up, I never took concussions seriously. That was no longer the case. They were now up there alongside a heart attack. After the recovery period, the aftermath went from bad to worse. Our once happy-go-lucky son was sullen and withdrawn. DJ went back to school but could not concentrate. Eventually, we had to pull him from regular school for almost a year and get him a private tutor so he could catch up. Initially, we were worried about him catching up, but as the year progressed that shifted, as we began to worry if he could keep up. After all, he was at an elite prep school and taking advanced classes. The timing was horrendous—this was his junior year, a crucial one, I learned, for college enrollment purposes. His grades took a real hit. His prospects with it. Candidly, at this point, I just wanted my son to be healthy and happy—consider me very afraid!

Eventually, DJ recovered, but it took a few long years, with a lot of sleepless nights. Concussions and their impact had been swept under the rug and not discussed for far too long. The dangers were not in the public square like they are rightly so today.

Health Scare

"A burden shared is a burden halved."
—T. A. Webb in *Let's Hear It for the Boy*

Those sage words went right over my head as I stubbornly shouldered on right down the rabbit hole. That mistake is the backdrop that my own internal threat matrix redlined. Some people state that God only gives you what you can handle. I disagree. I also do not want to hear what does not kill you makes you stronger. In the words of Roberto Durán, *"No más!"*

If there was not enough already on my plate to scare me to death, things got worse. I experienced my own health scare. We seemingly could not catch a break. I began to experience major discomfort in the form of crippling stomach spasms. It felt like someone was sticking a knife into my side. I knew something was wrong. In truth, DJ's illness had worn me out. To me, there is nothing more distressing than seeing your flesh and blood struggle daily. You simply cannot get rest. I worried constantly.

At first I tried to ignore the pain and play it off as being stressed and tired, anything to not accept reality. As the weeks rolled on, though, I knew all indications pointed to something serious. I was having trouble getting through a meal, and oftentimes I would resort to lying on my back in my office until the pain subsided. I was sleeping fitfully, and no matter the circumstances, sleep is a toll that eventually has to be paid. The scarier thing was that the knifing pains were intensifying. I went in for tests and a scan. The doctor was alarmed at the calcium buildup and concerned with the significant amount of inflammation around my prostate. Not the first words you want to hear. The guy did not have a great bedside manner. It did not help when he asked if I was sixty years old. I was forty-six at the time and was offended that this so-called expert knew so little about his patient. Future testing would be necessary. I self-diagnosed and feared prostate cancer. Sadly, I won the contest. We discussed options, but I did not like this man and went in search of a second opinion.

I don't know who said your greatest hopes and worst fears are never realized. I disagree with that person on the worst fears part. They had been viciously delivered and then some. With everything going on, I wanted to shield the family and handle this myself. I made this decision consciously, as I feared this could tip everyone over the edge. At the time I was thinking, *Great, just one more thing to compartmentalize.* I had outstripped my capacity to cope and did not even know it. Up until this point, it had always been Carol and me as a team. We had faced everything together, rain or shine, as the ultimate tag team. I was deviating from the script. It was a ridiculous move. It was also the beginning of my unraveling. It set me on a collision course that would end in disaster and change my life immeasurably.

I went into full research mode. I learned there was a specialist in Eastern healing methods who practiced in Vancouver. I made a call and was informed I'd need treatments twice monthly. I had rented an apartment for a strategic partner previously to grow out Canada and arranged to stay there while in town for treatments. Luckily, we had a lot of business in the area, and I could manage the company from there. What I should have done, right there and then, was take a sabbatical and gotten better. At the time, I thought I was indispensable, and I could not leave the business exposed. What utter nonsense. Total hogwash. If only I could go back and scream in that man's ear.

I was lying to everyone, keeping my illness to myself. I played it down with Carol and did not even discuss this with my family or friends. I was making mistake after mistake, digging a deeper hole by the day. I simply was not thinking this through rationally. I was trying to protect everyone and in fact was setting myself up to hurt everyone. Talk about a Greek tragedy.

After only a few short months, my weight had dropped to 165 pounds. I did what I could to disguise it, but there's only so much you can do when you are walking around like a bag of bones. I took to eating scoops of ice cream several times a day to try to maintain some weight and feed the calorie meter. Despite these efforts, people were noticing. I was being swallowed up by my suits.

Ironically, in one Kohlberg meeting, Sam Frieder, the principal, pulled me aside and told me that I was looking too thin. I almost told him I was ill, but something made me hold back. I just thought they did not care. I remember after my wife's breast surgery and the entire time she went through her treatment they did not send one bunch of flowers. Not one! I just felt they were all about the money. On this one, I hate being right, but at the time it was only my opinion. Verification would be much more painful.

Thankfully, a little later, I began the treatments. They could not come soon enough for me.

Temptation Is the Devil in Disguise

For the first time in my marriage, I liked being away from home. It was not that I did not love my family. I did. But being around them scared me, as it made me face the one thing I did not want to—reality. DJ was not improving, and when I looked at Carol, it made me sad that she was going to be taken. A disaster reel played on continuous loop in my head. I wish I could have slapped myself out of this at the time. I felt lost in my marriage. I wish I could report this was the worst of it, but fat chance.

While in Vancouver, out to a restaurant, I met an attractive woman while waiting at the bar for my table. We struck up a conversation. I knew I should have run for my life, but I didn't. The sadder part is, I knew nothing good could possibly come out of this. Sometimes it really, really sucks to be right. I rationalized it all away. I ignored the flashing red lights screaming, "Danger!" going off in my head. It was just fun. It was just a few drinks. Right. There was no drama. No misery. No sadness. There was no pressure, just drinks and laughs. There was also total denial. I was in fact not facing and fixing my issues but instead running away from reality.

In my life to this point, I have never regretted anything. I simply don't do regrets. Sure, I had made mistakes and have been disappointed in myself and others. But no regrets. Ever! That was about to change. There is no other way to put this: I made the biggest mistake of my life. As Amber Heard would eloquently put it, I had shat the bed.

After twenty years of being blissfully faithful, I let down the one person who loved and protected me more than anyone. I let down Carol—my biggest supporter. To this day, it crushes me to think of the betrayal and the heartache I caused this warrior woman. I honestly am not sure if I or she will ever be the same. It took a long time, a lot of tears, and tons of hard work for us to heal as a couple. Trust had been shattered. This mistake was costly on so many levels. I hope it means something that this has affected me so profoundly. My wife has forgiven me, but I cannot forgive myself. There are times to this day that I see the hurt in her eyes. I know this is not a good reflection on me. I could have left this out of the book, but I want this to be real and hopefully help others in a similar situation not take the same path I did. Don't do it!

I was in a very bad place and taking medication for severe depression. The pills helped level me out and dull the feeling of utter despair. I'm not stating this for pity or to make any excuses for my actions. I am stating what my frame of mind was at this time. Having a few drinks, which had previously been a welcome release, was now not a fix. Mixed with the medication, the combination changed my thought process further. And not for the good.

The truth was, my fling, if I could call it that, or more accurately the worst thing I have ever done, was over before it started, even though it took some time to unravel it completely. Way before the proverbial shit hit the fan. But the fact I let it happen in the first place and its ramifications would prove to have long-lasting impact.

Ten Days of Insanity

"Words are loaded pistols."
—Jean-Paul Sartre in *What Is Literature?*

After my life experiences to date, I felt fairly confident I was prepared for anything the world could throw my way. The events of the next ten days that I'm about to describe proved that was not the case. In fact, the next week and change were the craziest in my life. These were days and situations that I felt were not even humanly possible. If someone had told me what was about to happen, I would have thought they were, to put it mildly, "off their rocker" and wearing the appropriate tin foil hat. Sadly, for me it was real. Each day should have come with a health warning—"not suitable for humans!" and each day felt like I had been shot out of a huge cannon directly into a concrete wall.

The Raid from Hell

I was awakened by a loud noise.

Initially, I heard someone screaming but could not make out the words. It took a while for me to recognize the source of the noise and orientate to my surroundings. After a few moments, I realized I was in my Vancouver apartment.

So far, it had been an awful day. Earlier in the day, I had endured a treatment for my illness, and right then I was feeling like I had been run over by a Mack truck. It was not the kind of day you'd expect for the CEO of a multibillion-dollar company. But this day was going to get worse—much worse!

For a moment, I lay in bed and hoped the person making the noise would go away or was banging on a neighbor's door. I made my way to the door as the banging continued incessantly. Who the hell was making that racket and why?

As I got about ten feet from the door, the blood almost froze in my veins. I heard a loud male voice demanding, "Police! Open the door!" He repeated the message and added chillingly, "Or we'll kick the door down." My anxiety spiked as I processed the words. I could not believe this was happening. Those are words I'd hoped I would never hear in my life.

I walked quietly to the door and looked through the peephole. My heart almost jumped through my throat when I saw fully uniformed police lined up on both sides. While a quarter of a century had passed since my Frankfurt incident, the sight I was confronted with brought those long-suppressed memories flooding back like it was yesterday. My body tensed up. *WTF?* I thought. *Is this real? This must be a case of mistaken identity.* But that gave me little comfort as I thought of the group assembled on the other side of the door. We have all seen many times how these types of incidents can go wrong. My recurring thought was that I did not want to end up a sad statistic. It looked like they were ready to storm a suspected terrorist's hideout. It was obvious that they felt that there was someone very dangerous to take down. I was having trouble registering what my eyes were seeing. It was like watching evolution in reverse. It was terrifying. I was terrified. How could this be happening to me?

I quickly stepped back, walked into my makeshift office, and closed the door swiftly but softly behind me. Candidly, I was already in a weakened state and had to put my head between my knees and take multiple deep breaths. After composing myself and getting a hold of my wayward breathing, I called my lawyer. Thankfully, he picked up almost on the first ring, and I started to give an update when we lost reception. I wanted to smash the phone to pieces but somehow regained control.

I slumped down heavily in the office chair and stared out of the window.

It was a very bright sunny afternoon, but it could not have been further from my mood. In my mind, I was playing out the next few moments. I had images of the police busting the door down and charging in, guns raised—firing first and asking questions later. Was I going to be shot? Was this how I was going out?

After a few moments, the storming of the door did not happen. I sat there in disbelief. I walked quietly across the office, opened the door, and then walked back and sat in the chair. I spun the chair around so I faced the door and put my hands behind my head.

Then I realized my phone was vibrating in my hand. Thankfully, the device was still in silent mode while I was taking a nap and did not announce my presence. My lawyer was calling me back. I quickly hit the Accept Call button. My lawyer quickly instructed me to ask the officers if they had a warrant and to put the phone on speakerphone so he could hear.

I walked unsteadily to the door and did just that. "Yes, please open the door" was the stern reply. My lawyer asked me to ask them to give me a copy of the warrant, which they slid under the door. I picked it up and read it out aloud. Each word was crushing. My lawyer told me to do the last thing I wanted to do in the world—to grant them access and for me to step back and place my arms, with open palms showing, at my side. To say I was scared shitless would be a gross understatement.

The lead uniformed officer harshly instructed me to step back. I immediately complied. In seconds, a gang of officers pushed through the door and surrounded me in the kitchen in a loose circle. The lead officer stepped forward and said that they were taking possession of the dog. I stood there for a moment and could not believe what I was hearing.

They had raided my private residence because they had come into possession of materials that showed I had mistreated a dog. You have to be kidding. This was the type of treatment one would expect for a terrorist or a serial killer. How could the mistreatment of an animal possibly warrant such an orchestrated show of overwhelming police support? That answer would only come in time.

We spoke for around fifteen minutes. During the discussion, two officers had slowly moved into position at either side of me. They were clearly positioned to grab me if I made any type of aggressive move. It was surreal. It appeared they were almost goading me. I was not taking that bait and forced myself to relax and again stated the dog was not mine and belonged to a friend. They left me with a notice that the animal was deemed at risk and was being removed for its safety.

After they left, I deadbolted the door, applied the safety chain, and crawled into bed. I called my lawyer back and explained what had just happened. I felt totally violated by the whole experience, and it took me an age to calm myself down. In that moment, I felt as weak and vulnerable as I have at any time in my life. It shows you what the authorities can do to you at any time no matter who you are. I was bone-chillingly terrified and realized my entire body was shaking. I had no idea how my life was about to be shaken up. What had just transpired was nothing more than the opening salvo.

Just stop and think about what had happened for a second. My apartment was raided by a team of jackboots. They deployed the ultimate scorched-earth tactic. Only guns and flash-bangs were missing. But for what crime? Was I an El Chapo–type fugitive? No. A dangerous murderer? Again, no. Was I trading state secrets and involved in espionage or treason? Of course not. No, I had lost my temper with a dog, which I immediately acknowledged.

While this is not about whataboutism, consider the fact that twenty million people annually abuse and cause their spouse or loved one to miss work. That's millions of people who actually caused bodily harm and mental anguish. Do these countless millions of people receive the same treatment as I did? Not on your life. From the jump, everything about this was not right.

The Unfiltered Truth

"Do not give the devil a foothold."
—Ephesians 4:27

Warren Buffet once said all it takes is five minutes to ruin a reputation. Sadly, I can attest one can do it quicker.

Here is the unfiltered truth of what went down and not what got presented through a grainy security feed. I had had a few more drinks than usual that night, which was becoming a habit, and had taken various medications as part of my treatment. The stress of seeing my son struggling was debilitating, and I wish that worry on no one. Earlier that day, I'd seen my specialist and had a treatment and was feeling a little under the weather. I walked the dog late to help clear my mind, thinking the fresh air would be good for me.

As I was walking back to the apartment, Sade must have seen something and darted behind me violently, pulling the leash behind my back. The result was the dislocation of two of my fingers on my right hand. It hurt like hell. I wish I had counted to ten and done some deep breathing. The tape is evidence I did not. Instead, I pulled her by the leash when she dug in and refused to walk alongside me as we got into the elevator. Sade was wearing a body harness, so I lifted her off her feet to move her along.

Let's be clear: I was in the wrong. On all fronts. It was totally avoidable, but lifting her in this manner caused no pain, and more importantly I was not trying to hurt the dog. Discipline. Yes. Guilty as charged. But to harm? Never! I lost my shit for a split second but quickly composed myself. In truth, the best way to describe the entire incident is I had created the textbook definition of a *self-inflicted wound*. I did not try and hide the incident. I told my friend I had regrettably lost my temper with Sade that very same night. I stated I'd overreacted, but Sade needed some serious obedience training. I thought it was over. Oh boy, was I wrong.

That forty-two-second clip, from a grainy elevator feed, without being placed into the proper context, undid a lifetime of good deeds. It did not show things for how they were—me disciplining a poorly behaved dog—but rather gave the illusion of me abusing a dog. My reality was totally distorted. That short clip made me not just persona non grata. Worse than that, it painted me as an abuser, when in fact I had been a protector of others all my life. I can state that until this incident I had never attacked anyone with intent without being first provoked, and I had never actually disciplined any of my children. I left that to Carol.

The closest I had come to punishing my children was when I once swatted DJ on his rear end while visiting Disneyland Paris. Even after that I felt sick to my stomach. The Twitter mob and media played it up like I was the second coming of Joseph Goebbels. That I must be a wife and child beater. Maybe Beelzebub himself. Shameless. I was shattered. Truly. But I had to push on. I had to fight back.

Inside the Tornado

"The next part is very important. They're going to take you."
—Bryan Mills in *Taken*

The morning that I got off of that plane from Vancouver had already been the worst day so far in my life. And that's probably a gross understatement. I will never forget the look on my wife's face when it sunk in I had been unfaithful. I had broken her heart. The other topics were immaterial. The saddest thing about betrayal is it never comes from your enemy. The shame I felt at that moment is the worst I have ever felt. It stays with me and haunts me to this day. I have often told Carol that she is the best thing that ever happened to me. I will spend the rest of my life reinforcing how very special she is to me.

Eventually, after we had cried ourselves out, I hugged my wife. I asked for her forgiveness, which she said would take time. In truth, I knew it was going to be a long road back to earn back her trust, if ever. But even after betraying her, she stood behind me. The moment was not lost on me and cut deep.

Later that morning I called all senior leadership, and we assembled a war room and pulled in our PR firm. The grim looks on the faces sitting around the room only reinforced my dire situation. For the past few days, especially after the raid from hell, I had been bracing for this. It was an odd feeling to know you are walking into a predetermined ambush and at the same time knowing you could do nothing about it. I had hoped we could have avoided this, but deep down I knew it was coming. It was inevitable. Even so, no one, including me, who was braced for impact was ready for the sheer pandemonium that it set up in its wake. My tinderbox had been doused in gasoline. A match would have set it ablaze, but a flamethrower had been used. Kate Bush's eighties hit "Running Up That Hill" matched my mood perfectly. I was on fire and in mortal danger.

Even then, I felt we had a fine line to walk, but I was confident we would get through this. For sure, a little bloodied and beat up, but at least alive. The key was to not appear desperate. To show remorse but at the same time unity. If I stayed true to myself, I felt my authenticity would come through.

Next, I personally called our venue leaders and told them directly of what they were going to see and what I had done. I knew miscommunication leads to miscalculation and ultimately to misery. I never tried to deflect. I owned this. I was at fault. Anything less than this and misery would be delivered. I then called all our key clients and took my lumps and stated we would help manage any and all PR that bubbled up. After this, I called every member of the board and the principal of our equity group. To say those calls were uncomfortable would be the understatement of the year.

So many people I spoke with stated privately what they could not state publicly—the sentiment being thank God the cameras had not captured them at their worst moments, or what they had done was far worse. Their words, while comforting, would not provide a shield. I also remembered a quote from Stalin, who is not a great role model for life but who said, and I'm paraphrasing, "Show me the man, and I'll show you a guilty person." We all have secrets we are not proud of. All the while, the mob was mobilizing. Apparently, the radicals are always sin-free.

The day the dog story broke, I actually called Michael Strahan. Michael had most recently gone through a high-profile divorce. I wanted to get his advice and see who he had used to manage the media. Michael took my early morning call and said he'd make an introduction. Later that morning Michael called back and stated the firm could not take me. Unbelievably, they represented Lassie. The stars were not aligning.

Timing from Hell

"Let either of you breathe a word or the edge of a word . . . and I will bring a pointy reckoning that will shudder you."
—Abigail Williams in *The Crucible*

My timing was incredibly poor. Tragic, even. The tie-me-to-the-bed-and-set-the-house-on-fire kind. It was the last thing I needed, but in life you don't always get what you want. Boy, was that the truth. To set the stage, there had been two incidents prior to mine that set Vancouver up like a powder keg waiting to explode. First, after the Vancouver games in 2010, a dozen-plus sled dogs used in the games had been unceremoniously shot and buried. No charges were filed. Truly sickening.

This was followed a year later by an even more despicable act. A pit bull had been beaten almost to death with an iron chain, which along with the barely breathing dog was discarded in a trash bin and left to die. The owner was not charged. There was public outrage, and rightly so.

Unfortunately, it is against this backdrop that I now entered the fray. My incident reignited all those pent-up emotions in the community. To make matters worse, I was pitched as a young, rich, white CEO arrogantly doing what he pleased. Under normal circumstances, it should have been seen for what it was finally judged as in the court of law: causing an animal distress. My actions did not rise to the level of animal cruelty. It was never going to turn out like the sensationalized social media and press coverage headlines touted. But that did not matter. They had a villain who needed to be destroyed.

The more distressing thing was that the media, along with Twitter, took everything out of context and whipped up the mob. It felt like the Ministry of Truth from Orwell's *1984* had assembled, and I was directly in their crosshairs. The truth was quickly assaulted by over-the-top accusations. In this case, the Twitterverse at its worst. One could call them howling-at-the-moon crazy. I'm not going there. Okay, maybe I will. No, definitely I am. I stand by that characterization. They are totally batshit crazy.

It felt like a "turn on the cams and get the popcorn" moment. They wanted a pay-per-view experience. Exaggerated claims of serious jail time were being recklessly bandied around, stoking hatred. It was a feeding frenzy with no end in sight, and I was on the menu. All this noise and these hyped-up charges also did not help the board see things for what they were. The Twitterverse did not care they were destroying someone's life. Truth be damned. They did not take a second to look at the full person and what they stood for. They reduced my life to a single regrettable and out-of-character event that is not a true reflection of my life. They did not care that I had spent a lifetime helping others who were in need. There was no gradation of punishment for escalating offenses. There was no nuance at play here. They screamed for a one-size-fits-all punishment. Burn him at the stake! It's ironic that they used a totally different measuring stick because I was successful. I was in the wrong place at the wrong time but arrived at the perfect time for the British Columbia animal protection services.

Upon hearing I was a so-called "prominent businessman," the BC SPCA leaders, I was informed, were apparently "licking their chops." Allegedly, they could not have been more delighted. They could raise a lot of money off me. I was going to pay. They saw me as a high-level target ripe to further their cause. I was to be their poster child—their villain. They wanted me to burn for all my sins.

My legal team quickly reached out to the organization through back channels and offered to set up a fund. I would also personally engage and help raise money and awareness for their cause. Our outreach was sadly rebuffed. They saw dollar signs. They had a better idea. They wanted to use my incident as the centerpiece for their upcoming fundraising efforts. My incident was a simple case of third-party culpability, in which they could point at me for all the previous sins. In some twisted way, they laid all issues at my feet, and this allowed them to make up for their previous mishandling of past horrendous offenses.

Over the weekend, still reeling from the raid, I huddled with the team and laid out a PR response. While the BC SPCA might reject the offer of working with us, we were hopeful to present a compelling response to the public at large. From the jump I knew an apology of mere words, while important, would not hit the mark. I had dealt with animal activists in previous positions and knew everything with these radical folks would be blown out of proportion, radicalized to its fullest.

We had hired the best counsel. How good, we would find out soon. I asked counsel about the likely outcome in court. It's always good to hear lawyers answer a direct question. After what felt like a long tooth-pulling exercise, the prevailing thought, of course, framed with many caveats and warnings, was that this would not rise to the level of animal cruelty. Jail time was not remotely possible, no matter how loud the social haters screamed for it. The contorted consensus was most likely a small fine and no community service. That's if the Crown even proceeded to pick up the case in the first place.

Mob Rules

"Dialogue with Twitter is akin to a fireside chat with an AK-47."
—Sage person

In a matter of days, the story had gone national and then international. The Black Eyed Peas' hit "Where Is the Love?" framed the moment: "wrong information always shown by the media / negative images is the main criteria / infecting the young minds faster than bacteria." There certainly was no practice what you preach, and you can forget about turning the other cheek. We had by now issued our scripted response, but the press did not want to hear it. Why hear the truth when it does not serve their purpose? We were in the middle of a high-tech, digitally-led mob takedown.

The saddest part of all was that they did not know me. They saw me in a grainy feed, completely out of context, and simply determined that my total destruction was the only thing that could right the world. They tasted blood in the water and wanted nothing but vengeance. They were playing with a winner-takes-it-all and loser-is-left-crushed-and-small mentality. I had prayed for a bigger story to hit, but sadly my hope went unanswered. Like it or not, I was the story for the week. The power of Twitter was greater and more destructive than we had thought possible. Press was staked out at my home and workplace. It was surreal. I had been in the spotlight for years, but never like this. I have never been the problem. I now have an appreciation for how celebrities feel when hounded by the paparazzi, and I only had a week of that.

On Monday we had an emergency board meeting where I, of course, apologized again for the special session and for the incident in the first place. We agreed to weather the storm and keep positive. I saw my CMO and PR team struggling to manage the crisis. To me, they looked overwhelmed. At first I was disappointed in them but quickly realized I alone had done this. They were doing their very best in the most hostile of environments. They were working around the clock to protect me—the very person who had created this bloody disaster in the first place.

I knew we needed more resources if we were to get through this crisis. We were constantly playing catch-up. Our efforts felt like we were trying to keep the patient alive, reacting rather than shaping the narrative. There was simply too much rage circulating for our current team to effectively manage. A new twist surfaced on Twitter by the hour, each one more incendiary than the previous one. What I quickly found out is that you do not bring the Queensberry rules to a social media fight, not unless you want to be carried out in a body bag. I brought in another PR and crisis communication expert, Sam Singer of Singer Associates. I had gotten to work with and respected Sam when we experienced issues in San Francisco. Sam's guidance and sage advice had been invaluable. I reached out immediately, praying for a repeat performance.

We mapped out our survival plan. Sam and his team would manage the corporate messaging, and our CMO and current PR group would manage the issues that boiled up at the local level. This way we could divide and conquer and hopefully cover more ground without duplication. Time and our ability to swiftly respond to attacks were our primary enemies. It felt like we were playing Whac-A-Mole, and we were the moles.

The thinking at the time was if we could get through the upcoming holiday weekend, in spite of the coverage, the press would turn their attention elsewhere. They were fickle and possessed the attention span of a gnat. Somehow we had to take back the narrative and get ahead of the story. Success is all about momentum. We knew the same goes for disaster. We needed to get on the front foot.

Our clients were being pressured and attacked for their association with me. It was a totally humbling experience. I had always been used to being part of the solution and not part of the problem. I dispatched Keith to connect with our key clients and our CMO, COO, and PR team to handle others as they came in. Others, like John Vingas, Tre Lucas, Richard Ginzel, Adrian Dishington, Thomas Tazbaz, and Laurence Ruiz, among others, did exceptional work. I know I am missing people, but the love and support I received from clients and employees across the Centerplate portfolio—from Hawaii to Europe—was heartwarming. You will never know how much your efforts meant to me. Thank you.

In a sadistic kind of way, if you like pain, the best thing about the worst time in your life is that you get a front-row seat to how everyone behaves. In the famous words of Cyndi Lauper, "I see your true colors shining through."

One of the PR team recommended I read *Firing Back* by Andrew Ward and Jeffrey Sonnenfeld. It lays out how one can rebound after a major setback. Candidly, I was not in the mood for reading, but I dug in quickly and read that thing cover to cover. We further refined our playbook. It felt good to be doing something instead of scurrying around surviving heavy incoming fire. Another play was to collect a portfolio of support letters. A handful would do, I was told.

Within days, I did not have a handful of support letters. We received over fifty beautifully handcrafted notes advocating on my behalf. The letters made my knees buckle. There was nothing in this for anyone. Frankly, there was risk—they were knowingly putting themselves in the line of sight of the keyboard cowards on social media. Community leaders, business executives, not-for-profit CEOs, senior city officials, major client CEOs, past and current colleagues and friends. It was humbling. These people knew me and stepped up because they wanted to. I owe each of them a personal debt of gratitude. Like anything, having all the facts makes for a more informed opinion. Unfortunately, other elements entered the fray before we could mobilize and launch an effective counterresponse.

Dan Kim—the Unwanted Mob Closer

"And we gonna, gonna let it burn, burn, burn."
—Ellie Goulding in "Burn"

By midweek, just as we were getting our arms around the story and finally finding our sea legs, things escalated. As misery loves company, and to compound things further, Dan Kim, the founder of Red Mango, saw my video clip. I later found out this had triggered him and reminded him of a painful childhood experience, the specifics of which I do not feel are mine to tell. Dan was so affected he helped support a petition on Change.org to have me fired. Regardless, the witches in *Macbeth* could not have concocted a more deadly brew. It was a gut punch that went to a whole new level.

Dan's actions reenergized the mob and did the very thing we were working to prevent. His actions candidly had the same impact as lining up my own firing squad. He was a dangerous threat multiplier and threat magnifier. Dan breathed new life into the story and whipped the keyboard carnivores into a further frenzy. It was a sight to behold as they went medieval, and in the most savage of ways. In fact, the henchmen of yesteryear had nothing on this crew. They very quickly collected over a hundred thousand signatures for my head. Soon this same mob coordinated and started reaching out to our clients, pressuring them to terminate business with us. The issue was spiraling out of control. I was evil incarnate. It did not matter that my efforts had helped raise over $100 million for various charities and helped tens of thousands a year. This one incident, which I apologized for, in their frenzied minds outweighed all the good. There was no logic—only pure hate fueled them. Dan did more personal damage than all other actions combined. Dan served me up to the mob, and I watched helplessly. We released a follow-up press release with what we thought was an over-the-top series of self-punishments to try to control the situation, which by the second was becoming more like an out-of-control forest fire. In that moment, I realized my ability to survive had narrowed, but I never believed it had been completely cut off. By the same token, it was not lost on me that the odds had officially entered the danger zone.

Sadly, the campaign gathered more attention. The publications seemingly wanted in on the bloodletting, and in a bad way. Several articles hit the wire at the same time. It was worse than a parade of horribles. The worst offender was *Sports Illustrated*. The writer, who is not worth calling out, made it clear in his smug proclamation that jail time was simply not enough. Apparently, his reasoning was there was no one who had ever made a singular mistake. It was simply more convenient to assume the worst. The mental gymnastics he performed to come to his conclusions were staggering. I think someone had forgotten he was doing a fact-based investigation and not a fiction piece. Who knows—he may have been self-projecting. The screamers are usually the most despicable. Needless to say, I am eternally grateful this gentleman was not the presiding judge. I'd have been given the death penalty, and Mr. Deep Throat would have gladly tied the noose nice and tight. As the saying goes, karma is a bitch, and a few short years later they suffered their own crisis with major layoffs. Clearly, they never got the memo to stick to swimsuits and not hit jobs.

Also, in a funny twist of fate, I have since become friends with Dan. He even joined as an advisor for one of my companies. People ask why I would work with someone who caused me so much pain. I state it was my actions that triggered his. Dan has stated if he had known all the facts, he would never have taken the actions he took. That's something we would all be wise to take heed of before we react to any situation. From my perspective, forgiving is a major part of the healing process. We all can grow and evolve. Hate only serves to make things worse. If only all of us would take that to heart.

You're Out of Luck. I'm Out of Time.

The timing could not have been worse. First, it was the week of the US Open Tennis Championships. Every year we tried to take in as much of the tournament as possible. This year was no different. We had invited several family members and friends as guests. Our house was full. Clearly, I was not going to be watching tennis, but Carol stepped up and played host the best she could—even though she was going through her own heartache at the time.

Second, DJ was moving to Paris for college later that very same week. We had arranged our son's sending-off celebration for that Thursday night—another reason that family and friends were visiting. Prior to this story breaking, we were scheduled to travel as a family to drop off our son in Paris late Friday. By now I was working around the clock from my office but broke free to celebrate my son. Yes, things were extremely difficult, but I wanted to show my son that even when things are tough, you show that family matters. That night my son was celebrated. I have always put family first, and even in the cauldron in which I was now living, I wanted to be there for my son.

But it got real serious, real fast. Directly after DJ's celebration, I returned to the office. That next morning DJ had some last-minute supplies to purchase. My son, for whatever reason, took my car for the trip, which was unusual. Unfortunately, he was followed by one of the deranged haters, most likely stoked up by social media, when leaving our apartment building. We had arranged security in the lobby and on our floor due to numerous death threats. The whack jobs could not get to us inside, so they waited until we left the building.

My son was attacked when he stopped at the local Walgreens by one of the "nuts" the rage machine had weaponized; however, seeing that my seventeen-year-old son was clearly not a nearly fifty-year-old man did not stop this loon from attacking my son. Luckily, my son blocked his punches, got back into the car, and drove off unharmed but visibly shaken. It was getting crazier by the second. Who does this?

I decided I could not put my family or the company that I loved and its twenty thousand–plus employees at risk. They should not suffer for my actions. I thought long and hard, and upon landing called for an emergency board meeting and offered my resignation. The board accepted. That is the official version, but it's not the truth. How it really went down was different.

Over the weekend I spent countless hours with Sam, Keith, and others orchestrating our next moves. As the song goes, I wanted to see the condition my condition was in, and the reality is, I felt like dead man walking. On a personal note, I did not want my unfaithfulness to surface and embarrass my wife and hurt her further. This would also serve to breathe life back into the story.

We bandied around several potential scenarios: Do I take a leave of absence? Do I simply stay away from the office and keep a low profile for a few weeks and let this blow over? Or do I take the heat like I had been doing and soldier on? Both Sam and I thought the latter was the best option. The press and haters would eventually move on to another story. A show of support was needed by the board, or the story would build. I was optimistic.

Late that Sunday night, I called another emergency board meeting. Sam was on the call. We laid out the current situation. We outlined actions taken and proposed next steps. I thought we had an agreement and ended the call. Our thinking was we weather this through the long holiday weekend, and we will come out of this. Battered, for sure, but alive.

As the saying goes, you learn something new every day. Some more than others. This was one of those big ones. Less than an hour later, after I had made several calls to my team stating the board was supportive, I received a call from our chairman and my equity partner liaison. They stated the board had decided I was to be terminated but gave me the option of resigning first. That they deeply regretted this and that they did not believe my actions should have resulted in this. They then said the magic words: "But we have to protect our investment." They ended the call stating they needed a decision in twenty-four hours. To them, it was all about money and saving face. In reality, we had a handful of clients with issues, but I felt comfortable they could be managed. Candidly, the deer-in-the-headlights response from some, who will remain nameless, did not provide the confidence the board was looking for. It had little to do with my actions. All had said they had done worse. It was sickening. I had spent a lifetime defending those who had made mistakes. I believed in forgiving transgressions. I certainly did not judge someone on his or her worst moment. Here I was being kicked to the curb in my time of need. It was like an arrow pierced my heart. I had been betrayed, and by those who I thought had my back. I ended the call and stated I'd be in touch. It was no longer a crapshoot if I would survive. Without the board's support, surely I was officially dead on arrival.

Don't Leave Me This Way

"No greater grief than to remember days of joy, when misery is at hand."
—Dante Alighieri's *Inferno*

By now only ten days had passed since the raid from hell. It seemed like a lifetime ago. I would not have thought it possible, but each day was more excruciatingly painful than the one before. It was soul-crushing. The compounding impact was catastrophic. I was sadly living in my very own Luciferian reality. That was my frame of mind as I regrouped with my PR team and inner counsel. I was consumed by the thought that I had stepped into a big pile of shit. I could not shake the feeling that this may be my last drink at the last-chance saloon. In my head, I had played out all the different scenarios like I was Doctor Strange in *Avengers: Infinity War*. The paradox of choice was not lost on me. I was not concerned about my illness being public knowledge. My PR team actually wanted me to make this public, along with the fact I was on medication, drinking, and dealing with an emotional family matter. They thought I would be placed in a protected class. They were probably right, but I wanted nothing to do with that. I thought the truth would come out and, as they say, "Set me free."

The board sadly showed their true colors. They were weak. They had no code and less honor. One could make a case they were spineless. But I'm not going there. No, I will. They were spineless. Admittedly, they did not ask or want this. I had certainly put them in a bind, but where is the loyalty and the thought of having each other's backs? Members of the PE group had been trying for some time to get more involved. Until this time, I had successfully pushed back due to their lack of insight and relevance and our growing success. They saw this as an opening to gain greater control and influence. They were making good on the theory to never let a crisis pass you by. If it took my demise with it, so be it.

What concerned me was that my infidelity would become fodder for the public square. The board now knew of this, and if I got into a legal dispute, I knew they would most likely leak this to the press. It would not help their case, but it would harm my family, Carol in particular. Carol had suffered enough. Although I relish a good fight, I did not want my wife to suffer the indignity for my mistake. Carol did not deserve this. I had to protect her at all costs. There was too much on the line to be distracted by the implications to my career, even if I lost terribly in the process. So, like the good Doctor Strange, after the many manifestations played out, only one ended with Carol not being embarrassed: my resignation. It was against every fiber in my being. Even so, I knew it to be the right move.

There were many other mitigating circumstances that pushed me to this decision. Any litigation would take several months, possibly years, before being settled. I was battling my own illness and needed to weigh what was more important: winning in court or focusing on my health and spending time with my family. It's ironic that I did not realize I should have done just that a year ago. I should have taken leave. My family had recently expanded with the birth of our first granddaughter. I wanted to capture as many moments as I could. Litigation would steal valuable time.

There was a lot to process. It was the deliberation from hell. I truly loved the company I had helped grow immeasurably; however, while I bled Centerplate, and every bone in my body wanted me to fight, I knew doing the right thing meant doing something I hated the most.

The real people hurt by my resignation were the tens of thousands I was currently able to help who in the future, with no income, I would no longer be able to. I'm not talking about the causes we supported. I'm talking about helping others on a personal level. I could line up people around the block who I have personally helped. Dental bills. Health bills. College bills. Funds to survive. Housing. Helping others set up their dream ventures. Car payments and dozens of other things. Never for publicity. Never because I had to, but always because I wanted to. I would ask the mob now, "Who really suffered?" They never stopped to ask or answer that question. Pitiful.

Tomb of Memories

"Well, now pride's gone out the window. Cross the rooftops.
Run away. Left me in the vacuum of my heart."
—Duran Duran in "Ordinary World"

In the initial aftermath of my resignation, I simply checked out. As the song goes, I was living in a powder keg and giving off sparks. I was consumed with an endless stream of could-have, would-have, and should-have self-recriminations. All a day late and a dollar short. All utterly useless. In my life, I had dealt with extreme adversity, but this felt different. I wanted to erase the past year. To reboot. But I also knew alt, control, delete would not work. I feared gravely that something important inside me had broken. I was operating in a walk-of-shame mode. Well, truthfully, more shame than walk. For someone who had always been a positive "the glass is full" kind of person, right then it felt like I was swallowing shards of glass. My career was destroyed, and my marriage was in jeopardy. It was like I had been gut punched and could not catch my breath. The song that best frames up my state of mind at this time was "Can't Feel My Face" by the Weeknd. Truth be told, I could not feel anything. I'm not stating that I drank a lot, but I had a martial arts tenth dan in hangovers. Most mornings I woke up feeling like I'd spent the night bouncing around in the tumble dryer. I had not learned the bottle was never the answer.

A few days after my last board call, while still in Paris, I signed my resignation letter. As I inked the document, my thoughts were best summed up by the Pet Shop Boys' hit "What Have I Done to Deserve This?" To add injury to insult, I had also poorly defended myself through the process. It was the first time I did not seek legal counsel. I had too many negative thoughts swirling around. I did not think clearly through this period. Without going into too many specifics, let's just say my personal net worth took a major hit from these proceedings. Even in this moment, my thought was that this would blow over in a few years. Lose some now but gain some later. Now I needed to work on saving my marriage. The intent was right, but my execution was poorly thought out. This is one I wish I could take back.

I thought that with my resignation the story would quickly die out. How wrong could I have been? The social media platforms fueled the debate. Throughout my life, I had lived by the creed to never kick someone while they were down. I was on the receiving end of the opposite line of thinking from a swarm of keyboard assassins.

It seemed the more we learned, the less we knew. I hired a company for a small fortune and found out that incredibly a handful of trolls had actually reposted my clip over 120,000 times. In reality, 60,000 people had been upset—at the time, a fraction of the 140 million guests we served annually. I could get more people to swear they had been abducted by aliens than those who wanted my head. What made this more painful was that all the time these "haters" were assisted by a nefarious invisible hand. While I acknowledge I had gone overboard in disciplining the dog, I never hurt the dog. These haters were pure evil. They despise the world. I could be crucified on the hour for months, and that would never be enough. They were unhinged. *Forgiveness* was not in their vernacular.

I was being canceled and had not yet gotten the memo. The mob had spoken, and in their opinion the future is now, and I am not part of it. Then I was doxed. I did not even know that was a thing at the time. Let me tell you, it is a thing, and it is horrifying. It was a very traumatic period. My wife, of all people, actually received death threats. One was sent to Carol listing the properties we owned and saying they knew where we lived and that we were not safe. Just the message someone needs while recovering from breast cancer. I approached the police, but because the haters did not explicitly name the time, place, and means of the attack, they were power-less. We increased the security of our immediate family and especially our son, who was now in Paris. How could this be seen as normal behavior?

The radicals were out for continued vengeance. My resignation meant nothing to them. At the same time, the recruiter calls dried up. My life had been obliterated in front of my very eyes. I had been disposed of like human waste. "If someone is lost, they can be found." That's what I remember my mother saying, usually when someone was not going to church. I feared I was truly lost.

The waves of despair swept over me until I did not know if I could continue on. It was paralyzing. The haters just piled on. Prior to the incident, I had accepted a board position with the Stamford Youth Foundation. One reporter picked up on this and wrote a hit piece on why the Stamford Youth Foundation would appoint me to the board. Thankfully, the board stood by me in my hour of need. I was hoping this would be the first of many. I was soon to learn that others would not be so courageous.

Kicked to the Curb

"In the end, it is not the words of your enemies but the silence of your friends."
—Martin Luther King Jr.

Confidence and conviction are needed to successfully manage a crisis. When you lose either, you open yourself up to the worst of outcomes. If one panics, usually they all do. My equity partner had panicked. You have seen what happens to grocery store shelves at the mention of a hurricane or a bank run when there is fear they are going under. Utter chaos ensues. The mob follows the mob like lemmings off a cliff. I found this out painfully for myself. For my life, it had the same effect of someone shouting, "Fire!" in a theater—complete stampede-style panic.

By this time I had worked for Kohlberg for over a decade. They knew how I operated, how I comported myself, and how I represented their interests. Also, I was a great rainmaker for them, having delivered two of their top ten biggest returns at the time of transaction. As CEO, I had delivered on average $2 million in investment returns for every week in position. In total, hundreds of millions in value.

After a week of trying to decompress, I called them and set up a time to talk when I returned from Paris. I thought while they would be disappointed in my behavior, once they understood the context, they would be rational. They would get behind me and show their support. I had made them a boatload of money and served them well. Boy, was I wrong!

On the call, now a few weeks after my resignation from Centerplate, they, too, terminated me effective immediately. They stated they had gotten a few calls from concerned shareholders, and they could not afford ongoing bad press. There was no "I appreciate your situation and know what type of person you are." It was just "Get out of my life. We do not need trouble." It was pathetic.

Several times I had gone above the call of duty and helped them with fundraising and taking many prospective investor calls. I was also currently helping them attract investors with their latest fund. Not only did they state I was being terminated as an operating partner but that I would not be part of any future fund. While it was a big financial hit, it hurt much more on a personal level. It was betrayal.

The decision was more stunning due to the fact I had stood by them and helped them with two embarrassing incidents. The first was when one of their older operating partners was making inappropriate sexual advances toward members of my team. I did not stand for that nonsense and never have. I could have blown this up and made a real stink; however, I worked with them to remove the offender and handled it with dignity.

The second incident was when at the closing party for our Centerplate deal one of the Kohlberg executives got hammered and started lap dancing on guests, myself included. I could have caused real harm to them. I did not take that route but chose instead to stand by them. I naively thought they would have done the same for me. What a disappointment.

When I mentioned that I had stood behind them repeatedly and expected the same loyalty in return, they stated their hands were tied. It was truly sickening. What I thought would be a safe haven was my own kill zone.

One Kohlberg executive, who had a regal bearing to shame kings, who was as flexible as the IRS, and had a habit of saying my name like it amused him, stated I should make protecting animals my future cause. That this may help me in the future garner public approval. He talked about this stuff like he had read it in a book or heard it on a recent podcast. I was offended. After all this time, they obviously did not know me. I did not need to find causes to be passionate about. Charity is not a tuxedo I trot out a few times a year. It's certainly not a virtue signal and has never been a way for me to scream, "Look at me! Aren't I Mister Wonderful?" It's been a fundamental part of my life. I had, after all, raised a lot of money for worthy causes across the globe. I had already supported at-risk children, education, inner-city anti-crime initiatives, providing a second chance for offenders, child homelessness prevention, cancer research, protecting people against domestic violence, and so much more.

I did not need to fake being someone who cares. I cared. Apparently, that did not stop the haters from coming after me. My message to the haters is if you could see inside me, I hope you regret everything you have done to me. I realize the chances of that are slim to none.

Julius Caesar, Act II

"Et tu, Brute?"
—Caesar in *Julius Caesar*

Some say two times is better than one. In this instance, I think not. At the time, I was also serving on the board of Sbarro. My efforts had, in large part, helped them reemerge stronger through bankruptcy proceedings. My personal involvement had saved the company tens of millions. I called the then CEO to update him. The CEO stated he was already aware and that he was firmly standing behind me. His words were similar to what I had been hearing from others. I got off the phone feeling positive. At least there was someone with some backbone.

That did not last long. The next morning the same CEO called and said his equity partners wanted me out. He apologized and stated he was powerless.

I have made a career out of following my convictions and standing up for what is right and not what is convenient. I can tell you from experience at times it is very inconvenient. Many executives have survived ordeals due to my personal backing that I know others would have never given. In my opinion, tough times do not build character; rather, they show you have character in the first place.

One incident that underscores doing the right thing occurred in early 2012. One of our executives was arrested while traveling to Dallas. He was arraigned and transported back to San Diego, the apparent scene of the crime.

I was called late at night after midnight and informed of this. I took the call and was told this individual was being charged with rape. This is not the kind of news you want to let fester, and no matter the hour, the executive had done the right thing waking me. My initial thought was to wash my hands of the whole thing. Rape, in my opinion, after child abuse, is the worst crime one can commit outside murder. After all, I should know. I took a few moments and processed this and called the executive in charge of the individual. I said we needed to make sure there is due process administered. Nothing more. Nothing less.

I informed our board the next day. The mood turned grim, and support for this individual was flatlining, if not nonexistent. They wanted to manage the fallout. I wanted to protect our talent as well as in the process make sure we did not throw him to the wolves. If he was proven guilty, I'd have gladly done that and more. But what if he was innocent? He would serve time, and that I could not allow.

This placed me in a difficult position, as I had always liked the accused. I thought there was no way he would have done something like this, but we had to allow the facts and not emotion to lead us to the right outcome. We arranged for him to serve his house arrest with one of our executives while he awaited trial. Without this support, he would have most likely had to take a plea—his life forever changed. Through discovery, the legal team got a copy of the footage from inside the hotel on the evening of the alleged rape. The woman was walking down the corridor with three men. She was kissing all of them and removing articles of clothing.

Thankfully, I stood behind getting the facts. The tape clearly showed the woman to be a willing participant as they walked down the hotel corridor. The DA incredibly still wanted to press charges, but he eventually capitulated when the witness repeatedly changed her testimony. The facts simply did not line up. Our executive was free but now had the unpleasant experience of going home and facing his wife. I mention that story because there are not many who would have stood behind someone like that. I wish I had received the same treatment from Kohlberg and Sbarro. They all showed no backbone. They melted away like cupcakes in the afternoon sun. No loyalty. They had all caved to the mob. It was simply more convenient.

Is the message that when you make a mistake there is no way back—no possibility of redemption and absolutely no forgiveness?

Watching with Tears in My Eyes

"A watched kettle never boils."
—Ancient proverb

Naively, maybe foolishly, I used to think everyone loves a good comeback. I can tell you that I no longer believe this is the case, at least not with the press and the definitely not with social media platforms. They want clicks and eyeballs. If they need to lead a sacrificial lamb to slaughter, no problem. They'll gladly build more altars. The more rage they can generate, the better.

Overnight the endless pages of positive press I had accumulated over decades were replaced with the dog incident. If I did not see it firsthand for myself, I would have thought it was not possible. You could not do any type of search without my worst moment being center stage. The countless good I had done was barely a footnote, relegated to page ten, where news went to die. I suppose that was what the keyboard cowards were looking for: my death. If not physically, then at least digitally and professionally.

The first few months were particularly brutal. I was living in the "Wicked World" that Chris Isaak so painfully sang about. I felt every inch of his pain. At times I felt lost, defeated, and hanging on by my fingertips—and that was on my better days. This was a strange sensation for me, as I'd always been able to bounce back quickly from adversity. Usually, all I needed was to get some sleep. The next day I was typically back to normal, with my "mood monitor" reset to positive. This was not the case. It was terrifying. I honestly felt I was having a mental breakdown. I most definitely suffered an identity crisis. Carol and I were doing our best to support each other, but the challenge was unbelievable. We were both hurting. As a way of self-preservation, I decided it would be a good idea to change my look.

First, I grew out my hair. Then I took a crack at growing a beard. The look was old man trying to look young. It was tragic.

Even worse, I got heavy into online clothes shopping. I went all in. Anything I liked, I'd buy five pairs of, because who doesn't do that? It's true when they say you can have all the money in the world, but it will not buy you happiness. I only stopped when I filled up multiple closets around the house. If there is a silver lining to that activity, the local charity shops have benefited from multiple bags of unused clothes.

I am a fighter, and slowly over time I began to get the energy to fight back. I spent a lot of time, effort, and money working with various PR groups and marketing agencies to repair my reputation. I made an impact, but it was a David-and-Goliath battle. I have come to realize the social media platforms control what we get to see. A white Republican perceived to be a rich CEO who hurt a dog was someone who must be punished to infinity and beyond. Even in this period of darkness, somewhere deep down I was convinced this would pass and things would return to normal. Wrong again. It was a very costly mistake.

Thankfully, the hit pieces did not continue. Yes, the Twitterverse kept up their sick vigil for several years. Even today I get random hate notes from the most deranged. Sadly, Google displayed this incident like their life depended on it. It's ironic that since the incident there have been over fifty press releases on my behalf, but none took away Google's obsession to display my worst moment. Whatever happened to redemption?

Judgment Day

"Decisions, not conditions, determine what a man is."
—Viktor E. Frankl

As the saying goes, it's not over until a certain lady sings. You know the one, but I'm not going to add body-shaming to my alleged crimes. As fitting with this entire case, there was last-minute drama afoot. Early the morning of my day in court, my lawyer called. I could tell something was wrong. He was quite ruffled. The Crown, he told me, had just called him and were asking for house arrest, a larger fine, and a ban on me owning a dog in Canada. *Of course they were*, I thought. Why would I think this would go smoothly? Silly me. It was as if they had woken up and suddenly realized the terms we had previously agreed to did not satisfy the social media keyboard carnivores. I told him house arrest was not an option, or I would bloody fight to the end. I agreed to raising the fine to five thousand from five hundred dollars. After all, it was a fraction of my original proposal. Owning a dog in Canada was not relevant, as I did not live and did not plan to live in Canada. We finally had an agreement. Again! I simply wanted this behind me and settled. Get to court and get out of the city I had once loved.

Nine long months had passed since my resignation, each day being more painful than the previous one. My patience had redlined months prior; however, we had no option but to wait, patiently or not. For someone used to being in control, this was soul-crushing. It's an even harder thing to endure when garbage is being spewed at you daily. Throughout this period, my legal team did an admirable job. While we could not get a fair hearing in the court of public opinion, we could and would ensure we got one in the court of law.

The story, from the beginning, came in dirty but miraculously came out clean. I simply was unaccustomed to bathing in this level of filth. I was being bagged and tagged. The untruths from all corners continued to pile up. First the dog was timid and therefore had been harmed previously. Wrong! Next that the dog was mine, stated someone from the BC SPCA no less. Not only false, but the BC SPCA knew this to be untrue, as they had returned the dog to its owner. The dog was not being well looked after—terrible accusation and one that could not be further from the truth. In the media, my predicted sentencing was being wildly exaggerated. Unfounded! Excessive fines were to be levied. Not in your wildest dreams! Surely many others must have suffered similar abuse at my hands. Ridiculously false! Many other falsehoods were being bandied around like confetti. All unsubstantiated! This was hyperbole masquerading as the truth. They were ginning up the story to drive public condemnation in the hopes of raising funds. It was a coordinated and curated killing. It looked like a professional hit because it was a professional hit!

In light of the many false accusations, the social media crowd was clamoring for me to be burned or banished. Hell, if the accusations were true, I would truly be disgusted as well. In this painful case, they were all manufactured lies. The mob was elated but not sated when I was forced out of Centerplate. As I said, that was not enough for certain members of the press who tried to have me fired from board positions and the like. In truth, the press were novices compared to the relentless lunatics on social media. These people are unhinged. Let's not even get into the psychos in the comment threads. Can anyone say *cuckoo*?

Regardless, this was my day in court. This was my chance to have the facts fully aired. As the saying goes, I'd rather be judged by twelve than carried by six. At least I was still breathing; however, the final verdict was like a consolation prize. The problem for me was the keyboard carnivores had already forcibly grabbed the gavel of justice and had meted out their own brand of justice. It was completely lost in the media kerfuffle that the court's punishment, even with the attempted last-minute shenanigans, was much more lenient than my own offered-up proposal. In fact, the fine was twenty times less than I had offered. There was no community service imposed, where I had offered up one thousand hours. In her sentencing, the judge stated that after reviewing the circumstances of the offense, she concluded that it sat at the very low end of the spectrum in terms of "gravity." Wait. Stop the press. Talk about burying the lede. Where had this logic been for the last nine months? The reality is, the cold, hard facts did not count for a hill of beans. The social media assassins had already achieved what the courts could not. While they may be as sharp as a frisbee, their keyboards could cut deep. They had publicly executed me and gotten me fired, attacked my family, and hurt my business. It was akin to bathing in a tub of piranhas. These carnivores had served as the BC SPCA's foil, unwittingly manipulated by every "rage tweet" along the way. They had helped them get their man. Sayonara!

The sad thing about the case is that not one report out of the many made actually stated the true offense I had been charged with. They all screamed "animal abuser" or "animal cruelty." The authors of their previous hit pieces simply let the false claims previously made stand. The truth simply did not fit their false narrative. A few brave authors came out and stated my actions did not deserve the response or the punishment. I was thankful to those.

I was pleased, however, that we got to finally use the letters of support written on my behalf to be entered into evidence. All were submitted. The judge, in her ruling, even said I had been punished far more than warranted. While it was a good verdict in the courts, I was still a despicable loser in the court of public opinion. The facts did not trump their reality.

Ironically, immediately after the ruling, the BC SPCA had the nerve to reach out wanting to know if I was going to donate. They even took to Twitter and stated I had not made a donation. "Not a chance," was my response. They had basically set me on fire in the local square and watched my public execution. They had lost their opportunity to raise real money.

The Evil People Do

"My name is good in the village! I will not have it sullied!"
—Abigail Williams in *The Crucible*

Sadly, I was going to know all about being sullied. There was something wrong about this from the jump, from the initial heavy-handedness of the raid to every aspect of the incident. For the life of me, I could not put my finger on it. That would come, like most things, with time. For me, painfully so, but that is my perspective. I think it best if you come to your own conclusion. All I will do is provide you with the facts. Again, you be the judge for yourself.

I think it makes sense to give you a little recap of how things went down for my incident. This way we also keep things real and help place things in context as I unfold some new material for you to consider.

During my case, the chief prevention and enforcement officer (CPEO) for the BC SPCA either leaked or encouraged the tape to be leaked to the media. The BC SPCA press release mentioned me by name. They adopted a scorched-earth policy. You may be thinking, *Hold on a minute. That's how they handle all cases.* That's a fair point. I thought that at the time. Maybe you're thinking I may be a little biased. I get it. So let's investigate their practices a little closer. Are they consistent, and am I simply overreacting? You make the call. The media and the CPEO will provide the facts.

Four years after my incident, it was reported by Stephen Heywood of the *Penticton Western News* that a Victoria-area owner of forty-five dogs who surrendered on April 12 to the BC SPCA could be facing animal cruelty charges. This case was handled by the same CPEO who oversaw my case. So this will give us an opportunity to see how this case was handled and if done so consistently. The CPEO was interviewed for the article and made the following quotes. The full press release is also available in its entirety below for closer inspection:

> A member of the public reported the property owner on April 10. Officers with the SPCA investigated, and the owner surrendered the dogs.
>
> Workers and volunteers have been washing and grooming the dogs all weekend. They were found inside the home, she continued, living in unacceptable conditions including high levels of ammonia inside the home. The dogs' fur was severely matted with feces and urine, making any assessment of their condition troublesome. "It was hard to tell tip from tail."
>
> The individual appeared to have become overwhelmed by the number of dogs and was not sure how to find new homes for them.[1]

The CPEO acknowledged this was a serious case and went on to stress, "The dogs are not yet up for adoption, as their overall health must be determined."

What is different from my case is that the alleged abuser was not named, which is consistent with all their past and current practices. There was no leaking of the video footage of the animals suffering in this case, and there was no police raid. Instead, the CPEO went out of her way to protect the identity of the person in question. The CPEO's exact quote was: "The individual and where they live are not being identified at this time."

One incident does not make a pattern. Let's look at another incident from

---

1 Steven Heywood, "BC SPCA seeks cruelty charge after seizing 45 filthy dogs," *Penticton Western News*, April 16, 2018, https://www.pentictonwesternnews.com/news/bc-spca-seeks-cruelty-charge-after-seizing-45-filthy-dogs/.

2021 reported by CTV News Vancouver. This is about alleged abuse of over three hundred cows in Fraser. Was that handled differently?

"We immediately attended the farm on an unannounced visit and are reviewing more than 300 video clips as we prepare our case to present to Crown counsel," said the CPEO.[2]

The BC SPCA did not name the dairy farm at the center of its investigation in its statement. Allegedly, the CPEO did break the name of the farm to the media, but again the individual owner was not singled out. Again, my case was handled far differently and did not result in the mistreatment of hundreds of animals.

This last incident to compare was even more egregious than the others. It involved over one hundred dogs, and the story was reported by Denise Wong of the *CityNews*. Again, the same CPEO was involved. How did they handle this one? The CPEO said, "I can't think of a case in recent memory that comes close to this one."[3]

Even with not one case coming close in recent history to this level of animal mistreatment, the CPEO was *not* considering charges, and again privacy of the individual was maintained and there was not a police raid.

There are plenty of other examples I could highlight here, but they all would only further support that my case was totally mishandled.

I also want to be clear: The BC SPCA has important work to do. In fact, they have over eight thousand cases to deal with each year. The cases above, and many more, blatantly reflect that challenge. Their role is to protect animals that are treated by cruel and inhumane individuals; however, they should stick firmly to that.

But it does pose important questions on how they utilize their power and authority. Should their role be to persecute lesser acts with greater vengeance than the most egregious of acts? Should there be a graduation of response and punishment? Should they be abetting hate campaigns?

---

2   Staff, "SPCA investigating allegations of 'very serious' animal abuse at B.C. dairy farm," CTV News Vancouver, October 28, 2021, https://bc.ctvnews.ca/mobile/spca-investigating-allegations-of-very-serious-animal-abuse-at-b-c-dairy-farm-1.5643388.

3   Denise Wong, "B.C. owners surrender 119 dogs to SPCA," *CityNews*, March 15, 2021, https://vancouver.citynews.ca/2021/03/15/bc-dog-owners-surrender-spca/.

Should they have an obligation to go about their service consistently and not subjectively? Should they place coverage, potential donor contributions, and sensationalism over principle and honesty? Should they act like shock jocks contorting reality to fit their purpose? Should they instead hold themselves to a higher standard?

Not one of cases above was treated like my case, where I caused an animal distress, not cruelty. To be clear, this is not about whataboutism. I have gone on record and apologized for my behavior, and I'm not trying to deflect responsibility. I overreacted. I should have handled the situation better. What I am trying to call out is the discrepancy in how I was treated—for fairness.

Before you make your final determination, there is one more piece to consider. Is it fair for the BC SPCA to act as judge and juror? In addition to their fiduciary responsibilities, should they also do what is just? One would hope so. Let's examine a little further.

My initial donation would have been, as I stated, $100,000. That was really a down payment, but let's just cap it at that for this purpose. The BC SPCA, through its entire fundraising, brought in $600,000 in 2021, and they spent $300,000 to get that. For an entire year, their fundraising efforts netted $300,000. My contribution would have been over a third of their annual haul. Why would they forgo that just so they could crucify me in the press and release my name? Does this seem right to you?

I have never been big on conspiracy theories; however, by all indications, it appeared the press, social media, and BC SPCA were in each other's pockets. Or at least they were playing on the same team. And their takedown was sadly complete.

Warriors of the Wasteland

"Is life always this hard, or is it just when you're a kid?"
—Mathilda in *Léon: The Professional*

Sadly, bad acts were not just isolated to the media, the keyboard assassins, and seemingly their puppet master, the BC SPCA. Two incidents surfaced quickly that shook me to my core. First, a very good friend of mine was a friend of the president of a very prominent animal protection agency. My friend made the introduction to this person. I was hopeful I would get a fair hearing and that we could make lemonade out of this situation still.

This prominent leader, whom I have no desire to call out, called me while I was in New Orleans. I took the call while walking in the French Quarter with my sons. We talked for a few moments, and the man stated curtly that if I wanted their support to ever run a company again, then I needed to write a million-dollar check to his group. I was flabbergasted, almost speechless, which is quite the feat. There was no pretense—just a bold-faced stickup job. I was to be bent over and shafted.

After a momentary pause, I told him that I would not do this and put the phone down. As time usually reveals a person's true nature, this individual was swept up as a part of the "me too" movement months later and fired for several incidents of sexual inappropriateness. What I did pales in comparison.

A second incident came shortly after this, when one of my clients went out of their way to ridicule me for the incident. This holier-than-though executive was terminated for major financial malfeasance a year later. In the words of Jar Jar Binks, "Me thinks his moral outrage would have been best served on himself."

Since then there have been others who have fallen far deeper from grace, with one client actually getting into domestic battery charges, among others. I say this not to gloat but to remind people that we all make mistakes and to be careful not to throw rocks at others, especially when we live in a glass house.

I Can't Stand for Falling Down

"We deal in deception here. What we do not deal with is self-deception."
—Oliver Queenan in *The Departed*

I did not need to have finished top of my class to know what condition my condition was in. I knew it was grim. On my better days, I felt like I was a passenger in my own body. But more often I felt like I was better suited to playing a role in "One Flew Over the Cuckoo's Nest." My inner voice constantly pounded away, chastising me for my momentary loss of control with the seriousness of a prosecutor delivering their closing argument. I was no stranger to pain, but the hurt was not just mental—now my body ached. As each day stretched out, I felt my body shutting down, my emotions drying up, and my heart closing. One morning I awoke and felt a deep pain in the left side of my body and my back. Later that morning the doctor confirmed I had shingles. I felt like I was falling apart. The realization finally set in that after spending my life protecting others, I was now the hunted. The thought chilled me to the bone.

Watching Centerplate, the company I had helped emerge as a leader in the industry, flounder did not help. To witness firsthand the loss of account after account that I had previously won with the team was devastating. It was worse than the old Chinese torture of dying from a thousand cuts. Almost immediately after my departure, it was reported in the press that they became embroiled in an FBI investigation. This is never a good thing. This was a train wreck I saw coming and was powerless to prevent. It's funny that actual crimes did not warrant the social warrior's wrath. Pathetic. The board apparently terminated no one. Heads should have rolled, and rightly so. Their silence was deafening.

I do not blame the team, even though they made unbelievable mistakes. I blame the board. Even before my forced resignation, the board knew I was starting a search for a president. I was going to pivot and focus more on global growth and segment and business extensions to build out the growth diamond. There were gaps in the organization that needed to be filled. In order to do that, I realized my operations and marketing teams were not strong enough. We needed to strengthen the base, but I'll leave it at that.

Knowing this deficiency, it is still a head-scratcher to this day that the board never strengthened the existing team after my departure. In fact, they knowingly made things worse. Not only did they not hire a new president but they promoted the existing COO. The business needed stronger leadership. What it got was sadly lacking. To quote venture capitalist Fred Destin, "Good boards don't create good companies, but a bad board will kill a company every time." This board, like the song, was "Bad to the Bone."

Over the next few years, Centerplate accelerated in losing more accounts. If that was their strategy, to lose business, then they were highly effective. In spite of amazing leaders in place, like Keith and Hadi, the CFO, they fell short. Watching key players I had hired leave the company for other opportunities only crystallized my pain. It reminded me of the quote, "Everyone has a right to be stupid, but some people abuse the privilege." It was a truly staggering reversal of fortunes, and in such a short time: the San Francisco 49ers, Denver Broncos, San Diego Chargers, Kentucky Fairground, Florida Panthers, the Javits Center in New York, Notre Dame, Tampa Bay Rays, San Francisco Giants, Portland Timbers, Atletíco Madrid, Warner Bros. UK—the list went on and on. These losses alone equate to a staggering loss of easily over half a billion dollars in enterprise value. That's a hell of a lot of zeros.

I thought I could salvage things and worked with another equity group and approached Centerplate's equity owners, Olympus, about a purchase. We offered half a billion. I felt that was generous, due to their current performance. Our bid was summarily rejected. What I have learned in this space is there is always "dumb money" at play. The equity partner must have realized the jig was up, as shortly afterward they sold to Sodexo for a staggering $100 million more than Centerplate was valued at its peak. They then rebranded to Sodexo Live!. The losses merely continued under a different banner. A rebranding was not the silver bullet. People are your greatest asset. Talent was missing. They have excellent people still working there, but executive leadership was the missing ingredient. Regardless, to watch this from the sidelines was depressing.

I Guess That's Why They Call It the Blues

"The world breaks everyone, and afterward, many are strong at the broken places."
—Ernest Hemingway in *A Farewell to Arms*

It was like living in *A Tale of Two Cities*, but unlike those in the Dickens classic, mine were bleak and bleaker. There was no best of times, only the worst of times. I was a basket case. The more I tried to get out of the tailspin I was in, the more I felt like Tom Cruise after his jet spinout in *Top Gun*. Sadly, like Cruise, I could not find the strength to reengage. I felt like the Hulk had simply "gone smash," breaking every bone in my body. I felt I had nothing left. The pin was pulled. The proverbial fork had been put in it. Finito, really.

We had moved full-time to our mountain retreat. It was a way to escape the haters, but it felt like we were fleeing the fight. It did not sit well. What had previously been seen as our getaway place and my own sanctuary was now more like my prison. I felt like George Michael's "prisoner who has his own key." It was surreal. I could go anywhere, but I knew wherever I went, I would be contained in my own mental cell. To compound things further, I could not shake that I had fled the battlefield—and that, too, was eating away at me like a potent deadly virus. Even though I objectively knew why I had made the decision to resign, it did not lessen the pain.

We were isolated, living almost two miles high in the mountains. I went weeks without leaving the house. Carol was concerned, and rightly so. We were still healing and still coming under heavy social media attacks. Regrettably, I was now self-medicating nightly with alcohol. Sadly, I needed to numb my mind, and more importantly my feelings. Previously, I had thought there was nothing quite as divine as a good bottle of bourbon. After all, that's why they're called spirits; however, the spirits were doing nothing for me. I was in my own freak show. It was like I was in suspended animation. The combination of my nightly concoctions, while they would numb me, did not allow me to process and move on. I was not healing. I was feeling more isolated than ever. For several months, I bounced along the bottom like Wile E. Coyote getting this head hit on jagged rocks along the way.

I would receive hundreds, if not thousands, of posts, texts, and calls. All anonymous. All vile and hateful. It is crazy the number of nutjobs who are out there. Staggering, really. I did have a company track down a few of the more threatening repeat offenders. Against legal advice, I called those individuals personally. To a person, they denied any involvement; however, they knew they were caught red-handed, and they knew they were no longer posting with anonymity. The disgusting messages mysteriously ceased. Funny how that happened. True keyboard cowards. Go figure. I should have just disconnected and gone off the grid to heal and recover. That would have saved me $1 million in failed efforts to restore my online presence.

Far worse than the hit to my professional reputation was the private shame. I had dishonored my wife and broken my vows—something I thought was just not possible. It felt like someone had pulled all the fuses in my head and forgot to reboot. I was crumbling day by day and hanging on by the thinnest of threads. Some days I would have a hard time just going through the basic motions of life. I cannot tell you how many times I just wanted to fly off and go into hiding, or worse; however, I could not do that. I could not allow for my oldest son nor my youngest son, who was just starting his great adventure, to see me run. I was worried what it would do to them psychologically. My family needed to see me atone for my mistakes.

PART 5

REBIRTH

Just Like Starting Over

> "When we are no longer able to change a situation, we are
> challenged to change ourselves."
> —Viktor E. Frankl in *Man's Search for Meaning*

My recovery was a slow process—the watching-the-kettle-boil type. Just like Cher, I too wished in vain to have the ability to turn back time. At times I felt like I was in suspended animation and perpetual purgatory. At other times it was like I was an unwilling insect pinned to the mat for some type of unpleasant experiment. I could not shake the feeling of being an absolute twit. Disgust hollowed out my insides, but I pushed onwards.

Friends are few, and true friends fewer still. Bill Caruso was a true friend. By now many of my so-called friends had fled, but not Bill. About a year after the incident, Bill called me up out of the blue. I was holed up in the mountains. I had taken to Google-searching myself daily. Talk about the classic definition of *insanity*—doing the same thing and expecting a different outcome. I was like a rubbernecker who could not look away from an accident. In this case, it was my pileup. The only silver lining at the time was that my inflammation was finally under control, my treatment was going well, and I was at least feeling healthier again, if not out of the woods. Carol was there beside me every step of the way. Seeing that woman at my side, encouraging me, actually made me feel, if possible, like an even bigger heel.

Bill said he was contemplating selling his successful consultancy business but would be interested in continuing if I bought in. After some back-and-forth, that's actually what I did. We were fifty-fifty partners. I threw myself into the job, hoping it would help me move forward. The reality is, I needed more time to get my head straight. Most mornings I was a mess. My head felt permanently foggy, and I was racked with waves upon waves of shame. I could not forgive myself for allowing all this to happen.

My previous enthusiasm for life was snuffed out. I could not get the spark to reignite. My soul felt dark and barren. I did not think I would be happy again. Of course, I did not show others these feelings, just like I had done earlier in my life, when the Darkness walked the earth. Like then, I faked it. Regardless, I had hit rock bottom. I was also wallowing in self-pity.

Even in the middle of all this, for brief moments I was able to push the sadness aside. To focus on the business a little bit more of the time and less time on wallowing. We set around repositioning the company and setting it up for international expansion. At the time, we had two offices. In less than two years, we had eight offices strategically placed around the globe: Berlin, São Paulo, Philadelphia, Athens, Costa Rica, and Vancouver. The company was now truly global; however, at the time, these developments did not bring a glimmer of happiness.

We worked on approximately eighty to one hundred high-profile projects a year. Many were iconic buildings, like the Miami Dolphins' stadium renovations, the San Antonio Spurs, the Texas Rangers new ballpark, and so on. These were big projects, and our small team thrived and delivered. Each project added a little more spark to my life.

Saving a Life (Again)

There is a quote that if you can impact just one life, you have lived a good life. Helping others has always been a driving force of mine. I like to think I have helped save tens of thousands of lives through numerous fundraising efforts; however, actually saving a life one-on-one is special. Years ago I had saved the diner at Ashford Castle. Now it was time for Act 2.

Carol, DJ, and I were in Cabo at the Las Ventanas resort. DJ was on break from college. We had just sat down to dinner when an elderly gentlemen clutched his throat and fell off his chair. Talk about déjà vu. Again, no one was fast to react. I jumped into action. The man was clutching his throat. He clearly was choking. I positioned myself behind him and gave him my trusted move. Soon the food was dislodged, and he was breathing well.

A few moments later, another diner stepped up and asked if I was a doctor. I said, "No sir." He slapped me on the back. He said what I did was impressive, and a few moments later he sent over a message that a round of drinks were on him. These actions give me a lot more pride than many of my professional accomplishments. Success is measured in more ways than money. I was also silently proud that my son had seen me do this.

Little by little, I was reawakening. I was healing. My grandchildren were a great aid. We would visit regularly. Sofia was two years old and a ball of energy. Every afternoon I would put her in the bike seat, and we'd cycle for hours along the Strand on Manhattan Beach.

Luis had just been born, and I'd get him at night so his parents could get some sleep. Having that little guy lay on my chest was so comforting. His peace gave me peace.

Time to Exit

"Is it getting better, or do you feel the same?"
—U2 in "One"

Eventually, we had taken WC&P as far as we could. In truth, it was occupying about 25 percent of my capacity. That's not a criticism. It's just that I had been used to much more demanding assignments. We sold to the management team, and I exited the business to a wash on my return on investment. In essence, we knew we would have gotten a lot more if we ran an open process, but Bill and I wanted to reward the team who had helped us and set them up for success. It's awesome to see Young and Caruso continue to drive the company forward.

I was playing around with the idea for a business book and decided I'd place my focus there for a while. In truth, the executive recruiters who would call daily at one time had not made a call in over two years. I feared I had been canceled forever. My state of mind became more anxious as I hoped anyone would call. Simply stated, I was not in a good place. I had proven that I could grow a company and make money for investors. I was just having trouble connecting with the right leaders. My close friends told me to be patient, but I was internally losing hope by the day.

While I was still in a funk, I was in less of one. Candidly, I was so busy worrying about my life that I was forgetting to live my life. By now I had stopped the nonsense of doing my own daily Google search. That was a good thing, but still far too often than healthy I replayed my incident and the aftermath on a virtual closed loop. I never thought forty-two seconds could have such an impact. The thing is, I knew I did this to myself. If I could, I'd have never spoken to myself again, if that were possible. It was me who lost his temper. I honestly feared that the Des I knew and loved was dead. That I would be a shell of my former self. It was terrifying. I just seemed to be perpetually depressed, in a constant fog, with nothing but dark thoughts keeping me company. Yes, I would have dinner with friends, visit family, and travel, but I'd be faking happiness. The outside world would think I was as right as rain. The reality is, I was still in a bad place. Inside I was a ghost. For anyone going through their own adversity, it is important to make sure your worst enemy is not living between your two ears. Mine was for the longest time.

I'm Not the Man I Used to Be

> "Happiness can be found, even in the darkest of times, if only one remembers to turn on the light."
> —Albus Dumbledore in *Harry Potter and the Prisoner of Azkaban*

Sometimes things happen just when needed, for no reason and against your wishes. That's how I originally thought of the entrance of Dr. Patty Ann Tublin. I really wanted nothing to do with her and her witchcraft. But my wife insisted I speak with her. I lost that battle. Little did I know the effect this wonderful woman would have on me.

Over time the good doctor made an impact. The doctor got me to realize she was just like any other service provider in my life. I had someone to help in the gym. She explained she was there to help in the head. *Good luck with that*, I thought. After our initial session, I thought there was no way she could help. I'm not saying I was off my rocker, but I thought after speaking with me that my shrink would need a shrink. Slowly but surely, as hard as I fought it, we connected, and she helped me process my feelings. It was not a moon shot. It was a five-year process, but I finally emerged a better person. The passion I had previously lived life with had not returned fully, but there were glimpses. It may never return, but I am on the right path again.

Dr. Patty played a pivotal role in getting me right. The doctor gave me a copy of Viktor Frankl's *Man's Search for Meaning*. The story is horrific, but it was the right book delivered at just the right time. The essence of the book is that if you have a "why to live," then you can cope with any "how." I have read that book every Thanksgiving since then. It is a great reminder to put your own troubles into perspective. The head doctor joins my consequential list. Thank you!

The Power of Healing Hands

"Some of you are thinking that you won't fight. Others, that you can't fight. They all say that, until they're out there."
—Proximo in *Gladiator*

Along with the help from the head doctor, I had rebooted my exercise regimen. This truly was a lifesaver. One of my friends recommended looking into mediation. Carol and I worked on both together—exercise followed by meditation in the mornings and the same process repeated in the afternoons. These sessions were instrumental in my recovery. At this time, and for the next several years, we also spent three months a year in Paris. It did not feel like it at the time, but every day I was getting a little better.

We took our annual trip to Paris for the next several years. I made remote work fashionable way before the pandemic thrust that upon the world. Twelve weeks with different groups of family and friends staying with us for a week at a time. Paul and Shirley, Adrian and Jen, Carol's brother Jay and his wife, Ginny Sue, Tony and Stefanie Spadaccini, the Spadaccinis' boys, Keith and Jackie King, Steve and Jan Clark, and other friends. With each visit, we could feel their love flow to us, and it was special. It was rejuvenating. It was powerful. We toured the whole country. These memories I will cherish for life.

At the same time, Dante, our third grandchild, had now entered the fray. Now we had three grandchildren who visited us in the mountains for four to eight weeks each summer. Their joy for life played a massive part in my finding myself again. Thank you, rug rats, I mean grandkids.

Almost Landed It

"Yeah, baby, you're close, so close, but no cigar."
—Weird Al Yankovic in "Close but No Cigar"

I'm not saying I did not allow negativity to enter my mind, because I did. I just never gave in to my darker thoughts. Even when I felt things were hopeless, I pushed on. Onwards! has always been my mantra. I also felt that the head doctor was starting to make a difference. At this time I had been working with Durational Capital. We had Del Frisco's in our sights. Gerri Kies made the introductions. Over the course of a few months, I had put together the Plan on a Page and actually developed a global growth strategy for the brand. I was excited about taking this business to new heights. Carol and I were on a road trip traveling through Florida to visit our eldest son, Patrick, and his family. We stopped off at a hotel so I could sign my employment agreement as CEO. I was elated. After several years in the wilderness, I was finally going to be leading another global brand. I could not underscore how much this meant to me. I did not even realize until I experienced it. I could finally put the Vancouver debacle behind me. The phrase *aliquam proficiscantur*, which translates to "It's time to move on," sprung to mind. It was a blissful feeling. It was like a ton of bricks had been lifted from my chest. *I am not going to squander this chance*, I thought as "Tik Tok" by Kesha played full blast on the stereo to get in the party spirit.

In a cruel twist of fate, that party feeling was quickly snatched away. Just a few short hours after we pulled up to our son's driveway, I pulled out my phone and saw several texts regarding Del Frisco's. Durational Capital, for various reasons, was not going to make an offer for the company. I was stunned and consumed by the thought that I was doomed. It was a new low. I felt just like my favorite song by Mike Posner, "I Took a Pill in Ibiza," and not the good kind.

Houston Hero

One of the greatest joys for a parent, if not the greatest, is to see their children happy. Anything else is merely icing on the cake. On the same trip of my Del Frisco's disappointment, we watched the news of the deadly hurricanes set to pound the States.

Houston was ravaged by a monster flood—a one-in-five-hundred-years beast, the media screamed. Hundreds of homes were destroyed in its initial wake. People lost their lives, and many more were stranded.

Patrick volunteered to join the rescue party in Houston. We were all worried, especially his mother. We also knew this was what he had signed up for when he joined the coast guard. There would be no stopping him. Sadly, he was too old for time-outs!

Even before arriving at Air Force Station Houston, fighting though harsh winds and torrential rain while flying over a trailer park, Patrick saw two teenagers waving frantically. He and his crew swooped down, rescued the youths, and dropped them safely off to the National Guard on a nearby bridge.

Early the next morning, they were airborne again. It was also going to be a very long and arduous outing. There was an extreme sense of urgency, as there were many in need. The rain had not abated, nor had the high winds. Conditions were brutal, with ominous low cloud covering at three hundred feet. The low cloud cover was particularly troubling, as Houston has towers as tall as six hundred feet. At times they were flying blind.

The pilots were on high alert, as this one could very possibly be their last mission. This certainly upped the ante and their bravery. They got an urgent call that an elderly man in an apartment complex needed help. The man apparently had serious heart issues and needed immediate medical attention. Within a short time, the helo located the apartment. The rescue swimmer was activated, and then Patrick lowered the harness. The elderly man was hoisted up to safety.

While Patrick was hoisting the elderly man up, he heard there were others trapped and in need nearby. Patrick radioed the helo and alerted them of the situation. The diver went off in search of them. There he found a terrified young mother huddled with her infant child. Moments later the helo was above them, and Patrick lifted them to safety.

On the second day, Patrick's crew scoured the surrounding area for hours before he was pulled to help with maintenance. On Thursday, Patrick boarded a C-130 to head back to Miami, which was now in the path of its own hurricane.

We had spoken to Patrick every night. He had said only that he was very busy. He never mentioned his heroics. That was typical of our son.

Several months later, Patrick received the Coast Guard Commendation Medal for his actions in Hurricane Harvey. His medal was awarded by the commandant of the coast guard, no less. We were there, along with his entire family, to celebrate.

We will never forget that day for the rest of our lives. That young man makes us so proud.

Swing and Miss

Within a few weeks, Robbie Hahn, former president of the Colorado Restaurant Association, called me out of the blue. He told me that he was working with a start-up frozen smoothie product that I should take a look at. Robbie told me the company had good bones. What he should have said and didn't is that they had a whole graveyard full of them.

I met Robbie and the financial advisor, Joe Durnford, in Denver and tasted the product. It was great, and healthier products were certainly a growing trend. I met with the founder and current CEO, along with the COO, over the next few days. I joined as the chairman, with a financial commitment if I liked what I saw. I quickly realized I did not like what I saw. In truth, I should have run for the hills, but I wanted to get back in the race too badly. It was a bad move. Desperation is never a good look.

The company was managed like a child's science project. There was little coordinated effort. The leadership team was not aligned. They had misspent on building out a state-of-the-art production facility subscribing to the "build it, and they will come" philosophy. Everything they could have done wrong they did and more. The only thing going for it was the product itself, but even then, the cost structure was crippling.

I halved my investment commitment and agreed to take on the CEO role. The company was based in Denver, which was very convenient for me. I took to bombing up and down the mountains daily. The company was small and had their products in less than one hundred locations. The sales were nothing to get excited about. In fact, they were subpar, as was the leadership team. In fairness, there had been no real marketing effort behind the product. But it tasted great and was extremely healthy. The previous CEO, now a board member, had zero experience in the space—and that was more than the rest of the board. It was a classic situation of the blind leading the blind. To make matters worse, there was mutual distrust between all parties. The Hatfields and McCoys were everywhere I turned. No one got along with anyone.

Over the next year, in spite of the dysfunctional nature of the venture, with a couple of well-placed advisors—Renate Siekmann and Robin Michel—we started to implement a game plan. We repositioned the brand, developed new marketing materials, and designed more effective packaging. The company had previously hired FDM Marketing, a sales broker, and severely squandered the deployment of this very capable group. I met with their principal, Fred, and over a six-month period we zigzagged across the country and met with the category managers of countless companies. Long gone were the high-profile welcomes. The boardrooms were replaced with small cubicles. If there was no room available, we pitched our brand in the foyers. It was like I was starting my career again. While humbling, I knew ego had no place in the proceedings. Getting our product on shelves was our goal, and we quickly got approval to place our products with multiple major retailers: Walmart, 7-Eleven, and Safeway, among others. We had achieved critical mass and soon would be a household name, or so I believed.

Enter the Ambassadors

We developed a powerful go-to-market strategy. We deployed an ambassador program—the thought being, let's engage a few key influential dietitians to get behind the product. We reached out to the US speed skating organization and sponsored the team. One of the skaters, Joey Mantia, got behind the product.

Next, Beth Miller, a nutritionist at UCLA, came on board. Beth was a rock star and was quickly followed by other nutritionists. This was a major part of our grassroots endorsement program. It was powerful. It was also a lesson for all start-ups that creativity and finding the right asset to deploy, with the right message, can work wonders.

Next I strengthened the board, initially bringing on Joe Essa, a longtime friend and CEO of numerous food-service brands who at the time was global president of Wolfgang Puck restaurants. Then I asked Dan Kim, the very same person who organized my social media takedown at Centerplate, to join. I wanted to close that chapter and move forward. Over the coming months, both individuals provided invaluable insights and advice. We had liftoff!

Making Lemonade Out of Lemons

After a few months at the helm, it became known we were dangerously close to having hundreds of thousands of dollars' worth of product pass its useful shelf life. This little fact had been conveniently ignored and swept under the carpet by management. For any company, this would be a nightmare. For a start-up, it is deadly.

With the help of our COO, Charlie Walling, the only good executive on payroll, we were able to make lemonade out of lemons. Charlie contacted the Denver mayor, Michael Hancock, and we were able to send the short-shelf-life product to feed the multiple Boys and Girls Clubs across Denver. It was a win-win. We contributed $100,000 worth of product to those most in need, and we launched Froozer Cares at the same time. It felt great to be able to do good again.

Constant Power Plays

> "Nero fiddled while Rome burned."
> —Unknown

While that quote is not known to be true, it could not be more fitting for our situation. Unfortunately, the board was engaged in constant power plays. Remember the saying about the negative impact of an inferior board? The lack of decision and vision that Mr. Tears sang about—or maybe it was the other one, Mr. Fear—was sadly on full display. Either way, it was disconcerting. The founder disliked the now former CEO, whom I had replaced. The former CEO disliked the people I had brought in. The board members and other investors had deep disagreements with one another. It was a merry-go-round of disaster. *Harmony* was not in the lexicon. I had managed to keep them focused on most occasions, but while on a trip to LA it boiled over into the "silly" territory. After discussing this with my trusted network and a couple of the advisors I had personally brought on, I resigned, as did all the executives I had brought in. The company hired new players, but they were incapable of executing our plan, which should not have been hard to do. Simply bring on the retailers we had gained commitment from. It should have been a paint-by-numbers play. The former CEO, whom I had removed from the day-to-day operations, got involved again to the detriment of the brand. Sadly, Froozer goes down as one of those brands with great potential to be a household name that never made it. It also cost my investors and me $500,000.

Kissing the Fool

> "Anything that sounds too good to be true usually is."
> —Reynolds Balmer

As the saying goes, you have to kiss a lot of frogs to find a prince or princess. Of course, after asking for their permission! That had certainly been my experience. For every hundred opportunities presented, less than a handful were worthy of serious exploration. After Froozer, I went back to providing services for a few equity firms and combined with my own investments was making a living. Not a CEO compensation–type living, but enough to live comfortably. I was spending a considerable amount of time helping aspiring leaders launch their ideas. It felt good to help others, but I missed running my own show.

Throughout 2018, I had conversations over several months with the original investor in TurboChef, the infamous BB. Yes, that very same man who had previously caused so much chaos at TurboChef. In truth, I would have rather seen hell freeze over than see this man again. It's funny how the world works at times, or really what you will do in desperation.

For all BB's faults, though, and there are many, the man had a knack for finding diamonds in the rough. So I carefully listened to his pitch. Sometimes I am simply too optimistic and believe people can change.

This same man asked me to come in and run his latest venture. I thought about this hard and long. Maybe BB was the leopard that can change its spots. Upon a lengthy review and several demos with the leadership team, who were exceptional, I came to the belief that the technology he found could, in the right hands, be a breakthrough idea. I thought it could be special. I also knew the man well and knew he would royally screw it up if he did not get out of his own way. I agreed to join under the conditions that he would not engage in the day-to-day business, would not try to direct management, and would never ever participate in client pitches. I knew this man's flaws, and these were nonnegotiable demands. He accepted the terms. I believe it's okay to make mistakes, as long as you learn and evolve in the process. We started with a clean slate. I would have been better served to have listened more closely to the lyrics of "Love the Way You Lie," one of my favorites from Eminem and Rihanna. It would have saved a lot of insanity and misery.

VIPER really was a great fit to take advantage of my lifelong experiences. I had run large global retailers and knew their pain points intimately. I had earlier experience in designing and implementing software solutions and understanding what it takes to gain an organization's commitment. I had been responsible for all advanced technology launches at Maytag. Most importantly, I had built up a long list of senior executives who knew and respected me. Leveraging those relationships and their networks was going to be pivotal and directly proportional to our success. I could feel that in my bones.

Within a few months, I knew the man I had known from my TurboChef days had not changed. If anything, unlike a fine wine, BB worsened with time. I discovered he had actually changed the company name five or six times over a few years—all on a whim, with no logic or deep thinking involved. The man had actually received a cease and desist from a very high-profile retailer for sharing confidential information. He had not shared this with me prior to my joining, or I would have not made the move. Classic move by him, unfortunately. The man was toxic, and I doubled down on keeping him at arm's length.

BB's rantings were more out there than they were previously, and that is saying something. It was like having a daily front-row seat to the Dr. Jekyll and Mr. Hyde show. At times he was smooth, but more often as smooth as diarrhea. The guy speaks like he swallowed an arsehole. And a big one at that. To say he seemed aloof was like saying ice is cold. Interestingly, BB spoke in question and exclamation marks but few full sentences. The man was also long on recriminations and shockingly short on self-awareness. I'll stop there. My mother always said, "If you cannot say something good about someone, stay silent." I am doing my very best here. I still, in spite of it all, had confidence that if I could keep him at arm's length, we could be successful. Now who was being foolish?

Around this time, I also knew the technology was something special, and the company had some real talent in place. In December 2018, I presented with the VIPER team to Staples Canada. I had spent the weekend before whittling down their 180-page PowerPoint presentation. We got the message down to under thirty slides. We failed to secure the retailer, but we got very close. We also realized where we fell short. What we were missing was a credible reference.

There'll Be Sad Songs

"Don't raise your voice. Elevate your thinking."
—My mother

Pick up a business book, and somewhere in it the importance of aligning expectations will be highlighted. You have to define and agree on what success looks like. It's essential. Before even joining VIPER, I wanted to make sure the primary investor's and my vision were aligned for the company. If you don't achieve this early, the venture is almost certain to fail. Nothing good ever comes from that. For any aspiring leader out there, heed this warning well.

I spent a good month working the primary investor through my thinking.

Every day I would spend a minimum of an hour or more walking through the logic and planning. Every day, sometimes several times a day, we would go over the same discussion points as if it were the first time. It was like he had no short-term memory. I was living in Post Malone's "Circles" world. Before I agreed to even join, I informed the majority investor that the retail commercialization process would take at least two years. I asked if he had the stomach for this. He stated he did. I should have really pressed him harder on this. It reminded me of the line, "How do I know you are lying?" Answer: because your lips are moving. Regrettably, his actions did not match his words. A few weeks later, after providing the first-year plan, he blurted out that this was a CYA exercise. There was no pause for reflection—just a poorly thought-out determination. This period reminded me of one of my favorite Tears for Fears songs, "Mad World." I was thankful that this was a one-on-one session, as the current leadership had all told me that if I had not come along, they were going to walk. That the man was crazy. That I was hopefully going to bring some adult behavior to the proceedings. This was a very bad omen of things to come.

My forecast was not a layup. I had projected acquiring six clients in year one, building to fifty-plus annually over a five-year time horizon. We were beginning from a standing start, and this was a stretch target. Disappointingly, the investor stated that fifty accounts should be our year-one target. I patiently repeated that he had previously acknowledged this had a minimum of a two-year fuse. I explained that overnight success stories in my experience were in fact years in the making. Yes, it's great to sign up a major retailer, but others will come on easier and smoother once we can demonstrate proven results. Once we had a validating client, then we would ramp up, and quickly. I finished the review, stating that everyone loves massive returns and the luster of breakthrough innovation. The problem was it takes time, typically five to six years, for a product or a business to scale, and for a long time even some of the best innovations in the world can look like sinkholes where good money goes to die. At the end of the review, the investor agreed with the plan but insisted he felt we would do this sooner. I stated that no one would be happier than I for that to be the case. The writing was sadly on the wall. I just refused to see it.

Health Is the Mightiest Currency

Over the past few years, I also made a conscious effort to improve my personal well-being program. Previously, I had exercised four or five times a week, but I was doing that on fumes. I was sleeping less than four or five hours daily. I was not eating to adequately fuel my body. I was still drinking way too much. Basically, I was not approaching my personal well-being with the same vigor and dedication as I approached my professional life.

I knew VIPER was going to be the challenge of a lifetime. It would take all my strength, from a physical and mental perspective, to succeed. With the help of my trainer, we developed the "Best Ever" plan, which paired nicely with my favorite John Legend song, "Best You Ever Had." That was my mindset going in. No excuses. Like the Gillette commercial, I wanted to be the best a man can get.

At the outset of joining VIPER, every day I would carve out two hours for my "Best Ever" plan. Two hours seems like a lot, but it's really not if you plan your day out well. I would get up early, have my coffee, and hold my first of two fifteen-minute meditation sessions. The clearing of the mind and concentrating on my breathing were uplifting. It never failed. Years ago I used to laugh at this nonsense. Not anymore. Then I'd hit my gym, which I was fortunate to have set up at home. I'd do five strength-training sessions for one hour each weekly. Shower, breakfast, and hit the office. At five in the afternoon each day, I'd repeat the process—meditation followed by exercise. As any trainer will tell you, the number-one thing for anyone serious about their training regimen is consistency. To be honest, the exercise regimen was also a massive stress reliever and a major reason for keeping me in the game. I combined this with a balanced diet and cut down on the alcohol before finally eliminating it entirely. I knew staring at an empty bottle was not a winning path forward, and being able to cut it off was a major step in my personal recovery and future well-being.

Calling on All Ambassadors

With my wellness plan getting into shape, it was time to supercharge our VIPER efforts. The ambassador program used in Froozer was quickly reactivated and deployed as the VIPER advisor program. Robin Michel, an awesome retail executive and friend of twenty-plus years, who had helped put Froozer on the map, quickly made her mark with VIPER as well. Within a month, Robin had us in front of a retail giant where she had deep credibility. Within six months, we had landed a $5 billion annual revenue retailer. It was a big moment for the company. This was the first major client. We were elated. I felt that my comeback had been achieved. We did something in six months that the major investor had not been able to do in eight years. This was really a double-edged sword, as it also fed the primary investor's belief that all other retailers would quickly follow.

I also knew that any chance of a ramp-up was tied to bringing on board more credible advisors. So, after the success with Robin, we quickly expanded our advisory board. We hired, over the next year, twenty-five world-class C-suite retail leaders. It was part of our Bigger, Fewer, Better play. These executives built careers on trust and respect. They were all credible and added gravitas in any setting. To a person they were not afraid to voice their opinions and at times to serve to protect against our own impulses—the likes of Hank Mullany, former president of Walmart North America; Diane Ellis, former CEO of the Limited and president of Chico's; Ruth Hartman, former president of Lord and Taylor; Monica Woo, former president of 1-800-Flowers; and Matt Gutermuth, former CEO of Safeway e-commerce, to name a few. I also had the pleasure of linking up again with Sarah Palisi Chapin from my 7-Eleven days. One of the greatest gifts I was given was to be introduced to Glenn Backus. Glenn joined as an advisor, and from day one we clicked. Glenn possesses one of the sharpest minds, and I am thankful for his friendship and consider him a consequential friend. This was the A team and was by far the greatest group of people I have ever worked with—an advisory board for the ages. They were simply brilliant.

Birthing of a Brand

With our advisors now locked in, we developed our go-to-market plan, utilizing the Plan on a Page methodology. Bigger, Fewer, Better was again central and even more so in this venture. BB previously ran the team ragged, chasing any warm-body opportunity that moved. BB had taken fitting a square peg into a round hole to a whole new level. We quickly narrowed our focus down to retail only, with a major emphasis on the grocery channel. After all, the total addressable market was over ten thousand retailers globally generating in excess of $26 trillion in annual revenues. Within a year, the advisors were working on making introductions to over 150 retailers. At any one time, there were fifty-plus accounts being coordinated. A week did not go by without multiple client virtual meetings. These were crazy busy times, and we had a core team of less than a handful. We were doing the work of fifty.

Plague for the Ages

Like the rest of the world, in early 2020, we were confronted by COVID-19, the newly minted global pandemic. The timing could not have been worse for VIPER. Our core clients were some of the most negatively affected. To make matters worse, our primary clients, the grocers, were hit the hardest. They were deemed an essential service, and their operations were placed under severe stress. No retailer was thinking about our services at this time. They were scrambling to keep their customers and employees safe and figure out how to keep product on shelves. Optimizing profits was not given a fleeting thought. They were under siege. It would be seen as tone-deaf to approach them at this time. I understood this, but BB, disappointedly, not so much. In truth, BB had no experience managing large, complex businesses. BB simply did not get it.

Burn Rate

I again thought I was living in Dickens's "worst of times." The misery was not just in my personal life. Our newly signed-up retailer informed us in March 2020 that all third-party projects were on hold indefinitely. At least our client called me personally. Nevertheless, it was a gut punch. The client told me that they were being tasked with heading up the vaccination process for the entire state of Florida. To our team's credit, we pivoted and worked on other things to add value with minimum stress to our client. While the client liked what we were doing, we were no closer to getting what we needed—a high-profile retailer to validate our technology.

For the next two years, we operated virtually and had no in-person meetings. This certainly made the commercialization process a lot harder. We also closed our corporate offices and tightened our belts to survive the pandemic. It was important to reduce the *burn rate*. Those two words for start-up companies illicit the same fear as *corporate downsizing* to the corporate world. I took the biggest personal salary reduction, as I wanted to lead by example. This team was exceptional in every sense of the word. Everyone chipped in. In fact, every advisor gladly restructured their agreements if it meant we stayed in the fight. It was special.

Throughout this time, I would keep BB constantly informed with daily calls and detailed weekly updates. I wanted him to know the latest developments and be aware of the progress and challenges we faced. But you have to remember the conversations and actually read the updates to be informed. That was not BB's style. It was also a recipe for disaster.

I remember one exchange with BB that helps put an exclamation point on his mindset. Our accountant and Keith had worked tirelessly to secure a PPP loan, which was a lifesaver. We also worked on a small business loan (SMB) from the government. BB demanded that we should offer the US government a stake in our business instead of agreeing to an interest rate of the SMB. Read that again: BB thought the US government would entertain such a proposition. Simply delusional.

Going Totally Off the Rails

Over the past few years, I had disappointedly allowed myself to take abuse from BB. I am ashamed I allowed this to happen. I found myself enduring discussions and witnessing more erratic behavior by the day. Prior to my meltdown in Vancouver, I would never have tolerated any of this. It reinforced vividly how far I had fallen. Looking back, I suppose I wanted a win too badly, to get back in the game, and therefore allowed the mistreatment to continue. We all know what happens when you embolden a bully.

In the summer of 2021, the vitriol and volcanic behavior went off the charts. BB was back to his bad old ways. The saddest part is, we were now so close to our breakthrough. By mid-2021, despite the pandemic, we had gotten about twenty retailers into the closing stages of our sales process. Twelve of them we were either confident or very confident in inking deals with in the next three to twelve months. We had just gained a written commitment to launch a pilot across a billion-dollar division of a well-known retailer and had a contract out with another $5 billion-plus grocer. Things were starting to take shape, ironically in sync with my original timeline.

But BB wanted back into the business. That's when I knew I could no longer contain the situation. BB was becoming impossible to keep at arm's length. The fundamental disagreement was that he felt the pandemic should not have caused us delays. BB was in a party of one, but it was his party. Basically, BB was firmly advocating taking a confrontational position with our prospects. He believed the executives of our target clients should fear being fired if they did not deploy VIPER. Every advisor warned against this approach and would not subject their trusted relationships to such outlandish treatment. Crazy was truly in the house.

Final Hail Mary Attempts

I attempted a few intervention sessions with BB. I held numerous strategy sessions with Glenn and several other trusted advisors. Together we laid out our attack plan in full detail (not the first time we had done this exercise), and again asked BB for a little more time. Eventually, he agreed to see out the year. That was in July 2021. The cease-fire did not last long. Less than two weeks later, the threats were back and at a full-throated war cry. Ironically, by now the company, which had been valued at $5 million on my first day, was now valued at $100 million. My family had a sizable ownership valued at just under $8 million. We were in fact close to having multiple clients sign up, and the enterprise value would skyrocket further. I told BB that we had a potential unicorn on our hands and to stay the course.

Maldives Scare

"Just when I thought I was out, they pull me back in."
—Michael Corleone in *The Godfather: Part III*

As the world opened back up, it was time to celebrate a long overdue milestone birthday for my wife. Carol originally wanted to take the family to the Galápagos Islands, but the trip had been canceled for a third time. The Maldives was next on the list. Six of us took the trip—Carol and I and both our boys and their partners. It was a perfect spot. The resort came highly recommended and did not disappoint.

Two days into the trip, I was enjoying dinner when out of nowhere the stomach cramps I had experienced several years earlier returned. If possible, they were even more painful. I tried to tough it out, but for several evenings I had to leave after dinner and head back to our room in severe pain. I feared that my prostate issues had returned. This time Carol was beside me all the way.

Waiting Game

Talk about watching and waiting for the water to boil. Immediately upon getting back stateside, I lined up my doctor and had several tests done. How ironic. I had finally gotten out of my tailspin and was ready and once again excited about living. After all I had endured, was this the way I was going to go out?

I went in on Monday and waited for the results. The next couple of nights I had little to no sleep. Meditation helped, but only so much. Europe's "Final Countdown" played in my head. Truthfully, I was scared witless. I did not want to check out just yet; however, this time around I did not turn to the bottle but to my wife. We were again the team we had always been, except for my "crazy year."

On Wednesday the doctor finally called. I was already on pins and needles and knew something was immediately wrong when the doctor asked if I had gotten worse, and if so I was to rush to a hospital. What an opening statement. My heart was pounding against my chest, as if I'd just completed a bloody marathon. I asked the doc to hold for a moment, and I called Carol into my office and put the phone on speaker. Whatever we were going to hear, we were going to hear together. The doctor went on to state that I appeared to have issues with not just my liver but also my kidneys. That sucked the life out of me very quickly. Could I not just have one issue to fight? The doctor went on about other concerns, but I had checked out. What I do remember the doctor saying is that I needed to take more tests the following week. I asked, or Carol did, why not immediately and was informed that the inflammation had to come down first. Talk about déjà vu. I feared the worst.

The next several days ground on. At times it felt like I was in suspended animation. I felt like a prisoner on death row waiting for the inevitable to happen. Dickens's "worst of times" just kept getting worse. Carol and I had decided not to inform our boys until we had something concrete to discuss. I started to think about making sure that my affairs were in order. We had good lawyers, accountants, and financial advisors, so I knew that for the most part Carol would be in good hands. I thought at the time, *Isn't this ironic. I am just starting to feel like my old self, ready to move forward, and this happens.*

Finally, it was time for my appointment. I put on my game face. Carol drove me over to the doctor's office. After being jabbed multiple times, and with blood drawn, we returned home. Movies have always been our great escape, so we lost ourselves the rest of the day bingeing a new Spanish series on Netflix. The next few days were the most painful. It's amazing the power your thoughts can have on you. I made a life by beating the odds, and here I was, filled with dark thoughts. Whatever the diagnosis, I was readying myself for the fight of my life.

Friday afternoon rolled around. Carol and I were in the movie theater, still losing ourselves in the Spanish drama. The phone rang. I saw the doctor's name on the screen. Carol and I walked to the office, and I again placed it on speakerphone. I looked into Carol's face and said, "Okay, Doctor, have you good or bad news?"

There was a pause, and we held our breath. What he said next I knew would have profound consequences on my life and that of my family. The doctor seemed to pause for dramatic effect and then stated, "The tests all came back great. You are all good." I remember Carol and I jumping up and down like excited teenagers. I had the realization we were going to be okay. The powers that be had seen fit to give me more time. I committed to putting it to good use.

Heaven Knows I'm Miserable Now

"Woke up this morning and got myself a gun."
—theme song to *The Sopranos*

That did not mean everything in my life was going to be okay. That was far from the case. I had dodged one bullet to only stand in front of another. The very next week underscored that. Ego is a strange bedfellow and sadly oftentimes trumps logic. BB, by his own actions and demands of being involved in the day-to-day business, was putting the company, our employees, our advisors, and investors all at risk. It was like I was walking my own trail of foolishness. I had a decision to make: Was I more interested in protecting my money or doing the right thing? It was not even close. While I had hurt my reputation in a moment of anger, I would never knowingly hurt my reputation for money. Depeche Mode's "People Are People" resonated with me. The song was about how some people can get along so awfully. It was the perfect song to describe my relationship with BB.

Over the next several months, I tried to make it work and held more intervention sessions, bringing in the majority investor's longtime friend and second-largest investor in the company. We were hoping his friend, who was the former CEO of a large PE group, would see the dangers of BB's actions and advise accordingly. Along with Glenn, several other advisors, and my own management team, we laid out the precarious position the investor's actions placed us in. Nothing seemed to make the man see reason. I was what climbers would call "climbing heavy," having a harder time than I should moving forward. It was so sad. I simply refused to work under those conditions and was let go in early November 2021.

The exit experience was surreal but not totally unexpected. The investor informed me that I had actually been terminated a month earlier. That was certainly news to me and the wider organization, advisors, and in particular the retail clients I had been dealing with. Then, as his standard MO, I received a flurry of emails from the investor. In one, he stated I was fired for woefully underperforming and maybe for cause, and then another note a few minutes later where the investor praised and commended my performance and said that he had run out of money to keep me on board. That was life at VIPER—the wild contradictions and crazy mood swings of BB. I was glad to break the cycle of abuse and ridiculousness.

If I could do it all over again, I would not change a single thing, except to have totally sidelined BB from the business. In spite of BB's erratic antics, we almost put the technology on the map. If only BB had bloody listened carefully to Adele's hit "Rolling in the Deep." Talk about snatching defeat from the jaws of victory. For sure, it saddens me that the technology will never reach its fullest potential. Today I value my $8 million equity as worthless. I hope I am wrong, but as Joe Pesci famously said in *My Cousin Vinny*, I feel I will be proven "dead-on balls accurate" in this assessment. Time will prove that out. It's just a shame, but BB will always be the same.

Looking Forward

The VIPER exit was another body blow. I took a few months off to recover. I had invested a lot of my time and personal credibility in commercializing the technology. It hurt, and still does, to see those efforts go up in smoke. But I am once more moving forward and looking at future possibilities. In spite of it all, VIPER provided something special. After seven long years in the wilderness, it had helped me finally find my mojo again. Priceless!

It is funny how life goes in circles. Right now, while seeking out my next venture to lead, I have also turned my attention back to writing. My first business book is being edited, and I'm putting the finishing touches to this one. I have a draft outline for a suspense thriller on the drawing board. My ultimate goal is to have a fiction and nonfiction book simultaneously on the bestseller lists. If you dream, you might as well dream big. I spent my life thinking big, achieving the impossible at times, and taking risks. My philosophy is if you walk on thin ice, you may as well dance.

It's accurate to state that I have made my fair share of mistakes and have done some things I am not proud of. It's equally fair to say I've done many things I am tremendously proud of. In the end, we are all a combination of our total actions. Hopefully, the good far outweighs the bad.

I let my demons cause me immeasurable pain and inflicted unfair pain on my loved ones. Right now, in this moment, I feel I am a better version of myself, which is all we can ask of ourselves. For the first time in eight years, I feel joy slowly coming back to life. I feel more like my old self. For years I truly feared I would never recover. I felt that something was broken in me and that I would never be functional again. Recently, I was driving down the highway to my doctor's appointment and realized subconsciously that I was singing along to the tune and smiling. I had finally allowed myself to be happy again.

For my haters out there, what I did not realize for a while is that when they tried to bury me, I was a seed. The path back to sanity was not easy at times, but I endured. VIPER got my competitive spirits fired up. I now feel I am back. I no longer want to crawl under a rug and escape. I no longer walk around loaded down with shame and self-loathing. Instead, I move forward, knowing it's time for my reentry. I am finally in a place where the past holds no sway over my future. I want to share my experiences and philosophy on overcoming adversity with others who may need the encouragement to go on.

My loathing for the peddlers of hate on social media has not dulled with time. When all is said and done, has the Vancouver experience made me stronger? Absolutely! Would I want anyone to have to go through the same? Absolutely not!

As it relates to my feelings toward the BC SPCA, it is beyond a shadow of doubt that they seemingly had a biased and oversized role in my takedown. They could not have left more bloody fingerprints at the scene of the crime if they had wanted to. My response is nuanced, complicated, and conflicted.

First, I truly believe that when people do wrong they will eventually be judged. It may not be in the time frame one would like, but it will happen. I take solace in that. Also they will be judged ultimately by someone much more powerful than myself in their final reckoning. There are few things worse than consciously trying to destroy another human being. No one should take pleasure in that. It is a complete abuse of power and something I have fought against all of my life and will continue to fight. Sadly, we see so many do this, but that does not make it right.

Even after my total alienation and dehumanization at their hands, I strangely and inexplicably feel sorry for them. They have to resort to such disgusting measures and tactics to further their cause. They have to shill for dollars. They peddle in hate to survive, and that is tragic. I know I could not sleep at night if that was my lot in life. Deep down, I know who I am, and that has to be good enough for me.

I have always worked hard, even when it was very difficult to do so, to provide second chances. It's part of my internal moral code. I fervently believe you should never judge someone on their worst moments. This person at the BC SPCA needs the same forgiveness. What is life without compassion, forgiveness, and redemption? Is it right that a mistake is not only fatal but final? I believe this person was relatively new to the role. Maybe the moment was too big for them. Maybe they felt insecure and needed to get a quick win on the board or that the bright lights of acquiring fifteen minutes of fame were too great. One never knows what someone else is truly thinking or going through. What I would like is a public acknowledgment of their culpability in the matter; however, I'm not waiting by the phone for that call. The final word on this is that I forgive but will never forget!

Life Lessons

What follows are a few key learnings from my life:

- Family, loved ones, and friends are the most important people in your life. As Sinéad O'Connor sang so beautifully, "Nothing compares to you." Cherish them. Care for them. Be there for them always.
- Accept that we all make mistakes. All you can do is learn and evolve. Remember the words from Human League: "We are only human." Cut yourself and others some slack.
- We at times live in a world of greed and "what's in it for me?" We need to think more of others. Challenge ourselves to make the world a better place with our actions and words. As Michael Jackson sang, "We are the world."
- We only live once. Live in the spirit of Prince and party like it's 1999.
- For social media, as Phil Collins sang, there are at times too many people with too many voices—not every opinion needs a reaction.
- Pursue your dreams, believe in yourself, and channel yourself like Sia and be unstoppable.
- In life, you will face adversity. Know those difficult times will pass. Like Taylor Swift sang, we have to learn to shake it off.
- Never punch down. Care about people and be kind. Allow for forgiveness and redemption. Be someone the song "Lean on Me" was written for and not "Highway to Hell."

Second Act

"He who has a why to live can bear almost any how."
—Friedrich Nietzsche in *Twilight of the Idols*

Before looking toward the future, I need to recognize how lucky I am. If I could go back and ask my nine-year-old self what my life would turn out like, I can tell you it was not the life I have been fortunate to live so far. It has been beyond my wildest imagination. The people I have met, the experiences that I have had, and the love I feel from family and friends humble me. I am truly blessed. We would all be wise to think that our worst days are other people's best days. That's a sad and humbling reality!

I am fitter and thankfully healthier than ever. Like my go-to tune "Believer" by Imagine Dragons, I have confidence that I will have many more successes in my future. In truth, I feel I have already lived eight lifetimes, but like Oliver I ask respectfully for "more, please." In the words of Simon Le Bon, I have survived my own nuclear winter. In the immortal words of Dickens, I look forward to living in the "best of times," spending the rest of my life making my wife, Carol, who has stood by me through all my nonsense, feel loved, honored, and cherished. Steve Jobs once notably said, "You can only connect the dots in life when looking backward." What I didn't know then that I do know now is that meeting Carol back in Poland almost thirty years ago would be the most consequential meeting of my life. What a woman! What a friend! What a mother and absolutely my better half, always. I plan daily to make her feel like the center of my world while I have breath. I love you.

What I also hope came through in this book is that while life is serious, we do not have to always take ourselves seriously. Humor plays a big role in my life and how I live it. That I am even speaking to my elder brother through all his shenanigans should be proof of that. Sorry, Paul. You know I love you. To my family and friends, I adore you. To my detractors out there, thank you for helping me find the will to fight back and live. Your hatred for me actually fueled me. You will never beat me. Only I have that power. To channel the amazing lyrics of Christina Aguilera in "Fighter," criticism "makes me that much stronger / makes me work a little bit harder/ makes me that much wiser / so thanks for making me a fighter."

We need more people to have fun and not take themselves so seriously all the time. We are too intense, too ready to be enraged. We need to learn to chill a little and forgive. Also, never compare yourself to others. As Teddy Roosevelt one said, "Comparison is the thief of joy." My goal has always been to not be better than anyone else. My goal is to be better than I used to be. Take that message to heart.

We need to get out more and see the world, experience new things, and not judge others who think and act differently. We need to ask more questions and have an unquenchable passion for life and defining ourselves. For any aspiring leader out there who wants to do great things, I would tell you that you first of all need to invest in yourself. Read like your life depends on it. Acquire knowledge. Second, with equal vigor, invest in your people. Commit to making them the best they can be. You do those two things well, and you will practically book your ticket to the big dance.

As it relates to the big dance, if and when you get there, don't be an idiot. Enter with grace. Enjoy every moment as if it was your last. Take nothing for granted and always remember where you came from. Reflect on how fortunate you are. Respect all people, no matter title or position. Never act like you are better than anyone. The truth is, you are not. Instead, be humble, caring, and a positive force to all.

Chaos and adversity visit us all. It will rain, and I hope that you learn that when it does it's okay and dance in it. I also just read Brad Thor's latest book, *Rising Tiger*, in which he eloquently dropped some wisdom on happiness that I'd like to share: "Have something to do. Someone to love. And something to look forward to." This will help you in your pursuit of happiness.

Finally, I have spent a lifetime inspiring others. Now I'm up for the challenge of inspiring myself once more. As I start my next act, I relish my future and what it holds. I start with a blank canvas and intend to paint vividly. It has been my extreme honor and privilege to lead many great organizations. I hope I am fortunate to lead a few more before I hang up my hat. Truth be told, I miss it like the desert misses the rain. Regardless, I plan to move forward in the spirit of my family motto, which I find incredibly appropriate: "*Sans Peur*," meaning "Without Fear." I hope to live up to that daily. I am further inspired by this Hemingway quote: "You may talk. I may listen. And miracles may happen."

We all would be wise to remember that we all die. It's how you live your life that matters. Life will throw curveballs—just and unjust—at the least opportune times. Even so, it's never okay to play the victim. Victimhood truly debases you. Love, not hate. Being challenged in life is inevitable; being defeated is optional. I hope you took something away from my experience. I had many laughs and tears while living it and a second helping while writing about it. Through it all, though bent, I was never broken—and I'm proud to say *I'm still standing*!

Onwards!

ACKNOWLEDGMENTS

First, I'd like to thank the Amplify team, which worked tirelessly to bring this book to market. Thank you to Naren Aryal for taking a bet on a first-time author. To Brandon Coward, Caitlin Smith, and the entire team—you were amazing. Thanks for putting up with my constant rewrites and ideas. Also, a special mention to Jeff Hamill, who patiently listened to my ramblings throughout the process and helped me through so many drafts and never complained. You are a rock star!

I'd also like to thank the people who played a role in the rest of my life and were integral in bringing the book to life in the first place. From the top, I'd like to thank the small band of people who helped me survive some very harrowing times that no one should ever have to endure. To my four brothers: Paul, Dominic, Damian, and Neil. I love you more than life.

To my mother, Teresa—you were everything a child could ever want. I'm so sorry I did not get to spend more time with you, but your impact is still felt today. To my father, for giving me life and for eventually becoming a great grandfather to my boys.

Thanks to all my childhood friends, with a special callout to Daryl Ashbury and Kenny Macquire. Together we seemed to spend half our time getting in trouble and the other half getting out of that trouble.

Many thanks go out to two very special teachers. First, to Mr. Scarsdale for spending countless hours helping this numbskull learn to read. Second, to Ms. Reynolds, who got this young scrapper to see that a mind is much more powerful than a fist. I do not even want to think where I would be without your guidance and influence.

To Malcolm, for providing me a start in life and igniting in me an unquenchable passion for business. To Mark Hopkins, my first area manager at Pizza Hut, who launched me on my wild corporate ride. To Paul Clark, who gave me a shot and forever changed the trajectory of my life.

A special thank-you to the many executive teams I have managed, especially my Centerplate family: Keith King, Kevin McNamara, Hadi Monvar, Scott Marshall, John Vingas, Ashton Sequeria, Adrian Dishington, Laurence Rua, Thomas Tazbaz, Peter Matra, Gary Wattie, Steve Trotter, Paul Daly, Sal Ferrulo, Adam Elliott, Andrew Pollard, Steve Cahoon, Bill Greathouse, Chef David Skorka, Chef Reyes, Chef K, Chef Lenny, Chef Blair, Chef Leidy, Chef Prell, Chef Callo, Chef Hauser, Michael Barrett, Jerry Reed, Simon Pile, Paul McArdle, Jamiejohn Anderson, Mark Miller, Vincent McPhail, William McCully, Matt Long, Bill Donavan, Eric Wooten, Zach Hensley, Josh Prell, Greg Lesperance, Richard Ginzel, Nelson Drake, Anna Ference, the hundreds of general managers and support staff, and the tens of thousands of loyal employees across the globe who helped create extraordinary experiences on a daily basis and made Centerplate the leader in event hospitality. Your efforts are unprecedented.

To our unbelievable slate of Centerplate clients and suppliers who were the best in the world: A. G. Spanos and the Chargers; Jed York and the 49ers; Tom and Gayle Benson and the Saints; Steven Ross and the Miami Dolphins; Andy O'Sullivan and Tottenham Hotspur; Angel Gil Angel and Atlético Madrid; Chuck Armstrong and Kevin Mather and the Seattle Mariners; Simon Cohen and the Leicester Tigers; Dan Dark and Warner Brothers; Jim Mercurio, Angelo Anatasio; Howard Saffan; Carol Wallace; Bob Johnson; Bob Prattey; Gerald Andrews; Vince Purves of Sysco; Michael Hancock—mayor of Denver; Stephanie Rawlings-Blake—former mayor of Baltimore; Marc Silver and B&T; Deb Coldwell and Haynes & Boones; and Alan Steele and Peggy Daidakis, along with hundreds of other clients we were proud to serve.

To all the board members who supported me and the teams I was very fortunate to lead. I would also like to thank the numerous executive assistants throughout my career who made the trains run on time and enabled me to do what I do: Tammy at Whitbread, Marty at TurboChef and Maytag, Jane and Grace at 7-Eleven, Rachel at Hot Stuff Foods, Stephanie at Safeway, Gail at IHOP, Jill at Centerplate, Lara at Froozer, Sue at WC&P, and finally Kaity at VIPER. These ladies are all simply amazing. Thank you!

To Bill Caruso for being there for me in my ultimate time of crisis and who helped me pick up the pieces. To Brian Cornell and Joe DePinto—your continued support and friendship is something I will forever cherish. You both are giants! Also, a callout to my LinkedIn supporters. Your encouragement in recent years has kept me going when I so wanted to quit.

Also, a special callout to all the advisors whom I have had the extreme pleasure of working with, including Matt Gutermuth, Dan Kim, former NFL stars and Super Bowl champions Michael Strahan and Tracy Porter, ten-time NBA All-Star and two-time Olympic gold-medal winner David Robinson, Joe Essa, Robin Michel, Renate Siekmann, Glenn Backus, Lisa Walsh, Sarah Palisi Chapin, Gerri Kies, Monica Woo, Melanie Steinbach, Bonnie Siegel, Noel Matos, Peter Larkin, Ken Hamlet, Antonio Coto, Joe Essa, Tom Park, Miki Racine, Diane Ellis, John Harlow, Ruth Hartman, Lisa Walsh, Woody Bendle, and Ed Stagman. Working with and learning from you all has been the privilege of my lifetime.

I'd also like to thank the core VIPER team, who humbled me daily with their professionalism and ability to create excellence: Johnny Custer, Ernie Deyle, Andy Grimes, Keith Shoemaker, Agustin Falus, Desmond Hague Jr., Erich Smithson, Anthony Abbott, Ryan Andres, Todd Bruchnak, Laura Court, Wayne Crandall, David Demland, and Jason Nesbit.

To my core network of friends: Keith and Jackie King; Stephanie and Tony Spadaccini (now in heaven but never forgotten) and their two boys, Anthony and Paul; Scott and Nichol Marshall; Jan and Steve Clark, Ben Clark, and Grant and Ella Clark; Dave Brenner; Lisa Douglas; the Wolfman; Martin and Sarah Thorson; Tom and Dona Daniels; Bill and Lynn Byrne; Patty Ann and Mitch Tublin; Heather and Tom Scally; Greg O'Dell; Jeff and Rene VanderVorst; Jeff and Kathy Hamill; and Shelby and Peyton Prather. We have ultimately had enough fun to fill several lifetimes together. Thank you for the memories.

To my entire extended family, especially my daughter-in-law, Debora, my younger son's fiancé, Victoria, and my sisters-in-law—Shirley, Bonnie, Ginny Sue, Brenda, and Karen—and brothers-in-law Jay and Bill. You are the best. The way you opened your hearts and supported me in recent years is humbling.

To my two sons, Patrick and DJ—you always inspired me to be the best person and role model I could be. I am so proud of the men you have become and the great things you will achieve in the years ahead. Thanks also to my three grandchildren—Sofia, Luis, and Dante—who fill my heart with joy and make me want to be around to see the positive impact you will each have on the world.

Finally, to the person without whom I would be nothing—to Carol, my wife. You more than complete me. Thanks for putting up with me and all my nonsense for almost three decades. My wish is that I get to sing you our song for many more years to come and be your forever *Midnight in Paris* partner.

Onwards!

ABOUT THE AUTHOR

Des Hague is a highly regarded innovator in the international business community. For more than thirty years, his forward-thinking approaches as a high-level executive have achieved sustained growth and robust competitiveness for companies such as Centerplate, Safeway, IHOP, 7-Eleven, PepsiCo, and Maytag.

He currently serves as cofounder and CEO of Hague Enterprises, sits on the boards of MRGN and YoungCaruso, and is an active mentor, advising several start-up ventures and working with numerous private equity groups to create more than half a billion dollars in returns for investors.

Outside the business world, he has received numerous community leader awards and helped raise more than $100 million for a variety of nonprofits. He holds an MBA from the American College in London and resides in Colorado with his wife, Carol. They are the proud parents of two sons—Patrick and Desmond Jr.—and three grandchildren: Sofia, Luis, and Dante.